ADVOC
FOR
HUMANITY

MEDIA AND PUBLISHING

In dedicating this book, I would like to express my gratitude to all those who have crossed my path and left something for me or who have journeyed on the path with me for a time. You have helped me survive and are now helping me move into thriving.

In particular, I give thanks to my kids, Joshua and Kate, for their love and support.

Delivered Sunday 12 March 2023
Colossians. 3:12.
Dearly LOVED...
Well - Beloved by GOD Himself.

Praise for
A Journey Towards Acceptance

'As a senior leader in Australian media, I know the value and importance of storytelling. Jason tells a bold story: his story. It is a story that is, at times, uncomfortable for the author and reader, as his journey intersects family, communities of faith, sexuality and business. Jason's involvement in supporting many in the LGBTIQA+ and faith communities is often unseen, and this book explains the path of reconciliation for himself through his focus on faith, family and sexuality.

Freedom is being able to accept, and be, your true authentic self, and Jason takes us on this pilgrimage that leads to inspiration and, finally, hope.'

— **Manda Hatter, Head of Operations and Chair at ABC Pride, the Australian Broadcasting Corporation**

'*A Journey Towards Acceptance* is not your average coming out story, so it adds a valuable contribution to this genre.

Author Jason Masters has been incredibly generous in opening the door of his life to reveal the challenges of faith, family and society that he had to navigate in order to finally find authenticity and self-acceptance. Many would shy away from such personal self-disclosure.

People often think it is easy for people to 'come out' these days, but Jason's story demonstrates that this is far from the truth. It can be a lifelong journey and, depending on a number of factors, some never make it. Jason nearly didn't. One wonders how many more Jasons there are out there: gay, lesbian and bisexual people still living with unresolved, internal conflicts. They live in fear and shame behind a façade of overcompensation, believing that the truth would destroy not only them but also those around them. This is what makes Jason's memoir so important. The truth didn't destroy him; it set him free.'

— **Anthony Venn-Brown, Author of** *A Life of Unlearning: a preacher's struggle with his homosexuality, church and faith*, **Founder and CEO of Ambassadors & Bridge Builders International**

'Jason's story is a powerful lesson in resilience and humility, and it shows the courage needed to be true to yourself. His ability to reflect on his own difficult experiences, and to use what he has learned to benefit others, means that his voice is a powerful one, particularly for those struggling to reconcile their faith with their sexuality.'

— **Dr. Justin Koonin, President of ACON at acon.org.au**

'Jason's journey of self-discovery emerges in this raw and thought-provoking memoir, **A Journey Towards Acceptance**. He stopped allowing disruptions to get in his way, and he revamped his outdated beliefs. His endearing story will take readers down the many paths of his life where he faced challenging obstacles, and by overcoming these hurdles, Jason has stepped forwards as a champion in his journey. His simple nature shines through in a unique way with compassion and love as he acts as a voice for the LGBTIQA+ community, and his advocacy for this populace is commendable and steadfast. His book will bring awareness to every village, community, city and continent around the globe. What an amazing person!'

— **Cheryl Moy, President and Insurance Professional Founder of Moy Insurance and Author of** *The Origami Balloon: Becoming Mei-Rose*

Table of Contents

Author's Note

It might be helpful to understand what this book is and is not. As I journeyed through writing the memoir, I had so many ideas of what it might include and what style it might have, but many of those ideas died away naturally through the writing process.

For those hoping this book might provide a theological understanding of LGBTIQA+ Christians, I eventually decided intentionally not to go there. There are amazing books that cover the theology, such as Matthew Vine's *God and the Gay Christian* and Justin Lee's *Torn*, which are both biographical and theological. There is also the amazing work by Kathy Baldock, with her first book, *Walking the Bridgeless Canyon*, which provides a theological, historical and political context of the LGBTIQA+ journey from a non-LGBTIQA+ person's point of view—such as parents of LGBTIQA+ people. Her latest book to be published in 2023, called *Forging a Sacred Weapon: How the Bible Became Anti-Gay*, explores biblical translation and history on another level and how biblical errors have added to the pain for LGBTIQA+ people. For those readers from Australia seeking an Australian voice in this space, there is the work of Dr. Stuart Edser, *Being Gay, Being Christian*, and Joel Hollier's publication, *A Place at His Table*.

I also chose not to cover the issues of coming out and being LGBTIQA+ from my own psychological perspective.

There are many excellent academic pieces of work in this area. One such book was written by a therapist recounting his clients' experiences and is called *Velvet Rage: Overcoming the Pain of Growing Up Gay in a Straight Man's World* by Alan Downs, PhD. My copy of his book has the most underlining and margin comments of any book I have read—closely followed by Kathy Baldock's book. For those seeking another example of the intersectionality of faith and sexuality, particularly in the Australian context—although globally applicable—then Anthony Venn-Brown's book, *A Life of Unlearning*, is an important read.

My own book covers parts of my life journey; those parts that have had some intersection on my decisions to hide my sexuality and keep it hidden, and it explores what happens when the mental health consequences of that becomes too much to bear.

So, put simply, this is my story. However, I encourage readers to look at the works I have referenced above and the many others you can find through an excellent book shop or through your local librarian who is open to this genre of books. This is not a 'how to' book, it is not a therapy book, nor is it an academic or theological book. It is simply part of my life story.

For some readers, I hope you find this an interesting read. For others, I hope it might inspire you to consider justice in your own places of interaction: home, work or places of faith. For a few, it might provide some anchors and reference points as you go through your own journey and, if for only one or two readers, I would like to think that my story can provide you with some hope. For those who need hope and do find some encouragement from my story, then the purpose of writing my journey has been worthwhile.

If you are reading this book because you are on a similar journey, consider yourself a friend of mine. Please reach out to safe people for support, and if you can't find anyone, I can be easily tracked down on the Internet via my home page: **www.ajourneytowards.life**. You are too valuable and precious no matter how little you or others value you. You are much loved.

Those who know me know that I rarely swear in public, but in this book, I have used language that may seem unusual for me and may be offensive to some. This in itself demonstrates the intensity of this emotional journey.

To maintain the privacy of various people in my life, names have been changed as appropriate. I have, however, left out my ex-wife's name, but she is readily identifiable due to my profile locally in Australia. While I have attempted to fairly represent events, the words and representations are mine and mine alone, and I do apologise to her if she feels I have not fairly represented the conversations and events with balance and due respect. She is a private person, which has been one of the challenges for me in writing this narrative and for her in knowing of this project and the resulting work. So, to that end, I would be grateful if the media do not approach her for her insights or perspectives on this story. If her position changes, I will update the website associated with my memoir.

Also, in relation to my children, if the media has any questions, I would appreciate them contacting me to seek approval for communication. My kids have their own lives and are developing their own stories. I will forever be a part of their lives, and this book represents an insight to a part of their back story, but my journey does not, and should not, define them. My hope and prayer for them is to find their own place in the world and have their own passage of life, and we will always remain connected through our collective journeys.

Different readers like to follow stories in different ways. I have written this story chronologically; however, there are some flashbacks—hopefully, in context. For those who struggle with flashbacks (non-sequential), I hope the relevance of their inclusion doesn't distract you from following the narrative.

We are, I think, still a while away from seeing full acceptance in society of LGBTIQA+ people, and we continue to see many culture and faith communities rejecting LGBTIQA+ people based, in my view, on a misunderstanding of them and the misuse of religious texts—hence the ongoing importance of these stories.

This is my personal story, and no two journeys in life are the same. If you find yourself in any distress when reading this book, that might be a sign that it could be useful for you to contact a professional for assistance. One option might be your local doctor or general practitioner, who may or may not then refer you to another professional, such as a psychologist or psychiatrist, depending on your unique situation. There is absolutely no shame in taking this step. If, however, the distress becomes overwhelming, please call your local mental health crisis support centre by phone—such as LifeLine in Australia on 13 11 14—or visit your local hospital emergency care centre urgently. You are too valuable to be distressed.

This book connects my life as a Christian with my business life, my family life—in its various phases—my sexuality and my mental health issues. During the review of this book, and the various editorial processes, there was some feedback that suggested the pointers to my experience of emotional abuse didn't seem to marry up with the consequences that it has had on my life. However, I decided in writing this book that the main focus is not about emotional abuse, so I have made an intentional decision not to fully explore that. For me, emotional abuse has been one of the hardest things to accept, and it has had a dramatic impact on my mental health and its recovery. I hope you will accept the existence of this when it is referenced and accept my decision not to fully explore or share all the details. If this story leaves you wondering about the reality of the impact, extent or relevance of it, then I can only apologise up front, but there are some aspects of my story that I do wish to remain in full control of.

Throughout this book, I will be using the abbreviation LGBTIQA+, which is generally used more in Australia than anywhere else in the world, where the abbreviation LGBTQA+ is more common. LGBTIQA+ stands for Lesbian, Gay, Bisexual, Transgender, Intersex, Queer—sometimes Questioning—Asexual and other sexually or gender diverse people. The Intersex community tends to come under the broader banner for support in the Australian context, but this is not without its struggles and controversy at times. The Intersex community is different: they have straight and non-straight people, but in many ways, they are even less understood by the broader community than the rest of the 'letters'.

For the LGBTIQA+ people who have come before me—in particular, those of faith—thank you for your passion, fights and persistence. For those who come after me, please remember ...

'We can't change the past, but we can influence the future!'

With love,

13

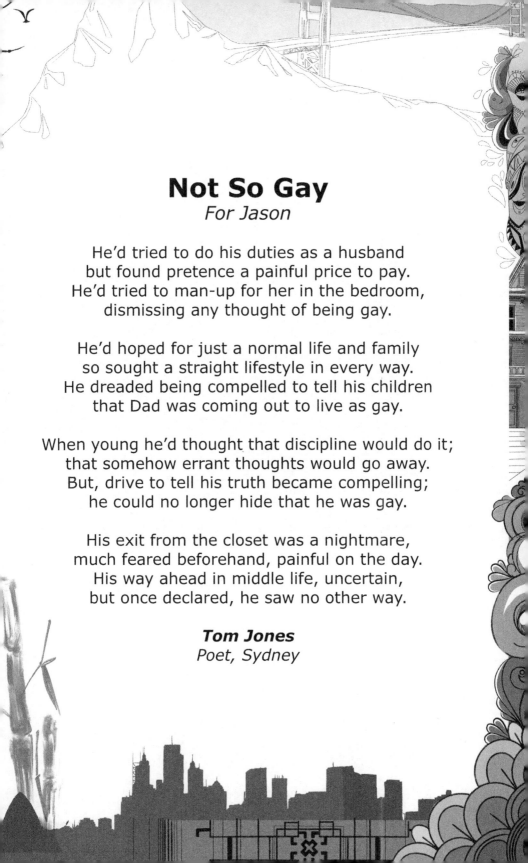

Not So Gay
For Jason

He'd tried to do his duties as a husband
but found pretence a painful price to pay.
He'd tried to man-up for her in the bedroom,
dismissing any thought of being gay.

He'd hoped for just a normal life and family
so sought a straight lifestyle in every way.
He dreaded being compelled to tell his children
that Dad was coming out to live as gay.

When young he'd thought that discipline would do it;
that somehow errant thoughts would go away.
But, drive to tell his truth became compelling;
he could no longer hide that he was gay.

His exit from the closet was a nightmare,
much feared beforehand, painful on the day.
His way ahead in middle life, uncertain,
but once declared, he saw no other way.

Tom Jones
Poet, Sydney

The Christian Assembly Fiasco: How Did I Get Here?

My head was exploding. There are only so many times you can survive a metaphorical hammer hitting your head, especially after the ordeal I had been through.

Whack.

Whack.

Whack.

Cars and trucks were streaming down the multi-lane highway only metres away as I grimly held on to a thin tree and tried to remember how to breathe. But did I really want to breathe? Would it have been simpler not to have grabbed on and continued to move towards the road instead … and then in front of the line of traffic moving past?

Yet, holding on, I heard voices getting closer and closer.

'Jason, please stop! Jason!' They were panting as they ran towards me, trying to make me stop ahead of the traffic that was literally beside me. I had kept going as they'd chased me, but now I was stationary, unsure of my next move, and the voices got closer.

Why am I here?

The hammer in my brain kept beating.

For some reason, I had seen the thin tree and grabbed on to it before I got to the footpath, before the road.

I was struggling to breathe.

I held onto the tree for dear life.

I concentrated on my breathing.

I tried to reconnect to my present surroundings and breathe again.

One of the state leaders, puffing and panting, called out, 'He has stopped! He has been stopped!' He tried to reassure me, and the other people who had chased me, after I'd stormed out of the meeting, kicking open and damaging a large, wooden door at the back of the conference room as I went.

Trying desperately to comfort me, my pursuers, who had now caught up, helped me to slow my breathing and relax while I still gripped on to the tree. When I finally came back mentally to where I was and oriented myself, my first words were, 'Well, I have made a right, royal example of myself now, haven't I?'

A church minister I had not met before—although I vaguely knew of her on Facebook as being an LGBTIQA+ minister from Victoria—broke the ice. 'No, Jason. When I did, several assemblies ago, what you just did, the ABC TV News was filming. They recorded the lot and played it on the television, seemingly for days.'

Slowly, I released my grip on the tree, and I was guided back to Lower Hall of the large Town Hall complex in Box Hill. As we walked, the ministers tried to help me calm down and gather myself as I sought to find that critical internal safety that I so desperately needed.

As I sat in Lower Hall, people milled around in the exhibition space as the catering team geared up for the dinner break. I could sense that everyone knew what had happened, and I imagined that they must have been talking about me. My constant companion, whom I called 'shame', reappeared. I was swamped with berating thoughts as the negative emotions unveiled themselves and continued to pierce my heart. It was a bombardment of guilt.

You've made an absolute fool of yourself.

You've destroyed the advocacy objectives you came here for.

Even the other LGBTIQA+ people will be nervous of being seen with you now.

You know this outburst will get back to your professional world with all of the negative consequences involved.

You looked like a raging idiot.

The hammer started its destructive melody in my head again.

Whack.

Whack.

Whack.

Box Hill Town Hall, dating back to 1872, was the meeting place of the Uniting Church in Australia—there was no church facility large enough or with the flexibility of space and number of rooms needed to run the week-long meeting—and it hosted the tri-annual Assembly in the winter of 2018. It was also where plenary meeting sessions were held for the national parliament of Australia's third largest Christian denomination. It was day six of the week-long Assembly meeting, and I, like most people, was clearly already exhausted from the discussions, debates and voting, all based primarily around whether or not the Uniting Church should allow same-gendered people to be married in the Church.

You might wonder why this was all so important to me. Well, at 54, I separated from my wife of twenty years, as the continual rejection of who I was became too much. In the previous years, my mental health had suffered as I struggled to come to terms with something that is now obvious and has been since before I was even ten years old: I was gay. But being gay was not acceptable on so many levels. After coming out, I entered into what seemed like a war zone of LGBTIQA+ issues in Australia, with marriage equality taking centre stage the very next year in 2017 and then this Assembly in 2018.

Three weeks before I was holding on to the tree in so much distress, I was at home in Sydney with a bout of influenza, sitting in my lounge chair with the air conditioner on heat mode because winter was in full force. I was feeling physically challenged and rather sorry for myself when the phone rang. 'Hi Jason,' said the caller from the Synod Office (State Office). 'Would you be available the week after next to attend the Assembly meeting? One of the NSW/ACT members can no longer attend, and you are next on the list.'

Without thinking, I said yes, as I knew that my diary was relatively free, and although I would have to cancel a couple of meetings, I knew this Assembly would be important. Six months before, after a horrendously stressful national public postal vote, the Australian Parliament had changed the Australian Marriage Act to allow same-sex couples to marry. The public voted strongly in support of marriage equality—so strongly, in fact, that many Christians must have voted in favour.

The Uniting Church came into existence through a merger of the Methodist, Congregational and about 75% of Australia's Presbyterian Churches in 1977. While considerably smaller than the Catholic and Anglican Churches in the country, it remains the largest provider of social welfare and aged care in the country. Theologically, it is more progressive than its larger counterparts, but with pockets of strong conservatism within, it makes discussions around LGBTIQA+ people at the national level usually quite challenging. This has been the case for its forty years of existence, but it had never been personal before. So, when I received that phone call, I knew that marriage equality was going to be on the Church's agenda, and I really wanted to take up the opportunity to participate in the discussions.

I pushed the physical implications of my illness aside

and commenced with travel arrangements, filling in various forms and downloading apps to start reading all the papers that were to be associated with the Assembly. There were a considerable number of reports and an even larger number of proposals.

As the weekend drew closer, my anxiety returned from having campaigned the year before in the only public postal vote in Australia's history on a matter of social justice—I will speak more of this later. At the time, as a vocal campaigner in my local federal electorate, I had received many harsh, negative messages via social media and even some death threats. However, I was determined to take part, and I discovered that, a few months prior to the upcoming Assembly, a working party compiled a report after they had spent the previous six years researching, consulting and studying the issue of same-gender marriage. Finally, this report and its proposal were made available on the Assembly's website for everyone to see: it recommended changing our definition of marriage from being a legal agreement between 'a man and a woman' to 'two persons'.

On Facebook, I saw some very negative reactions from the conservative end of the Uniting Church to the recommendations. There were threats to leave the denomination and a general rejection of the report.

Why do these people seem to hate me and the LGBTIQA+ community so much and with so much venom? was all I could seem to think. *Why can't they see that I am also fully formed as a Christian?*

Based on prior Assemblies that addressed issues of LGBTIQA+ inclusion, I realised that I would now be caught up in the same issues. These talks had previously been described to me as 'full and frank' discussions, yet others might have described the approach and antics as 'ugly church politics'.

As I ruminated over these thoughts, my anxiety levels

increased, and I needed to do something about it; I only had a week to go until I departed for the meeting.

Fortunately, on the Monday before I had to leave, I had an appointment with my psychologist, Michael. We discussed my general progress and, towards the end of the session time, I raised the issue of the imminent, week-long Assembly meeting. We chatted about my anxiety and techniques that I might consider using to help manage what would be a highly emotional period. Also, one of the issues we had been discussing for a while had been my perfectionism traits, and we considered what implications they might have for me at the Assembly.

As a professional, I would never want to walk out of a meeting. Yet, for the sake of my own mental health—which had taken a battering over recent years—and looking at what might happen, I realised that I needed to give myself permission to leave the meeting if, at any point, I felt that my well-being was at risk. I knew this would be hard, but my professionalism and my self-imposed standards would have to come second to my own health for the first time. This was a new skill that I had to add to my toolkit of survival techniques.

I also talked to a theologian and friend about methods I could use to survive Assembly, but one suggestion I had to reject. It was the concept of building a community with other LGBTIQA+ members, but I knew that if I became distressed, it would likely rub off on them too. So, I needed other communities with whom to build bonds within the membership of the Assembly, and some ideas were explored with regards to how I could achieve this support—I couldn't shake the feeling that my professionalism, spirituality, sexuality and my mental health were all going to intersect in an explosive way during the following week.

The first few days were very hard because they included me sharing a small part of my personal story—part of my own life experience—with the entire Assembly and all the visitors. 'I hope none of you here,' I said, 'have to make the choice that I had to make, which was for my kids to either have no living dad or to have a gay dad.'

After my short speech, I needed to retire from the meeting for the first time in order to take a small break; I hadn't anticipated how stressful it would be telling even this little part of my story in under three minutes, yet it was such a strain to be vulnerable in this very public way. I was eventually found by a chaplain, who provided valuable care and support as we talked through the evening's presentations and speeches. Stories are a key part of the biblical narrative, and storytelling has been used from Jesus' days to convey messages of hope and love from God. So, why shouldn't I use the same methods when explaining my support for marriage equality in the Church? Some people there did see the human side, and they acknowledged that we weren't discussing some theoretical, esoteric, theological construct; we were discussing the connection between LGBTIQA+ people and our God.

However, the day after my personal and emotional speech, I received numerous responses. Some people were not able to look me in the eye, while others came up and thanked me for sharing. They went on to admit that, with a number of other short stories they'd heard from LGBTIQA+ people and their allies, they recognised they needed to rethink their position and theology. Some were scared, but, having heard the stories, perhaps they knew that they needed to shift their conservative position against the idea and become more open to the possibility of supporting same-gender marriage. Many of these people came from theologically conservative parishes or organisations, and it is my belief that they felt their employment or roles would be at risk should their vote for the possibility of same-gender marriage be visible.

Apart from the committee commissioned by

prior Assemblies to review the theology and make recommendations to this Assembly, many other members had put forward their own motions for consideration. The proposer and seconder were both given an opportunity to present their motions and encourage support. It was interesting to hear.

There was one motion from two LGBTIQA+ people calling for same-gender marriage, and there was another from a group who thought the matter should be referred to every synod, presbytery and parish to vote upon. To me, this was simply a ruse of sorts because this issue had already been deferred from prior Assemblies. In my mind, this stemmed from former Australian Prime Minister Tony Abbott, who came up with the idea of forcing a national vote to change the Marriage Act as a delaying tactic when Parliament could have simply passed the legislation on marriage equality.

There was another motion for same-gender marriage, which was sponsored by a non-Anglo person. This was encouraging, as there had been a perception that the non-Anglo members of the Uniting Church would be against the proposition.

Then there was the expected proposal from the very conservative arm of the Church to enforce the current, archaic definition of marriage. These people worked very hard to try to frustrate and stall the discussions on marriage in the Assembly, which became a challenge for me.

I was surprised at how negatively I responded to another presentation from the non-Anglo community to reject the changes and retain marriage between a man and a woman. It was hard to read their proposal, not only because of the grammar, but because of the theological intent. When they presented, the speaker lacked confidence to deliver their position in English, and their message was via a translator. Sometimes, messages get a little lost in translation. However, like many others in the hall, I recoiled at the harshness of their intention to oppose marriage equality in the Church.

Then, finally a proposal was made for Assembly simply to defer, with a list of justifications provided; from my perspective, this was yet again simply a delaying tactic on this issue.

The main proposal from the working party and all of the additional proposals showed that we were going to be in for a challenging and difficult week.

The next day, there were a number of conversations about safety. Members of the Assembly heard the stories of their LGBTIQA+ peers and from members who had LGBTIQA+ children or siblings. God's spirit was moving among them, and with that came threats to their relationships and even to their employment.

Feedback was provided to the leadership of the Assembly, and a subsequent motion was put to the members that, from that point onwards, all discussions on the issue of marriage would be held in private—under the orders of the Uniting Church, a meeting of any council can be held in private. This means that only members of that council, and others permitted by the members for the orderly running of the meeting—such as the video and audio support staff—can be in attendance. We usually make decisions by consensus through voting cards; however, there is the option of formal voting by secret ballot. At the time, I thought this was necessary, but it was only when I started writing my story here that I discovered the limitation.

As the week progressed, there was movement. The theologically conservative members didn't want any change. Another group of traditionalists, I think, sensed the mood of the meeting, and they started a series of negotiations. This group wanted to be able to return to their parishes and say, 'We retained the 1995 decision on marriage between a man and a woman.' The trade-off was a second marriage rite that would allow same-gender marriage in the Church and its building if a minister's theology allowed for it and only if that parish allowed such marriages. It was a step away from a new, single marriage rite, but maybe this was the way forward to allow some Uniting Church ministers and some parishes to allow same-gender marriage within the Church.

As with all compromises, people at each end were not happy. Even though the conservatives would not have to perform a marriage of two people of the same gender, the fact that other ministers in the denomination could do so sent some of them off the deep end; it was as though they would fight to the death to prevent others from exercising their theology and conscience.

Some of the LGBTIQA+ community—myself included—saw the six years of study and reflection by the Assembly's working party as a good and balanced outcome even though that didn't meet full equality—it was already a compromise. But further compromises had to be made, and in the end, what was being negotiated, in reality, wasn't too far from the original recommendations.

As the week progressed, I found myself getting more and more worked up as I became angrier and more resentful. There were sessions when it seemed the conservatives were speaking endlessly, fighting to ensure that marriage equality within the Church would not happen. Many delegates from the state where I grew up in South Australia formed a seemingly endless queue to speak to the Assembly as they tried to justify why we shouldn't be allowed to marry within our much-loved Uniting Church. Each speech was like a hammer hitting my brain.

Whack.

Whack.

Whack.

Following my psychologist's recommendations, and for

the sake of my own mental health, I walked out of the Assembly meeting for the second time. As I walked around outside after collecting my afternoon tea, I decided that my main goal was to stay away from people as much as I could because I was getting increasingly distressed.

During the Assembly and apart from the plenary sessions, we were placed in working groups of around fifteen or so people. This allowed for more intimate discussions on complex issues and for people to listen more closely to matters including the theological and faith views of others. My diverse working group consisted of several LGBTIQA+ people or allies, an Aboriginal person, a person from the South Pacific and others from the progressive through to the very conservative end of the Church. The debate went on.

Whack.

Whack.

Whack.

The hammer in my head was striking its familiar beat again.

Despite being on the opposite side of the debate, one of the conservative members from my working group and I had genuine, open conversations to try to hear and better understand each other's perspectives. As a result, we developed mutual respect for one another. Eventually, as I hid outside after wandering past the electrified railway tracks, this conservative member, who was a fellow South Australian, saw me wandering discombobulated, and he offered some comfort. He tried to assure me that I would still be welcome in South Australia and that there were parishes that would be affirming of same-gender marriage. He prayed for my peace.

Reluctantly, after prayers, support and encouragement, I went back in to hear the rest of the speakers. Negative again. Where were all the allies—those who were supporting the concept of marriage equality earlier in the week—and why weren't they speaking now that it was later in the week? The hammer continued to beat.

Whack.

Whack.

Whack.

In most sessions, members are reminded that all are welcome at God's table in the Church and that Bible studies guide us towards inclusion and hope. The welcome and inclusion at this particular meeting was meant to include LGBTIQA+ people. But something happened on the Friday afternoon—as it happened in a private session, I am not allowed to disclose the details of what transpired in the room. The rules of private sessions, which are designed to protect people to follow the calling of the Holy Spirit, have been turned on their proverbial head. As a consequence, I am not allowed to describe what I believe was abuse towards the LGBTIQA+ community by one of the speakers.

What became even more frustrating for me was that part of a confidential session involving me and my reaction to the speaker was discussed on a Christian news website. One writer was factually incorrect—and not in the room, so someone else breached the confidentiality of the meeting to them—and another, who was a member, was attempting to correct the facts. This meant that the privacy of the session had been broken. However, I, the injured party, was not allowed to write or talk about the event that transpired, and, for me, this became another form of abuse and actually further traumatised me. But, as with my journey of life, I continued to try to be acceptable to others. The oppressors broke the rules and seemingly got away with it, but I, looking for that acceptance, continued to diligently follow the rules yet again, adding to my own hurt and mental health consequences. My emotional state in the meeting was already so fragile, and this event became the proverbial straw that broke my camel's back.

I want to explode. But I can't. My safety seems to be the most critical thing. How can I be acceptable in front of all these people? Am I not Christian? Am I not acceptable to God, to my church and to the community?

My very existence was now being challenged.

I was prepared to debate the theology of marriage, but, in my mind, the theology of the reality and acceptance of LGBTIQA+ people in the Uniting Church was settled thirty years ago. I was tired, exhausted and emotionally drained, so I stormed out of the meeting place, using my foot to kick open the old, heavy wooden doors, and my face scrunched up in utter discontent. Apparently, I damaged the doors, but I felt no pain and did not care.

As I walked through the foyer, my mental health was in grave danger. I could sense the heat and absolute rage boiling up inside me. I barrelled my way out through the foyer where there were people mingling and wandering around, looking surprised or shocked as I fumed my way through. They had no way of knowing what had just transpired in the private session behind those heavy doors.

I suppose the speech I had given earlier on in the meeting, where I had shared my vulnerability and where I had opened up about my occasional suicidal tendencies, caused people to follow me out of the meeting hall, calling my name. I ignored them. I stomped through the front doors of the building and across the portico, across the grass, and I headed straight towards the busy main road. Vehicles were moving at speed down the lanes. There were cars, buses and trucks, and their noise was dulled in my head by the hammer smashing against my brain. The issues of my acceptability, my very existence, had come into the debate.

Whack.

Whack.

Whack.

My body burned with rage. I had no fear—not even of walking right out into the middle of the road and into moving traffic.

Three ministers from varying levels of the Church hierarchy were careening full speed across the grass as they chased me, as was a member from my own parish—one of the chaplains who had been supporting me. I knew I was causing a bit of a scene, but all I could think was, *I don't fucking care!* What had happened was, in my mind, simply unacceptable. The hammer in my head was smashing my brain and my brain was screaming out from the pain I was feeling. I was mortified. I was angry. I was distressed. Oh, God, how I was distressed! And, I was heading towards the main road.

'Jason, please stop! Jason!' the ministers shouted. But, I just kept going.

Why am I here?

The hammer in my brain kept pounding.

Eventually, the people who chased after me helped me to calm down by talking to me, and they helped to guide my breathing from shallow and dangerous breaths to steady breaths that eventually slowed down my heart rate. After I was able to release my hands from the trunk of the tree, they guided me back to Lower Hall to further recover from this dramatic episode. They found a chaplain to sit with me, and for a while, we talked; otherwise, we sat in silence. My seemingly unavoidable companion, shame, had arrived in my head once again.

After some time, the senior state leader came to me and said, 'The president is asking for all members to return to the meeting as we are getting towards the voting stage, and the process is commencing.' So, I headed back into the plenary hall. We agreed that, rather than sitting at the front table where I had originally been, I should move and sit at one of the back-row tables with the chaplains. There, I would also be surrounded by some of the ministry leaders from my state and an LGBTIQA+ minister from my synod, who was one of the key LGBTIQA+ leaders in the debate.

There were various procedural motions, and as my head continued to spin from what had happened earlier, I struggled to understand—high-end church procedures are complicated at the best of times! Given that my head was still reeling, I wonder now if I voted in the most optimal way, but, in the end, it didn't matter; the decisions were clear. Any tactical voting 'mistakes' I may have made didn't change the overwhelming wave of moving forwards.

Assembly broke for dinner, and I still felt somewhat isolated. Talking to my spiritual mentor the week before attending this event, we had discussed who I could seek support from when I needed it, and he naturally raised the suggestion of the other LGBTIQA+ members. I'd said they would be supportive, but if I was having issues, I knew that even the more seasoned LGBTIQA+ people would be struggling in their own ways with the challenges of being part of a minority; I didn't want to lean on them for support—we were all becoming weary and weak.

Six months earlier, we had finished the horrendous campaign in Australia regarding this very issue of marriage equality, which had been passed in Parliament during the previous December. Many of us had been actively involved in that campaign, with some of the LGBTIQA+ leaders taking a national leadership role in the Australian postal survey for marriage equality. Now I was basically just trying to exist.

My mentor had looked at the list of chaplains, and he had identified those who would be allies of the LGBTIQA+ community. He recommended that I seek them out early, so they could get to know me in case I needed them, and it was well and truly obvious now that I desperately needed them. I continued to feel isolated at dinner, but it was potentially self-isolation due to my own self-imposed lack of acceptability of my very public outburst, which I worried had damaged our cause.

Shame. Shame is a regular visitor to members of the LGBTIQA+ community, and shame had reappeared to what it saw as its rightful place in my life.

The meeting continued, and it remained very tense for me as we wound our way to the final voting process. My heart pounded and the metaphorical hammer was cocked, ready to smash my brain some more if the vote was lost.

Eventually, after a very tense meeting session that evening, the result was announced. The Church would allow two forms of marriage rite: one being the pre-existing practise that the conservatives didn't want changed, and a second rite that permitted same-gender marriage.

This was extraordinary. But I could feel nothing—it had all been too much.

The previous November, I had celebrated in the park when we had watched the postal survey results being announced. Later that evening, Oxford Street—one of the main streets of the amazing Sydney Mardi Gras Parade—had been closed at the last minute, as there was a spontaneous march down it in celebration. I had finished the night strong, doing what I never did as a youth, which was sitting in a park with my friends and drinking champagne straight from the bottle.

Yet, after campaigning for months during the national postal survey, I'd later received some horrible communications and messages about my direct campaigning, and I'd had to sustain months of abusive and false advertising by those against marriage equality.

So the night this new result regarding the marriage rites was announced, there was no celebration, no relief, no feeling, no nothing.

After the finalities of the Assembly on Saturday, I flew home to Sydney, but I needed to be with people. I had dinner that night with some LGBTIQA+ Christian friends, and then I had drinks the next afternoon with a friend and ally.

The next day, I made an appointment to see my doctor, who was understandably worried about my state of mind and health. In the middle of the week, I also managed to see my physiotherapist, as my foot and leg were becoming increasingly sore since I had kicked my way out of that meeting. Thankfully, nothing was broken, but there was probably some bone bruising in my ankle. I also made an urgent appointment with my psychologist, Michael, and we talked about the week's events. As usual, he gently challenged me on the words I used, and I revealed how surprised I'd been by my emotional reaction to telling my vulnerable story given how well prepared I was. Other than two other people, I had never told anyone about my suicide attempts, yet at the Assembly, I had told the group of over 260 people about some of my darkest moments.

Michael and I talked about the 'hammer' in my head and the metaphorical reality of it, and we talked about the voice that wouldn't go away. I cried yet again as I talked about the speech that had led to me kicking the door. But, would I do anything differently in that context? Actually, probably not. I was struggling with perfectionism, and that meant I was looking to have the perfect performance at the Assembly. Yet, I had to remember that I was the new LGBTIQA+ kid on the block—I had only admitted my true orientation just over three years earlier, I was working through my divorce and I was still finding out who the hell I actually was. Additionally, I was supporting my kids as they finished their secondary schooling and started their university lives. Many of the other LGBTIQA+ people at the Assembly had been through this before, but maybe they had the experience to present and appear both ambivalent to the process and passionate for the cause at the same time.

Several weeks later, in the middle of a cold, dark and gloomy Sydney winter, I found the narrow staircase to the meeting rooms associated with Pitt Street Uniting Church, which was right in the heart of Sydney and a block away from Sydney's Town Hall. This meeting was for the members of Uniting Network, the LGBTIQA+ group within the Church, who worked on engaging with the denomination on theological and pastoral issues as they related to LGBTIQA+ parishioners.

As I walked in, people asked me how I was. I responded, 'You know it has been a full-on Assembly when afterwards you have to see your doctor, your psychologist and your physiotherapist!'

Their acknowledgement to my response raised concerns, especially when someone said, 'Well, that is what can be expected. It can be a very *robust* meeting over seven days.'

The New South Wales (NSW) State Parliament is known throughout Australia as the 'Bear Pit' because of the unruly behaviour of members of Parliament towards each other during Question Time. I had hoped a church parliament would be better, but maybe that was because this was my first time attending Assembly, and I was rather naïve. There had been success through the pain and the anguish however. Uniting Church had given ministers and parishes the right to hold same-gender marriages, if performing them was within their conscience.

People were very appreciative of the efforts of the LGBTIQA+ people at the Assembly, so, as they continued to ask how I was, I responded, 'I have had my first good-ish day since returning, but I still have a way to go.'

They told me to look after myself, but for me it was unnervingly raw; my life was still so fragile and new to me. I had only come out a few years earlier after being married for twenty years, and in my journey, that is relatively only a minute since coming out. During the

Assembly, the innocent and new 'me' had been on display in response to the rawness of people pushing against the LGBTIQA+ community.

I still have so much to resolve and learn about myself. I can't be ambivalent, yet what people see is my simplicity. It isn't perfect—I am not perfect—but it is what it is. It is who I am.

I am gay.

I am a Christian.

I am a father.

I have been a husband.

I am still a businessman.

I am who I am.

In the past, I had not been able to accept who I was, but, as I write this, I know that I am starting to be able to do so now. My life of acceptance had to start with accommodating my self-worth and knowing that my local parish church was there for me regardless. My kids believe in who I am, and they support my journey as I continue to seek a life of acceptance. But, what the hell happened in my life, and how did I actually get here?

Humble Beginnings: Childhood

I was born in August, 1962, at Calvary Hospital in North Adelaide. Apparently, I broke the record for birth weight. There had been concerns that Mum might lose the pregnancy, and she had spent most of the last trimester on bed rest under doctor's orders. According to Mum and Dad, my life had a rough start.

My parents married in June, 1961, just over a year before I was born. When she and my dad went on their first overseas trip, Mum was very pissed off to discover she wasn't actually an Australian citizen. You see, my maternal grandfather had travelled to the UK during World War I to try his hand at being an Air Force pilot. However, after regularly crashing planes, he was transferred to driver duties for the senior officers, which, to me, seemed like an odd risk to take! Soon after that, he met and married a nurse, had Mum and then returned to Australia when my mother was about two years of age.

By the time my dad met Mum, she was a divorcée, which was a relatively rare event in Australia during that time. I was told that the solicitor who had managed her divorce was a female—also rare—who later became the first female governor of South Australia, so I have some famous connections.

Mum had moved to a house that was a couple of suburbs

away from Dad's, and she worked in the local grocer's shop post her divorce—it was here that my parents met.

Mum was a strong-willed woman, who certainly didn't need women's liberation, but she assisted the movement simply by being who she was. Later in life, I wasn't willing to use this model or philosophy for my own benefit because, whilst I had her model of being independently unconstrained by any liberation movement, it always seemed to be a step too far for me. There were plenty of strong visible women in society, but I never saw a visible LGBTIQA+ person until much later in life. Even then, the complexity of my multiple traumas meant that I couldn't replicate her model of life for myself.

Mum was in the fashion industry most of her life, and if she wanted to wear trousers, she did. Her early feminist tendencies came out in the 1950s when she had to attend a meeting with the family's business bank manager. She was furious because she had to take her brother along, as the bank manager wouldn't talk to her due to the fact she was a woman—in those days, banking was only for men.

Mum's passion was the rag trade, and she did her apprenticeship with the Myer Emporium in Adelaide. She then managed to find a role in Flinders Lane, Melbourne, which was the epicentre of high fashion in Australia. It must have been handy to be there during the 1956 Olympics in Melbourne; she told me that she had thoroughly enjoyed the games and consequently insisted that my family attend some events at the 2000 Sydney Olympics.

My earliest memories were of her running a dressmaking business at home and having to deal with the mess that I no doubt made. She had a housekeeper, who came in a couple of days a week and who spoke to me in German, as Adelaide had a large Germanic population. As a five-year-old, I could speak the language, but as none of my schools taught it, I unfortunately lost a skill that ultimately may have been useful in my later career.

Seeing the unreliability of income from her business, Mum returned to working at a clothing factory when I was nine years old, as I needed to be moved to a private school from the beginning of Grade 5. Soon, the owners discovered her expertise, and she was moved from the factory floor to an office, where she became the personal dressmaker to the owner's family.

Moving on from there, Mum landed a position at Vogue International as a specialist cutter, and later, she became the first seamstress at the newly developed Flinders Medical Centre, which was connected to Flinders University of South Australia. This role managed all uniforms, adjusting them as necessary, and made special cloths and coverings that were required for operations or other patient needs. This was not far from home, and she remained there until she retired.

Dad, on the other hand, had a very different history, as he came from a troubled family. He grew up in Glenelg, which is a beautiful seaside suburb, and he was an only child. The atrocities of World War I and nuances of post-traumatic stress disorder (PTSD) had resulted in my paternal grandfather turning into an alcoholic. As a consequence of his addiction, his family regularly didn't have money and were forced to move from rental to rental. This meant that they never had a single home they could call their own. My grandfather was in the Gallipoli campaign, which was the ultimate military disaster, but it created the spirit of the Australian and New Zealand Army Corps (ANZAC) in Australia.

ANZAC Day is a deeply significant day in Australia. The commemoration of the failed landing in Gallipoli is Australia's veterans' Memorial Day, and great marches take place through each town and city. Dad had a love-hate relationship with the day, as I think it reminded him of the pains of war. Rarely did he march, but when he did, he would be angry and often drunk, perhaps just like his father had been.

Dad was born in 1925 and was a teenager during most of WWII. He became a King Scout and ran the local Scout troop during the war. Before his eighteenth birthday, he joined the Royal Australian Navy and completed his training at HMAS Cerberus in Victoria prior to moving to Sydney and heading out to sea. When my father was just six years old, the Australian flagship destroyer HMAS Australia visited Adelaide, and an old family photo shows Dad standing aboard the ship that would later have a devastating impact on our lives.

In January, 1944, Dad joined the very same HMAS Australia, which, while not having the fame of other European and Pacific war stories, was notable for a number of key events. For example, in 1942, two Australian Navy men were charged with murder for allegedly killing a fellow sailor, who was going to blow the whistle on their homosexual relationship. Although this was a year or so before Dad's arrival on the ship, the event created significant, international tension between Australia and England. The men were found guilty of murder under British Admiralty law, which was an offence punishable by hanging—this would not have been the case had Australian Naval law applied.

In October, 1944, and soon after my dad had joined the ship, it was hit during the first kamikaze attack of WWII by Japanese planes. Thirty people were killed and more than double that number were injured.

In January, 1945, after a rebuild by the Americans, HMAS Australia was attached to the American Fifth Fleet as part of the campaign for the liberation of the Philippines. Between the 6th and 9th of January, the ship was hit by five kamikazes, and Dad was injured in the attacks. An official telegram was sent to his mother, and his name was recorded in *The Advertiser*—the main morning newspaper in Adelaide.

From the end of the war until his discharge on the 15th of May, 1946, Dad was deployed on several ships, primarily moving around the Indonesian and Borneo regions. Their role was to scout for any Japanese troops who had not yet heard that the Japanese had lost the war, and Dad helped to formalise their surrender, location by location.

Post-war, my father returned to the railways, where he worked for the rest of his life.

As in my grandfather's time, there was no understanding of post-traumatic stress disorder during my father's era, but I think it is highly likely that Dad suffered from it. Like many Australian veterans at that time, he headed 'out bush', working as an assistant station manager in South Australia's country towns before eventually returning to Adelaide, where he met Mum.

For most of my life at home, Dad suffered from stress, and he spent some time in and out of the Daw Park Repatriation Hospital—for war veterans—which was not far from home. His stress added significant pressure to both Mum and me, and his ill health later showed up as kidney and heart problems.

During his working life, Dad worked his way up to middle management in the railways, from starting out as a clerk overseeing the planning of *The Overland*, which was then the daily overnight train between Adelaide and Melbourne. He finished his career as Australian National Railways' marketing manager for Passenger Services. The main benefit I received as a young boy was travelling on the special steam train trips, as he was the railway coordinator with the Historical Railway Society.

Our family, like many other families throughout Australia and around the world, lived for years with the consequences of both world wars. The injuries and scars of the wars, both physical and mental, played havoc with Dad's health and his relationships, particularly with me.

While Mum had some Christian connections through

family friends and through attending Sunday school, she showed little active faith. However, she was supportive of Christianity and encouraged my involvement. Dad, on the other hand, had challenges with religion, with one of his parents being Anglican and the other a Roman Catholic—in those days, it was not acceptable in society to intermarry between different arms of Christianity. During his work life in the railways, employees either needed to be a Catholic or a Mason in order to be promoted, so he reluctantly joined the Masons. As such, he was never a great supporter of my Christian journey.

Dad died in August, 1991, on a caravan trip, two days before visiting me in Sydney on their return to Adelaide from Queensland, where my parents often travelled in the Australian winter—the Australian-Florida escape. He was being interviewed by an author writing a book on HMAS Australia, and he had shared a significant part of his story. Sadly, the book was never completed and published, and the budding author no longer has the audio recording of those interviews. I would have loved to hear more about his life experiences, as he rarely spoke of them with me.

My mother battled on after my father's death, and in 1995 moved to Sydney, where she lived quite happily. It was a special time for her, as she was close to my family for the birth of her two grandchildren. Sadly, she was then diagnosed with breast cancer, which she recovered from after a mastectomy and various other treatments. However, a few short years later, she discovered that she was riddled with secondary tumours, including a brain tumour. She passed away in her sleep in May, 2003.

The Boy Down the Road

Mitchell Park was a quirky suburb, with many of the street names originating from children's names within the Mitchell family—this was the family responsible for subdividing this part of Adelaide to create the suburb in 1912. We lived on the corner of the unusually named 'Thirza' and more commonly known 'Richard' avenues. Most of the homes in our section were subsidised through Defence home loans, and they all looked pretty much the same, with timber frames and asbestos cladding.

Socioeconomically, Mitchell Park was quite poor, but everyone seemed to have a good life. The suburb, however, was split by multiple pieces of infrastructure. The ten blocks surrounding where we lived was completely cut off from the rest of the suburb, but you could always get through by foot or bicycle.

As my parents had married relatively late in life—compared to others in our part of Mitchell Park—I was one of the youngest kids in the area, with the exception of the family two doors down the road, who were of German descent. Our mothers spent time together, and their son Zachary and I would regularly play together, despite me being two years older than him. It wasn't unusual for us to spend the night at each other's homes if something unexpected happened or even if our respective parents just wanted a child-free evening. Occasionally, our mothers would alternate in taking us to the beach, which was a great place for swimming, splashing, being outdoors and making sandcastles.

On one particular weekend when Zachary slept over, the night was uneventful and, in the morning, we woke up and chatted. Then, it was time to change out of our pyjamas and into our clothes for the day. Like most kids, we had seen each other naked many times over the years when we had shared baths and changed in front of each other. I can't remember the exact age—I suspect it was when I was around eight or nine and a prepubescent boy—but we began to look more closely at each other and speak about our private parts. There were a few occasions where we actually touched each other.

My father used to breed fox terrier dogs, and he built a large, fully enclosed puppy kennel behind the shed. Some days when Zachary would come over, we would go to the kennel and pull our pants down, touching and fondling each other. We were aware of the pleasure this brought each of us, but neither of us understood why.

That hot summer, we became more daring down at the beach. The beauty of the Spencer Gulf beaches lies in their limited swell and waves—they really aren't for surfing, which was safe for us. We had goggles and would use them to swim and look for shells and other items on the sandy bottom. As we started to get more daring, we would go out into an area with less people. One of us would dive under the water, pull down the other's bathers, look, touch and then resurface for air. Then it would be the other one's turn.

For some reason, though, these events seemed to just peter out, and that was that. But, we kept playing until I moved schools, and all of the extracurricular activities and new friends of my own age seemed to separate us.

I was about two years old when Mum grew very concerned about me. She would call out my name and I wouldn't respond, so our family doctor referred me to see an Ear, Nose and Throat (ENT) specialist. I was diagnosed as being 'hard of hearing.' In layman's terms, I had 'floppy ear drums', which meant that my hearing would go up and down like a yo-yo. Consequently, I had several minor operations as a young boy. I was taught from an early age to avoid knocks to the head, which, I suspect, is why Mum enrolled me in basketball when I was six years old rather than letting me play Australian Rules Football (AFL). AFL was one of my father's preferred sports, and it had far more physical contact, but little did Mum know about the real levels of contact in basketball!

Due to my hearing issues, I was exempt from the compulsory, annual, medical examinations in the public schooling system. My specialist also wanted me to be seated in the middle of the classroom because my concentration—or lack of—was an early indication that my hearing was heading in a downward spiral. However, the teachers kept putting me in the front of the classroom, so my parents never received the feedback both they and my specialist required.

During recess and lunchtime, there were segregated playing areas for each year or age group. I was pretty much the tallest in my grade at school, and I tended to play mainly with the girls, often engaging in jump-rope games with them. One day, a teacher, who must have been new, told me to stop playing with the girls in the Year 4 area and to go to the oval with the Year 6 and 7 kids. They obviously assumed that was my year group. No matter how much I protested, I was marched off into what felt like 'no man's land'. Needless to say, I was picked on and roughed up. All of this was too much for me and, unbeknown to me, also for my parents, who were already working on a plan to move me to a private school. At the start of Year 5, I was moved to the local, boys' Methodist school, Westminster School, where I was so much happier. There were definitely new experiences in store for me there!

Starting in Year 5, boys were encouraged to commence playing inter-school sport. I took up tennis but didn't make the team in Year 5; however, I did by Year 6. Happily, I did make the basketball 'A' team in Year 5, and I'm so glad I did because basketball soon became one of my passions—later in life, I started coaching basketball for some of the local youth in the community. Even today, although I am unfit, I am still a technical official for the local premier competition in my city.

The next several years went by uneventfully; changing and showers just became normal and nothing special or unusual to think about. The only downer was in prep school and senior school where I was bullied a lot, and I never understood why. Looking back, I have no recollection of anyone taunting me about being 'gay'; in fact, I don't remember anyone being teased like that.

In some ways, though, I was different, and I was easy to 'set off'. I used to physically fight back in the most uncoordinated way, which only seemed to inspire the bullies more. Like most parents of kids being bullied, Mum tried to teach me all the techniques to try not to react: count to ten, 'sticks and stones won't break my bones' and so on. In the end, none of that really seemed to help me. Still, the bullying at my private school was much less than at the public school, so that was a significant improvement and relief.

One school holiday during Year 6, I attended a combined, private school choir camp held at my school's boarding house—this was my first and only experience of living as a boarder, and only for a week, as I was a day boy at my school. Throughout the camp, I was bullied a reasonable amount, and at one point, someone thought it would be funny to put pepper on my pillow. I think it must have been white pepper, as I didn't see it, but the impact was horrible—pepper going into your eyes is extremely painful and very distressing. I remember crying my eyes out, trying to find someone to go to for help. A teacher was eventually found, and they washed out my eyes and the pillow slip was changed. That night I didn't sleep well, as I worried that someone might try something else to hurt me. In the end, it made me feel more isolated and more separated from the other boys. No one was identified as the culprit, but I got through the week although it meant that I never wanted to stay in a boarding house again.

By Year 9 (ninth grade), the bullies had nicknamed me 'Chuck Chunder', and it stuck. Oh, how I hated that nickname! To 'chunder' in Australian vernacular is to vomit or throw up, as my response to being teased or bullied was to 'throw a fit', and that seemed to be the connection. I had developed a good, small group of friends from school and would often spend part of the weekend with them, but the only person outside of school who accepted me was Zachary.

It was around Year 9 that I had another sleepover at Zachary's, and in the morning, we stood facing each other as we undressed, taking off our pyjamas until we were both completely naked. I think that was the first time he had seen another boy whose body was going through puberty.

We obviously didn't bother with scientific terminology and anatomically correct thinking then, but, basically, I had a larger set of testes, a growing penis and the beginnings of a small bush of pubic hair. He seemed to catch himself, a little embarrassed; however, for some reason, I let him know that it was actually okay. I suggested that he came and had a closer look, and I was hoping to get a closer look at him to see where his development was at.

He allowed me to look. He was just starting puberty, and there was a single hair showing. There was tension in the air but still no understanding of its origin. We looked, we studied and then we got dressed. A little spark had been rekindled, and the next time he came over, a little nervous, we went back to the puppy kennel, and again we took turns in lowering each other's pants. This was the beginning of roughly six months of regular 'studying', with neither of us understanding what was happening or why because neither of us understood anything about sexuality or sex.

Every other weekend, and more often during the school holidays, we met in the puppy kennel. My father must have become suspicious at one stage because he would come around more frequently, and we had to pull up our pants quickly.

Over the weeks and months, we became more adventurous. Sometimes, rather than going to the kennel, we would ride our bikes and find somewhere outdoors—maybe a house under construction where we could find a protected spot or a vacant housing block with high grasses and overgrown plants that we could hide behind, staying out of view of passing traffic or pedestrians.

Sometimes, Zachary was nervous of being caught outdoors, but we would continue looking, touching and stroking. Towards the end of this period of adventure, he became braver, and I found it odd that he liked me gently caressing the cheeks of his face with my penis. It was exhilarating, as his soft, smooth, hairless cheeks were like nothing else, but again, our total innocence stopped what would have surely been the next phase. In the mid 1970s, well before the Internet age, neither of us knew about masturbation, so we never discovered that pleasure together.

One day, unexpectedly, he said he wanted to stop, and I never found out why. We decided to have one last adventure, and we got naked in various places in his backyard when his parents were out. His neighbours on the other side were painters, so their backyard was an open storage area, and we jumped the fence and carried on in there. But, Zachary's family had a telescope, which, during those months of exploration, we sometimes got out to look at each other long distance through the windows. That day, we lost track of time, and when Zachary's parents came home looking for us, they found his younger brother with the telescope. Needless to say, fear overtook us all. Zachary and his brother were told to go straight inside, and I was told to go straight home. Zachary's dad was a policeman, and I remember trembling as I hid in my bedroom. The fear that welled up inside me confirmed that what we had been doing was probably not 'normal'.

Indeed, I recalled in that moment the time when I'd been nine years old, and I'd heard about a homosexual university lecturer because he was in the morning newspapers. He had been murdered and his body thrown in the Torrens River, which runs through Adelaide. At the time, the Premier of South Australia was Don Dunstan, whom my father detested with a passion—although I always found it funny that my father also wore those awful safari suits that Dunstan wore. Premier Dunstan decriminalised homosexuality in South Australia in 1975, just after I had turned thirteen. South Australia was the first state in Australia to do so and was possibly one of the first jurisdictions in the western world to make this move. I remember that, at the time, my father had been against this and seemed angry. However, in my innocence and lack of education, I didn't see the connection between these events and who I was. I was so naive.

I know that my father only wanted the best for me, but his own model of life meant that his desires for what he thought was for the best were destructive; a destruction that carried through my entire life. As a thirteen-year-old in distress, I had earlier already approached the chaplain at school wanting to know how I could build some positive connections with my father, and now here I was, terrified about the ramifications of being caught with Zachary.

As I sat on my bed, I heard someone arrive at my house—one of Zachary's parents I assumed—but I didn't know which one, nor did I hear the conversation. Trying to be acceptable had already become an overwhelming driving force in my life, and nothing I had ever done seemed to be good enough. Now, I would be a major disappointment.

Eventually, I was called to the lounge room. It was evening, so the curtains had been pulled, and the room was black and foreboding. Mum sat in her lounge chair on the left side of the room looking towards the television, and Dad sat on the other side. There was a heavy silence as I walked into the room, and I went to sit near to Mum. The air was thick, and panic rose within me as Mum started to talk about Zachary's parent's visit. I just wanted to die and go away; I didn't want to be there. I wanted to disappear. Mum's comments had a sense of balance, but I remember her disappointment that Zachary's younger brother had become involved.

My recollection is that Dad didn't say much, but the little he did say made it clear that these events were unacceptable—I was unacceptable—and 'such activities' were absolutely not to happen again. In fact, he said, 'It would be best if you didn't play or socialise with Zachary from now on.' Looking back, I wonder how much Dad's experience on HMAS Australia, and the stories about the murder of that man at the hands of homosexuals, influenced his context and his attitude. I couldn't explain to my parents why I did those things with Zachary, and I couldn't tell them it made me happy because it seemed that these events were bad and horrible. Therefore, at least in my mind, shame reared its ugly head once more.

Zachary and I saw each other around the streets, and as much as I felt bad at the loss of our connection and our friendship, I could see in Zachary's eyes that he'd had it worse. Was that the consequence of him being the son of a policeman? The South Australian Police Force, like so many around the world at the time, would poorly—if at all—investigate gay bashings and, in some instances, may have even contributed to the occurrences of gay murders. For context, the murder of the Adelaide university lecturer remains unsolved to this day.

Our family were great believers in the growing Australian cinema industry, and we would often go to the movies. A new film called *The Devil's Playground* had been released in August, 1976, around my fourteenth birthday, and it was the first major film by the now internationally acclaimed Australian director, Fred Schepisi.

I don't think Dad had read the reviews, as there were a lot of themes in the movie that related to my time with Zachary. The key protagonist was a thirteen-year-old boy, Tom Allen. At the core of the movie were the rules around puberty and sexuality. In an early scene, Brother Francine found a boy showering without his swimmers on, and he stated how disgusting it was to shower naked. Yet, in the movie, we learned that Brother Francine, while displaying his strident focus on sexual purity for himself and the boys, secretly went to the baths—the local swimming pool—to stare at the women and fantasise about swimming naked with them.

Tom's friend Wazza regularly wrestled Tom, and the winner got to do whatever he liked to the other. There was a subtle sexual undertone, but Tom didn't want anything for his victory.

In a later scene, Wazza and Tom wrestled again, and it seemed that Tom was over the innuendo: he told Wazza to get on with it. Wazza moved to the bushes, dropped his pants and underpants and asked Tom to hold and squeeze his penis. Then, he asked Tom if he could do the same to him. This was very familiar territory. But then, Tom taught me something new when he asked Wazza, 'Is that all?' Wazza was further confused when Tom said, 'Do you want to pull?' and I, sitting in the cinema next to my dad, desperately trying not to squirm and wishing there was a place to hide, had no idea what he was talking about. Yet, I was intrigued even though I clearly needed to ensure that I showed no interest in what was being explored on the big screen. So, I feigned disinterest as Tom explained to Wazza about the benefits of holding on and rubbing up and down the penis until the 'white stuff came out'.

As soon as the movie was over, I my father said, 'I hope that you and the other boys at school have never done that!' I could honestly answer that no, I hadn't, but I had now been given information and knowledge that I desperately wanted to explore. Alas, however, I never would do so with another boy at school, or with another male, for a very long time.

A few days later, and home by myself after school, I entered the bathroom and tried to perform what Tom had taught me. The first time was so scary. My head felt funny, and there was this white stuff that Tom had talked about in the film. However, I was more nervous than anything because my penis seemed to thicken, and I was worried that I had broken something. But ultimately,

Tom began for me what became a life of masturbation; sometimes with me feeling good but, more commonly, with me feeling guilty.

We lived in a close neighbourhood, and it was a community of sharing. Everyone thought they knew everyone's business, but fortunately, no one else knew of the experiences between Zachary and me. The final part of this chapter about the unacceptability of my experiences came when Zachary's family sold their home and moved away without the usual community farewells. At neighbours' barbecues, people asked why they had gone. Why so sudden, and why no farewell? No one knew. But it seemed that I knew—at least in my teenage mind— and I also believed it was my fault, as their family could not be around me anymore. It was yet another vote for the unacceptability of my nature, but this time, it was self-imposed.

Zachary is someone who I often think about, and I wonder what he is doing now. He was one of the first people who seemed to understand me on a different level. He was my very first and last gay experience until after I came out to my family and when I allowed myself to begin living with some semblance of self-acceptance.

Year 10 (Tenth Grade): What a Year!

With my hearing problems and other developmental challenges, I struggled through most of primary school and then into high school. English continued to be a challenge, with the full gambit of writing, spelling and comprehension. I was fortunate that my school had a support unit, and I spent one and a half years of lower high school in the remedial English unit. When returning to my main class in Year 10, I was then able to cope with English studies and subjects that required a lot of writing.

Being at an all-boys school, and with all the sports, changing and showering that we did, sometimes it was a challenge to remain under personal control. We were all a massive, gangly group of raging and uncontrollable hormones, and we were testosterone-filled lads. There seemed to be an unstated rule in the changing shed, however, which allowed for no derogatory comments about bodies.

I became aware that I kept noticing things, such as who was more advanced on the puberty journey than others. Some days, I was aware of going to the showers semi-erect, and I would become scared that others would notice and accuse me of something. This was my own negative consciousness set in motion by my father. The voice in my head was telling me that I was unacceptable, but I still didn't fully understand why.

The year 1977 was seminal for all sorts of activities and reasons. In term one, we had a major, sixteen-day Outward Bound adventure camp. My discovery of masturbation the previous year had become a high frequency pleasure, and it was almost part of my routine when going to sleep every night. Therefore, camp was going to be a challenge for me. My dorm had seven boys in it: me, two others who I got on okay with—but not my best friends—two boys I could tolerate and two who I really didn't like at all. That seemed to be the pattern across all four dormitories.

We had several expeditions, and on those occasions, we all had to share tents. It quickly became obvious to others that I masturbated each night no matter how much I tried to hide it. Most of the boys I didn't worry about sharing with, but there were two who I wondered if something extra might just be possible because of comments they had made over the years. Would I be willing to take the risk?

Towards the end of the camp, I managed to share a tent with one of those friends who had been in another dorm group—our two dorms were working together on this particular expedition. I wondered if this would be the night where we had a rumble in our tent, and I was hoping we would be able to explore and see if we could 'play'.

However, when I got into our tent, I was disappointed to find him already there in his sleeping bag, and I couldn't see any clothes around. I asked him where they were, and his reply was that he was sleeping in them. My heart sank with a thud, but I took my shoes off and hopped into my own sleeping bag also with my clothes on—it was the only time during the sixteen days that I slept fully clothed, and it was an uncomfortable and disappointing night on many counts.

My dorm seemed to have a greater diversity of boys and a greater intolerance for each other compared to the other dorms. We were generally coming last in most competitions, and I was the only boy in the entire class not able to complete the 13 kilometre night run, which only brought more dissent within the dorm. Eventually, somehow, we agreed that there was no way that we would ever all like each other, but there was no reason why we couldn't work together and win some of the camp's competitions. Early reconciliation and some emerging leadership were evident among us. So, with this new purpose forefront in our minds—that we could be symbiotic without friendship—we schemed and became far more tactical and strategic in our approach in all of our remaining activities. Identifying and knowing our own weaknesses, we started to work out how to cover our gaps—or at least minimise their impact—and we commenced the burying of our egos and the playing to the strength of each individual.

We romped to a strong win in that evening's competition, and we became the strongest dorm rather than the weakest. In one of our last competitions at the camp, we divided up the tasks. One lad and I did the orienteering exercise, as we both seemed to have a good grasp of space, geography and time, and we won. While it took until the final term of the year, the realisation of tolerating and working with others became the biggest change in our class moving forwards, and this started to make my life easier. By the final two years of senior school, the bullying had pretty much stopped.

I had always been a better-than-average basketball player, and I always played in my age group's 'A' division at school. In Year 10, playing in the under-fifteens, we often trained with the Open squad, and I managed to make the Open A team for an interstate school carnival in Perth—the capital of Western Australia—in the holiday break after the first term had finished. I suspect my inclusion was partly due to some higher ranked players being unable to go and partly because I could play chess and was willing to fill in for volleyball if needed—multi-skilling outside of the AFL and basketball teams seemed important for selection to make the trip, and it was a fun and enjoyable experience.

My school was well known for its balance between academics, sport, arts and spirituality, and it had a focus on Christianity. It was also well known for its music program. I had started piano lessons when I was younger and was progressing reasonably well. I knew by the end of primary school that I wanted to be in the school orchestra. While there were several of us who played piano in primary school, it was recommended that I continue piano in high school—as well as learning many other percussion instruments, with the whistle being one of my favourites as it often brought a laugh in a concert. The school band undertook a major performance tour each year, and there were lots of rehearsals in the months leading up to this week-long trip.

I never understood why, but one Friday, I was removed from school to see a psychologist, and I had to run through lots of tests. The end result seemed to be that I wasn't intellectually impaired, which was nice to know, and, in fact, it showed that I had significant potential. As this had been a visit through most of the lunchtime and into the early afternoon, I had changed out of my uniform into casual clothes before being taken to the psychologist by Mum. But, when I then turned up after school for a band rehearsal, I felt a little out of place. Everyone else was in their school uniform, and I was wearing my mid 1970s, green, corduroy flared trousers and matching top. My mother's understanding of fashion allowed me to be a little different from time to time. Heck, I was probably the only teenager in my group who owned a purple suit!

At this point in time, the school orchestra had only toured in South Australia, alternating between the western peninsulas of South Australia and the south east. Our school had strong connections with rural communities throughout the state because it was a partial boarding school. As an experience for the day students, and to gain a better understanding of country living, we would be billeted with local families as we toured the country.

My first band tour was to the south east of South Australia, and our initial night was spent in the Coonawarra—what a pity we were too young to drink the globally acknowledged red wines from the region. We hit the first town late afternoon, where the community provided us with a huge country dinner in the community hall. Then, we set up for our opening performance, which ended up being a little rough around the edges. We soon learned that our music master could provide us with 'interesting' signals behind his back while being ever so nice, polite and bubbly to the audience. What the audience didn't know!

While not up to our usual standard, it was good live music that people in country towns would not get very often, so our performances were honestly appreciated. We were allocated our partners from the band, and late in the evening, we all piled into our billets' cars and drove off to their homes. We arrived in the pitch black of night, and that special darkness of Australia is where you get to experience the Milky Way and the grandeur of volume and depth of the stars. As city boys, these were infrequent visual experiences.

It turned out that our host was only expecting one boy and not the two of us who had been assigned to them, so the room we were given had a double bed. In the country and poorer areas, it was common for brothers to share beds, so they saw no issues, and the other band member, who had grown up in the country, seemed fine with the arrangements. I, however, felt strangely uncomfortable. My brain was saying, *If I share a bed with another boy, what would this mean?* This was a completely self-imposed fear—where did this come from?

We got through the night and, in the morning, my band buddy seemed unusually rude. I started to take offence for some reason, but the reality is that I probably didn't see that he may well have been reacting to my self-imposed protective attitude that I was completely unaware of at the time.

We moved to another town, and I shared the billet with the same band member, but fortunately not the bed this time. Again, there was a real strain between us, and, I would accept, it emanated completely from me. Was there a subconscious, self-protection mechanism in play that I didn't see or wouldn't acknowledge?

As we got ready to board the bus for the next town, it surprised the school staff to see the band member and me arguing—something neither of us had done in our entire school life—so we were separated for future accommodation.

Soon, it was another town, another billet, and this time I was sharing a room with one of the boys in the family, who was a year or so younger than me and who attended the local, rural high school. We walked around the town together after school with his friends. Just in the way that he talked with his group of friends, which included guys and girls, I could tell that he seemed so much more sexually advanced than me.

After dinner, his mother ran him a bath and suggested we share, and again this was not uncommon in the country for teenage boys. Many of us on the tour had not showered ... me included. When you're a fourteen-year-old boy, why bother showering if you can get away without having one? So a bath was definitely needed; however, the boy was very cute, so I felt it would be too awkward to bathe with him. I was offered a shower while he was in the bath, but I felt I needed to reject that as well.

After his bath, I cleaned my teeth and changed into

my pyjamas. This was the night that I also discovered pornography. Under my bed was a box full of porn: magazines with pages and pages of pictures of young women, and not a man in sight. His mum unexpectedly came into the room because she was concerned that, with all the boxes stuffed under my bed, I would be uncomfortable. We were both terrified, and the boy started to reassure his mother that the boxes weren't a problem. I really didn't trust him and was worried that I would get into trouble at my own school or, in the worst-case scenario, be sent home if the pornography was discovered. So, I helped him to convince her that I was comfortable, and she left. Then, we continued to look through the contents of the box, but I didn't really like it. I'm not sure if it was the dishonesty, the inappropriateness or that I just wasn't keen on looking at women's bodies. The picture that is embedded in my memory is of a young girl. She must have been younger than us, as she had no pubic hair and no breasts, but she did have searing eyes. I hated that picture. It was exploitation—that much I knew—but that picture gave me the excuse to stop looking at the porn in the box.

During that year, as well as band experiences, I found myself involved in a huge amount of extracurricular activities. In the midst of this, I asked Mum if I could join the youth section of St John's Ambulance. For some reason that I did not understand, she thought I was doing too much, and she actively discouraged me. However, it still took a visit to the family doctor for me to be convinced that I should not add St John's to my extensive list of activities.

It is interesting, for me, looking back at the patterns of one's life. It is now clear to me that the major periods of mental health issues also seemed to relate to periods of significant activity—I was avoiding things. Not only my sexuality, but also my father, who, in my mind, and no matter how hard I tried, never felt that I was doing well enough. This would result in devastating explosions during two later stages in my life. Unfortunately, doctors weren't as well trained in mental health and family dynamics as they are now. The bullying at school had died down during the year, but there were still a number of other significant events during this time period. Looking back to these moments in my life, I wonder if I was already starting to develop one of my survival mechanisms of travel and generally getting away; perhaps, just like the WWII veterans heading to the bush upon their return.

I loved going to Broken Hill. I don't think Poppa—my grandfather on my mother's side—played favourites among his grandchildren, but I was a very regular visitor and was always made to feel special. I have since learned that families often have patterns that repeat. I discovered later in life that Poppa had run away from Broken Hill when he was about 15 to the West Coast of South Australia—the inference being there was some troubling family dynamic, but the real issue was never disclosed or known. After the death of Mamma—his wife and my grandmother—when I was about four, he remained in Adelaide until he decided to marry a woman he met who was also formerly from Broken Hill. They decided to relocate back there because she still had a lot of family there. They made the move just after I came out of hospital, around my ninth birthday, and I was in bed when he arrived to share the news. I heard his voice, so I ran to the lounge room to say hello. However, Mum sternly told me to say hello and go back to bed. After that, I heard lots of loud voices, so I hugged my teddy bears as I worried about what was going on. I did hear Mum complaining about him not visiting me in hospital or doing anything for my birthday, so I imagine that was why she was cross.

From the Year 5 September school holidays, I started travelling the seven and a half hour trip to Broken Hill by bus on my own, where I stayed with Poppa and his second wife, who I had named Nana May. Broken Hill is an old desert mining town. All around is that famous never-ending red soil, and the kerbs in the town are very high because when it rains, it really pours. One day after a massive rain storm, we drove around to see the damage. I called out to Poppa, asking him what the red metal on the road in the distance was. As we drove up closer to it, we discovered it was the roof of a Mini Minor. The road had collapsed and the water had swollen up around it.

I found travelling to Broken Hill with Mum and Dad more challenging; it always seemed to be stressful. Maybe it was having to travel in the small car up and back, or maybe I picked up on the strained relationship between Mum, Poppa and May. But when I went by myself, it was always bliss; I was away from home. There was a tree house in the backyard, and I could spend hours up there dreaming and playing. Sometimes, Poppa would come out to see if I was okay. I think he wondered how I could play by myself for so long.

Other days, we would go out to the Royal Flying Doctor Service, the School of the Air, or further out to Silverton before it became famous from the *Mad Max II* movie. Or sometimes, we drove to the Menindee Lakes. Once, we did a mine tour and almost got blown up due to a safety break down!

Poppa and Nana loved playing bowls, so some afternoons, I would go with them and watch them at the bowling club, then we would have dinner. After that, I would sit around whil they played the poker machines.

On Nana's side I had a few step-cousins, one of whom was my age. I saw him a lot because he would also come to Adelaide. Another step-cousin was a year or so older, and I liked to spend time with him too. They provided some other wonderful experiences as well whenever I visited Poppa. The step-cousin I liked the most would play golf with me on the South Broken Hill Golf Course, where the fairways were red dirt, and all bar the last hole's greens were actually fine grey sand from the mine slag heaps. The 18th hole did have a proper green though.

Many times, I spent the day at my other cousin's, and a certain memory from those days probably triggered my interest in justice. Whenever I was with them on pay day and it was getting towards the end of my uncle's shift, we were all put in the car and driven to the north mine gates. Then, we would wait outside with all the families to pick up my uncle. One time, I asked my auntie why we only did this on certain days and not on others. She said, 'Broken Hill has more pubs and poker machines per head of population than anywhere else in New South Wales. If the men aren't picked up'—remembering in those days that people were paid in cash—'they would go straight to a pub or club and drink all their wages or put it into the pokies.'

As the summer of 1977 came to an end, Poppa got very sick. One early morning, while I was up and practising my piano, Dad came into the family room to let me know that Poppa had died. Poppa's death was the second funeral in my life; my first had been a friend from school, who I had known since I was nine—he had died in an accident a year earlier. With my friend, I was encouraged to attend his service at the school chapel, but I wasn't allowed to go to his burial. This time, though, for Poppa, the family travelled together to Broken Hill for his funeral and his burial.

There are two major memories of this for me. The first was after our arrival when we had put our bags in the rooms we were going to be sleeping in at Poppa's and Nana's and I walked into the lounge room. It was full of men, and I recognised all of them except one. Being a tired and a brash teenager, I asked the stranger, 'Who are you?' It turned out that he was my Uncle Jack, Poppa's son and my mum's brother. I really couldn't be bothered to be embarrassed.

The second memory epitomises the many unique things about Broken Hill. As Poppa's funeral cortège drove down Argent Street, the main street in town, all the shopkeepers pulled down their blinds and everyone walked out from the buildings and stood as the funeral cars drove through with their lights on. It was a very poignant moment in saying goodbye to a special person in a special place.

Our First Nation Aboriginal people often talk about their connection with the land that they never actually ceded. As a descendent of free colonisers, horrified about what was done to the Aboriginal people, I have a small insight into the connection they speak of. For me, getting out into the desert and being in Broken Hill, as I have continued to make sure I do even since Poppa's death, has been an important phase of my journey of self-reconciliation.

There was also a change in direction of my Christian journey during this period of my life. Like many kids born in the 1960s, starting school often meant starting Sunday school. In my case, I was sent to the local Presbyterian Church, but it didn't have much of a Sunday school. So, when I was moved to Westminster School, I then joined the far more active, local Methodist Church Sunday school, which I enjoyed. As high school went on, however, it became less trendy to go to youth groups, so I slowly dropped out. Fortunately, I still had a good spiritual connection through Westminster's Chapel services and scripture classes for the remainder of my schooling.

The final 'highlight' of the year was to accompany one of the girls from my friend's aunt's school to their formal. I was reluctant, but somehow I ended up going. We danced to one song, and then she disappeared. I spent most of the night alone and bored out of my brain. I told Mum that I would never do that again because of the way I was treated by the girl. It turned out later that she was expelled, as she was found smoking and doing other things during the night while leaving me alone.

Somehow, I had survived Year 10.

Senior High School Years

The turbulence of Year 10 had passed, and we were all growing up quickly. We were allocated our main academic streams in preparation for our graduation year. I was focusing on Maths—two courses—Chemistry, Physics, Economics and Technical Drawing, which I then dropped as I headed into the final year, but this still left me with a heavy academic load.

Despite all the struggles I had with English throughout my schooling, I successfully completed my matriculation, and I am so grateful for the remedial English teachers at Westminster School for their efforts and encouragement. They gifted me the skills of my language for more than survival.

The big change at the beginning of my senior year, and a shock to our system, was that our school went coeducational—girls entered across all year grades at once. My Year 11 grade then consisted of roughly ninety guys and eleven girls. To me, these were some of the bravest girls that ever existed on the planet, as they were changing schools in their last two years of secondary education and doing so while being heavily outnumbered by boys.

I continued to play tennis in the two summer terms, and in the winter term, I played basketball. However, in

Year 11, I had a dispute with the new senior coach and left the squad. I was encouraged by the school to coach the under-fourteen basketball teams that year, which kept me connected with the sport. It also kept my skills up—as I was teaching junior high boys—and I began learning the new skill of teaching others, which became a lifelong passion that ended up being a parallel activity to my professional career.

One of the greatest aspects of Year 11, when most of us turned sixteen, was the chance to get our learner's permit to drive cars. I was not able to get mine on my sixteenth birthday as it fell on a Sunday, but first up on Monday morning, I was eagerly waiting for the doors to open at our local motor registry office. I passed the written test and received my precious learner's licence. This opened up new opportunities and also new dangers.

A week or so after my birthday, Dad and I drove off to Renmark—which is on the Murray River and just on the South Australian side of the border with Victoria—and I did a lot of the driving. Then, Dad drove from there to Mildura, where we spent the night in the Grand Hotel, which was an older-style building with large bars, grand dining rooms, impressive bedrooms and solid brick walls with high ceilings. As Dad fell asleep, his snoring echoed around our hotel room, and I struggled to sleep. It was then that I realised why Mum and Dad slept in separate bedrooms at home.

In the morning, the hotel still maintained a travellers' table where people travelling by themselves could sit and engage with others over breakfast rather than eating alone.

After staying a day, we headed to Broken Hill for a further day or two, and then we headed home. Dad had a short drive to the point where New South Wales met the South Australian border, and then I took the driver's seat and drove home for the next seven hours. As I hadn't driven in city traffic at all since getting my licence, I almost crashed when hitting traffic in Adelaide. It was like a baptism by fire!

Years earlier, when I had spoken to the school chaplain about how to improve my relationship with Dad, one of the suggestions he had made was to find a place or activity that Dad and I enjoyed safely together. That turned out to be Australian Rules Football (AFL). Our home was in the South Adelaide Football Club catchment area, but the border with Glenelg, which was Dad's team, was at the end of the street, only three blocks away. The 'agreement' struck between Mum, who was a North Adelaide follower, and Dad was that I would be encouraged to be a South Adelaide supporter. As it transpired, however, Dad didn't keep to the agreement, and he secretly made me a Glenelg fan. I remember that, when I was a kid, Glenelg had experienced some really lean years, although fortunately not as lean as South Adelaide, but they eventually broke a long, losing streak and won the South Australian National Football League (SANFL) grand final.

Unfortunately, despite this interest in common, Dad and I still had our problems. One Saturday after a huge relationship breakdown with him, I jumped in the car and sped off down the street. I'm not sure how I drove for the first few minutes, as I was so angry and fearful. I didn't know where to go, so I ended up at my best friend's house in North Brighton. I really don't know how I didn't kill myself—or someone else—with my uncontrolled, erratic, emotionally-charged driving. My best friend's parents were supportive in their own way as they tried to calm me down, but very few people knew what was happening in our family. They called my parents to let them know that I was safe, and then I eventually drove home. That evening was very quiet, as this had been the first and only breach of the family secrecy until many years later.

Another Saturday, around the same time, I came

home from playing sport, and the house was eerily quiet. As I moved past the lounge room to the dining space, I noticed a large hole in the dining room wall. Dad had never been physically violent to me, nor, to the best of my knowledge, to Mum, but this was getting very close. There was an uneasy tension for days despite Mum trying to assure me that all was okay. The challenge with repairing plasterboard walls is that even when a whole panel is replaced, as we did, it can be very hard to get a completely flush finish. I was always able to see the lump where the new piece in the wall was, and this reminder of Dad's outburst was permanently ingrained in the house and visible at every dinner.

It was around this time that Dad's health was up and down. As I mentioned before, society and the health profession were either ignorant—or didn't have an understanding—of PTSD, even in the 1970s. Mum and I were forever walking on eggshells at home, and any slight slip up on my behalf seemed to set off Dad's huge verbal tirades. However, I clearly remember during one time when Mum and I were visiting Dad at the Daw Park Repatriation Hospital, the specialist took Mum and me aside and sat us down for a discussion. The message from the specialist was that neither Mum nor I could continue to walk on eggshells because it was having a significant impact on our own health.

People often remark how, in earlier periods in society and in the Australia of my 1970s youth, we could play in the streets. Or, if your house backed onto bushland, the kids could disappear for hours and only reappear when called in for dinner. It was fortunate for me that times were different back then, as it also allowed me to use one of my survival techniques before I could drive a car, and I could ride my bike around the neighbourhood for hours on end. Getting my driver's licence meant that I could drive much further, however, and being out of our home was a safer place to be.

In my final year of school, physical education (PE) changed, and I very much regret that the school—I assume under parental pressure—removed this aspect from its weekly program. Rather than having two double lessons of PE a week, we progressed to having Wednesday afternoons off, and it was compulsory to leave the school campus and participate in an approved activity. I suppose the school was gifting us independence and encouraging us to try activities beyond high school—I learnt windsurfing, horse riding and golf. Tennis continued as my interschool sport in the first term, and I also returned to the Open A basketball team. Much to the frustration of the school, though, I eventually dropped tennis in the final term.

Two of the girls who entered our school in Year 11 decided to join the group that I hung with; we were a mixed and eclectic collection of people, and by our final year, we had become experts in the card game, bridge. Even though this game is usually considered a conservative activity for older people, I suspect that we were the only group activity that year in the school to be closed down and banned for one week for being too raucous—we forgot that the classroom we used was above the teacher's staffroom, which didn't help.

Now, being a coeducational school, it didn't take too long for rumours to float around that a friend of mine had gotten a girl pregnant. But, for me, the girls were just other people in the school. As Year 12 went on, my feelings of being different became stronger again. Over a month or so, a friend of mine would occasionally come over to play snooker after school. He wasn't as good as me, as I played regularly during the week at home. However, I became aware of an ever-growing tension in me, and I knew that I wanted to get close to him. Maybe he needed my help. What if I leaned over his back, body to body, to guide his shots? What if he felt the same tension as I did?

I did want to explore his and my body together, but what if Mum came home early from work? From time to time she did, or, even worse, what if Dad came in? The fear and tension were unbearable at times. I think it was only my naïveté of who I was and what it was that I was feeling that saved me from doing anything stupid. But, why did I think helping my friend was stupid? Why did I think my feelings were stupid? A message had well and truly been planted in my brain that whatever these feelings were, they were unintelligent and downright *unacceptable*.

One lunch time, my friend and I walked together towards the creek at the back of the school where there was one or two trees. As we stood on the creek side, hidden by the foliage, there was, yet again for me, a sexual tension. There wasn't much talking, but it was as if there were questions hanging in the air, at least from my perspective. Who was going to make the first move? What about that sexual risk? If I did make a move and I was wrong, what would happen? It was here for the first time that I felt the broader risk of being ostracised for 'being different'; a difference I didn't understand. If I made that first move, gave that first signal, and I was wrong, would my parents find out that I still had this unacceptable idea of 'playing' with a boy?

My father's reaction to *The Devil's Playground* came flooding back into my head. Time seemed to stand still. Would I take the risk? But the risk seemed to be far too great, and the pain and fear of rejection was so much. So, in the end, nothing was said by either of us, and then we simply walked back the way we had come, with me feeling that I was slowly sinking into the grass as part of me closed up. We walked back to the structure of the buildings: the bells, the routine, the uniforms and the uniformity. Blandness, compliance, normality. Greyness. The moment had gone. That moment had gone.

Seemingly after this walk to the trees, the afternoon

snooker games at home also stopped. So, was that particular walk the reason? Decades later, I still wonder what would have happened had I said something or made a physical move.

It was also in these years that an interesting family dynamic appeared while my relationship with my father continued to deteriorate. One night, we were about to go out as a family when I was asked to join Mum and Dad in the lounge room. There was an obvious tension in the air, so it seemed the conversation was going to be important, but there would be limited time for discussion, as we had to go out to a function.

For me, this experience had an air of darkness similar to the night when we had the family discussion about Zachary, the boy down the road. Even the main light in the lounge room seemed dimmed, and my mind began searching. While I still thought about boys at night and had been masturbating a number of times each day, I couldn't for the life of me think of anything I had done that would lead to this oppressive environment.

At that time in South Australia, there were strict rules regarding when you could apply for a concession card. Up until that point, I had been too young, but because I was always a tall kid, it was often assumed that I was older than I actually was—which was helpful when getting into clubs in Sydney, but that's another story. As a result of this misassumption, Mum started the conversation by saying that I needed to carry my birth certificate with me to prove that I was eligible for discounted travel, student prices at the cinemas and so on. This seemed an odd place to start a conversation because I knew this already—for a year or so I had been carrying an extract of my birth certificate in my wallet, and it was getting more and more crumpled and ripped through regular use.

Mum moved on to say that I might soon need my full birth certificate, and they needed to let me know about some information on it. I can't really explain why, but my brain immediately leapt to our next-door neighbours, who were a quiet couple that I knew couldn't have children, so they had adopted a girl. Surprisingly, for that period of time, they were open with her, their friends and their neighbours about her adoption. Suffice to say, I had some understanding of adoption through this experience.

My brain also computed that birth certificate extracts in South Australia didn't have any information about parents on them; they simply stated who you were and when and where you were born. And suddenly, I understood what this conversation was about. Yet, why were they telling me something like that right before we had to go out for dinner? I'm sure it was a tactical move on their part because then I wouldn't be able to make a scene at the event. Suddenly, it all made sense … why Dad struggled to accept me as I was. He couldn't cope with the fact that I was adopted. Maybe Mum had pushed for him to go through with it, and it hadn't ever been his choice. This information rushed around my newly enlightened brain, and the explanation as to why, for me, I couldn't connect with my father made complete sense, but it seemed that Mum was struggling to say it. So, I said, 'It's all right. I know that I'm adopted.' Then there was silence and confusion in the room.

Eventually, Mum spoke up to break the heavy atmosphere. 'No, you're not adopted. I was married and divorced before I met your father, and my previous married name as well as my maiden name appears on your full birth certificate.'

So, my dad *was* actually my dad. I couldn't use the lack of a blood connection to understand my strained relationship with my father. The great relief I had felt moments earlier having supposedly discovered the obvious reason for the issues between Dad and me had suddenly been withdrawn; the rug of explanation had been pulled from underneath me, and I was back to square one, wondering why the man who had given me life after all couldn't accept what he had created for the person I wanted to be.

The conversation that night was never spoken of again until years after my father's death.

I was under a lot of pressure from my dad to do well. I wanted to be a doctor, an anaesthetist actually, although not too many people my age knew what that actually was. As a ten-year-old, I had been probably one of the few at that age who could pronounce *anaesthetist*. This undoubtedly reflected the number of relatively minor operations that I'd had as a kid, and I was always intrigued by the power this special doctor had, who could make me magically fall asleep on command.

With the pressure to study, Dad initially wanted to check in on me more. Unfortunately—or maybe, in fact, fortunately—Dad became more and more distant over the months and spent a lot of time in his study, so Mum then took over the checking in on me. Years later, she told me that she had insisted on doing this because sometimes she would find me asleep at my desk, which hadn't been acceptable to Dad, but she had taken the view that if I had fallen asleep, I probably needed it, and she left me alone.

School classes came to an end, seemingly the beginning of the end of a life chapter, and then we had study leave. This was followed by exams, of which I had five. The only day that caused distress was when I was sitting the chemistry exam. Our school's first headmaster had just passed away—we were probably the last group of students to really know and remember him, so it was a very hard day. The school had attempted to delay our exam, but the State's School Examination Board wouldn't agree. The classroom where we were seated was on the same side as the school chapel, and the funeral was so big that the service overflowed onto the grass area towards the foundation stone, not far from where we all were. We could hear the entire service through the outdoor speakers. It was my toughest subject, and while I don't think I did any worse, it was one of the most emotional exams I have ever undertaken.

After the exams had finished, we had our school speech day and valedictory service. I was surprised that I was awarded—along with the boy school captain—a general service blue for my service to the school. What an amazing way to finish my schooling!

In early January, I received my matriculation results, which were pretty much as expected and allowed me to get into a realistic course at the university I wanted. This caused yet another dispute with my dad, as I could have gone to a 'sandstone' university—a similar concept to the Ivy League university in the USA—to do the same course, but I didn't want to. Being the first in the family to go to university wasn't enough for my father; apparently, going to a prestigious university was more important.

The journey towards the end of my childhood was fading as the voyage into adulthood commenced.

Growing Independent, Failing and Exposure

When I commenced my higher education at seventeen and started the slow journey of moving away from being under the control of my parents, I felt a sense of freedom. On a simple level, I didn't have to wear a uniform anymore, and I seemed to have more free time. However, the shift proved to be a big change for me.

There was pressure—mainly from Dad—to be successful; whatever his idea of success was. He took it upon himself to impose his thoughts on most of my academic options, which he believed would be the right base to launch into a successful career.

At that point in time, there were only two universities in Adelaide, with Adelaide University being the sandstone campus I mentioned earlier. Established in 1882, it is a member of the prestigious 'Great Eight' or 'G8' universities in Australia. Some eighty-four years later, in 1966, Flinders University opened in response to the push from around the country for capital cities to have a second major institution of higher education.

So, there were three main things that drove me towards choosing Flinders University. Firstly, my dad wanted me to go to Adelaide University because of its prestigious reputation in our city, and that was almost enough in itself to encourage me not go to there. Flinders University was known during the Vietnam War as a place where people would go to avoid the compulsory ballot draft into the military, which forced young men to fight even if they didn't believe in the cause. That was one of the many reasons Dad had a disdain for Flinders University.

Secondly, some of Flinders' research was about fifty years ahead of its time, as they were investing heavily in studies for electric vehicles. Dad considered this to be a complete waste of money. How times have changed!

Thirdly, when I toured the two universities, I felt more comfortable at Flinders. The Flinders' campus was more modern—some might say it looked like contemporary, utilitarian, concrete boxes—with lots of open spaces. It is nestled in the Adelaide foothills in Bedford Park on two sides of a valley, and the views still mesmerise me. The central buildings are at the bottom of the campus, including buildings such as the library, the student union building and the university administration. Looking up the hillside, spanning to the left and up one side of the valley are the humanities sciences buildings, such as arts, economics, history, social sciences and psychology. A man-made lake in the middle separates the other side of the valley, and on the right side are the sciences, where the mathematics, physics, chemistry and environmental sciences buildings are located.

Lower down and on the right side is the Flinders Medical Centre, where Mum had worked since before it opened in 1976 as their inaugural charge seamstress, helping to set up the facility before it opened to patients.

Under the Whitlam Government, university tuition fees had been removed, and free university was now available. In hindsight, I think this was the only thing that Dad approved of in the Whitlam Government.

The final reason for me wanting to attend Flinders was related to the economics facility. At that time, the economics school was considered number two in the country, and that was good enough for me. All of my friends from school who went on to tertiary education went to Adelaide University. So, manoeuvring my way around the various faculties on my own was challenging as well as exciting. Economics was my core subject, and the syllabus required all students to do Maths, even if it was at a minimum level. I chose to do the standard, full, first year Algebra and Calculus maths program. Furthermore, besides my core or major subjects, we had to choose another subject outside of studying economics. The university board implemented these principles to ensure that the students would obtain a broader, more liberal education. I chose to study geography, as I thought that there may be some crossovers into economics, particularly in the human side of geography rather than the physical. I loved researching about different cultures.

These subjects left me with little social time, and I spent most of my evenings at the library or at my study desk at home. Since I was only seventeen, I could only go into the union building's cafeteria for meals; I couldn't enter the bar because I was not yet of legal age. So, my yearning to find something outside of university led me to the Rotaract club, which was for eighteen to twenty-six-year-olds. This was a natural progression from the Interact club I had been a member of at school, which had also been sponsored by the Marion Rotary Club. We had been given invitations in our senior year for a meeting to see if we wanted to join the Rotaract club after we had graduated high school. My desire to find a place to fit in and to have some structure to enable me some social time instinctively led me to go along. From the first night, I realised that the club had a great bunch of people, and unlike university, it felt familiar, so I signed up straight away. By the middle of the year, I had been voted onto the board, which in hindsight was odd; I technically couldn't be a member until I was eighteen, and I was still seventeen. Back then, it was also illegal to be a director of an incorporated association in South Australia if you were under eighteen. But I suppose we worked on the 'don't ask, don't tell' policy.

Life at university started with me mainly trying to find my way around and making it on time to my economics, geography and algebra or calculus lectures. I kept in touch with my old network of friends from school, and most of the time we played bridge and continued to have cards nights throughout the year. Sometimes, we headed out to movies and the occasional dinner. I was developing new friendships through my Rotaract club, but I wasn't really making any friends at university, which did make me feel lonely and somewhat isolated.

During my time at university, my weight surged rapidly, so I decided to join a gym off campus and started jogging occasionally with a mate. After a while, my mate introduced me to a friend of his who was an editor on one of the student newspapers. The more time I spent with this new editor guy, the more I started to wonder if he was gay. I was still masturbating a lot and thinking about guys when I was pleasuring myself, but I continued to struggle with the potential identity of being gay; it induced a lot of anxiety. Even the thought of looking at, or thinking of, other men had me in a spin, and again it made me wonder where my place in the world would be. During my childhood, it had been made very clear to me that being with another man was unacceptable. I hadn't really made the connection with religion and sexual sin at this point in time, but I was already doing a good job of rejecting myself. I would regularly be in the student newspaper office with the junior editor, and I started to think of all the questions I could ask him, just to get some queries off my chest.

Should I ask him if he is gay? If he says yes, then what next?

I wanted to ask, 'How do you know if you are gay?', but I put off the conversation for ages because I was afraid that he might ask me the same questions; a risk that, in my head, would jeopardise my time at university. The thought of Dad finding out sent shivers down my spine because I knew in my heart of hearts that, if there was any news out there that I was gay, then my father would surely pull me out of university and maybe even send me somewhere for 'help'.

My mind started to race, thinking of the consequences of my curiosity and the potential ramifications of asking the editor questions about his sexuality. Questions popped up in my mind. *Maybe I can deflect? But, what if I can't? What if there are follow up questions, and I can't keep track of my stories and get tangled? What if the editor asks if I am gay?* I knew I could try and deny it, but would I be effective at doing that?

Trying to detract from prying too much and ultimately getting into trouble myself, I would often fill the space and conversation with some other topic, making sure that the conversation would go elsewhere. I do remember staring at him a lot, wondering everyday if he was indeed gay. As a matter of fact, I am pretty sure that my curiosity— which thankfully didn't get the better of me—was my way of finding out some answers for myself.

At the end of the day, I never found out if he was gay or not because I was too fearful of even asking such a question of him. The risk I saw in a follow-on conversation was too great, and it could have potentially blown the door right off my closet. As I was relatively uninformed about the gay community and people hiding their identity, I was very successful in putting my sexual orientation in the closet and trying to find a box to store it in forever.

As the months wore on, I needed to prove to my father that my education at Flinders was a good choice. As the first semester came and went, I was getting a good sense for how the system worked. My exam results were good by the end of the first term, and I was relatively happy.

During university, I continued to have opportunities to travel. I considered myself quite the traveller, which gave me new-found independence every time I went back to the normality of my everyday life. My parents had purchased a caravan for holidays, as they were planning for longer trips when they retired, so I'd bought their small car from them. They then purchased a much larger, second-hand car to pull the caravan. Our neighbours diagonally across the road also travelled a lot, with more international travel than my family. They had kids that were older than me by quite a few years, who were both working as school teachers. Michelle, who was the older of the two children, was a friend as well as neighbour. During the year, conversations about summer holiday travels came up between both families, and somehow, over the months, an idea was hatched that Michelle and I might do a three-week road trip around Tasmania. In the end, my parents agreed that it would be safe for us to go together, and travelling with a female neighbour for three weeks didn't faze me at all because I just saw her as a platonic friend.

In the final days of getting organised before departure, Dad had a strange conversation with me that didn't really make any sense. I remember distinctly how the conversation began. He didn't pounce on me with his words; he was calm and collected with a strict tone in his voice. 'You're travelling with Michelle, so you need to be careful,' he said.

'Careful of what?' I responded.

'Well, you're travelling with a woman, so you need to be careful.'

'Careful of what?' He still wasn't answering the question, and I felt naïve.

'Well, Jason,' my dad said, 'I don't think you would do anything inappropriate, but if you do, ensure you have condoms and whatnot.'

Why would I want condoms? Condoms? I haven't thought of those since playing with them as part of sex education in Year 10 at school. Why would I want condoms when travelling on holiday with a family friend? Suddenly it dawned on me that Dad was worried I might be planning to have sex with Michelle during our three weeks away or that she might want to with me, and I should be prepared. 'No, no, it's okay,' I responded, rapidly and nervously, and I didn't say much more than that.

I never bought condoms for the trip, as I never contemplated having sex with Michelle on our three weeks away, and never did the thought come up again for either of us.

However, following my trip and back at university, as with many of the 'issues of the week', there was a new display, but this particular one seemed very strange to me. Dad would have been mortified if he had seen the condoms blown up like balloons around a meeting space in the union building. This wasn't the only display on that week. There were some cultured art displays as well. It seemed that the condom décor was some form of gay collective that were trying to make a point, but the display made me uncomfortable.

As the days went on, I would grab lunch and sit near the display area, trying to see or listen for some signs to tell me if I was actually gay, or if I was just feeling awkward about myself. The strangest feeling hit me when I found myself not even being able to look at the condom balloons floating around the hall. I'm not sure if it was disgust or just a central feeling of shame tied to my traditional upbringing. There were some subjects that were just untouchable. It was pitiful; I was pitiful. Even at university, where hardly anyone knew me, I was scared shitless about even being seen around a gay collective display. This was another addition to my tightly sealed box of life, which was being closed a little bit more and an extra nail or two hammered in.

The mid-year exams started, and, in true form, I was feeling confident about all of my subjects except algebra and calculus. The School of Mathematics had very liberal rules, and they were obliged to provide you with at least three semester tests for every exam. So, if you failed an exam, there was an option for you to take a re-sit within a number of weeks. I used this option a couple of times during university to get through the year when nerves became my biggest obstacle. In hindsight, feeling bent out of shape and extremely anxious during my university days could have been signs of the onset of my slowly declining mental health.

One day, I completed an economics exam, and I felt good. After that, I confidently made my way to sit the geography exam, but I walked into a quiet, empty room. No one was there. I found my pocket calendar in my bag and realised that the exam had been the day before. *Oh fuck*. The thoughts of failure and what my lecturers and my dad would say to me put me in a mental meltdown. I could feel the stress building up in my body as a slew of thoughts hammered around in my head.

I have failed an exam because I stuffed up the days.
What the hell is Dad going to say?
What will this mean for me?
Can I go home?
What the hell am I going to do?

Panic, distress and fear were the only things I could feel. I was not able to calm myself down. The fear of being judged by my father was making me feel even more anxious. Some voices in my head tried to pacify me, but the voices of rejection, fear and anxiety ruled even louder.

What shall I do now?
Should I drive off and crash into something and kill myself? Then no one will know if I missed this stupid exam and how much of a failure I am.

The vortex of words swallowing me up felt like a horror movie, and I was sinking into a black hole. I can't remember what it was that jolted me back to the present moment; it could have been the sound of a bird or a student walking by. But, thank goodness, I managed to snap out of my suicidal thoughts and make it to the student support services. This was the first time they were concerned for my well-being because they could see I was a wreck. They asked me a few questions, and all I could say was, 'I am a university student, nearly an adult, turning eighteen in a matter of weeks, and I am a mess.'

I started crying and, within a matter of seconds, I was out of control. The counsellor on duty that day tried to talk to me while asking me to make coherent sentences at the same time because I was making no sense. In my head, all I could think was that I needed to be successful and prove myself to my dad. I had attended every lecture and every tutorial, and I had submitted every piece of work on time. This is what I was trying to say, but the words were just stuck. They had probably seen this before and understood similar family dynamics, but the fear around my father was all that I could express even if I could not explain it.

In the end, when they could at least get me to sit down and take a few deep breaths, they were concerned enough to call my mother at work. Fortunately, she was at the hospital down the hill on campus and within walking distance. And, unbeknown to me while I was waiting for Mum and at the request of the student services, a handful of university faculty had started negotiating with the geography department. They agreed with the recommendation that I be offered a supplementary exam.

When Mum arrived, I was still a mess, but then news came through that I would get the chance to sit the exam in the next few days. Mum and the support staff met, and it was agreed that Mum would ring Dad at work to tell him what had happened and to help me follow up with the next steps. I was grateful for Mum's intervention again, as it minimised the chance for Dad to blow up at me.

When everyone agreed that I was safe, I was then allowed to drive home. Mum went back to work to collect her car, and then she headed home straight away as well—this meant that I wasn't left alone for long. When Dad got home later—although earlier than usual—my parents went into a separate room to have a conversation. It was one of those times when Mum realised something wasn't quite fully right with me and the whole situation. It was just an exam after all, and my outburst must have confused her. When Dad spoke to me later, there was minimal discussion on missing my exam, and it was quickly over with. I'd stayed in my room for most of the time and collapsed into bed early.

The following week, I re-sat the exam and the geography faculty were amazing. They didn't give me any special treatment; however, they understood that there were some mental health issues that needed to be explored, possibly at a later date. During my university days, mental health was never discussed because such issues weren't talked about in the 1980s. Nevertheless, I had passed yet another exam, and I momentarily felt somewhat free from the tyranny of my father.

University, Work and a Health Scare

One Friday afternoon, I dropped by the union job centre, and they mentioned they had just been called by a tobacconist and gift shop in the city's Adelaide Arcade who was looking for a sales assistant. I gave the shop a call straight away and went in for an interview, which went well, and I started immediately. I had this job for the remainder of my years at university, working Friday evening and Saturday morning each week and then full time during the university holidays. The extra cash gave me some freedom to explore and travel.

By the middle of the year, I was a board member of my Rotaract club, had a job that was working for me and was doing reasonably well academically at university. Summer holidays, which in Australia are between December and March, rolled around, and our final exams were over. The period between Christmas and New Year was definitely peak season at the shop with tourists, but it had been a busy Christmas trade in the previous weeks as well. I had been rapidly learning all about the different types of tobacco products and pipes, and the fun part was explaining the different variations of pipes that ladies were seeking to purchase for their husbands as a Christmas present. I enjoyed talking to new people and connecting with different cultures, but I never used the products myself.

One morning, during this week between Christmas and New Year, I got up as usual and had my breakfast. As with any normal day, I went about my standard morning routine, not realising that the day was going to have a major impact on our family and my life. I walked the two blocks to the local railway station and then boarded the train to the city. As I got off the train, I felt a sharp pain in my stomach, but it passed almost as quickly as it arrived. However, the sharp pain kept coming and going, and I wondered about my breakfast and what could have caused these excruciating cramps.

Trying not to let the pain take over, I walked my usual route along King William Street and into Rundle Mall. Outside Myer, one of the mall's three department stores, a dagger of sharp pain caused me to double over in agony. I tried to compose myself and desperately held onto the window ledge, which was being transitioned from Christmas displays to the New Year sales. I straightened myself up after the pain eased a bit, but I was still out of breath. After a while, I finally managed to walk on, hoping and praying that no one was watching me.

When I arrived at the shop where I worked, I told my supervisor what had just happened, but I reassured him that I'd be all right. My supervisor was a kind man and he was definitely concerned, but I carried on because I didn't want to let him down. Later that day, when I made my way to the staffroom in the basement, another sharp pain ricocheted through my body. My colleagues sensed that something was up and saw my pain, but I convinced them that I would be okay. After all, I was made from the 'carry on regardless' stock.

Then, later in the day when I was in the souvenir section, I had another major stabbing pain, and I nearly knocked over an entire aisle of displays. I saw concerned customers near me as staff came running over. One of my senior colleagues mentioned that I should see a doctor right away. So, once again, I called Mum and headed to catch the train home. It was only a thirteen-minute train ride, but it seemed to take forever. The pain was getting worse, but Mum had already managed to get home from work before me, so she rushed me to the doctor. With every poke and prod, I winced or even let out the odd, pained yelp. It was a diagnosis of appendicitis. The doctor called the local private hospital where an operation was scheduled for me a few hours later. A surgeon was organised, and I was sent home to get toiletries and a change of clothes. Then, I was driven to the hospital and admitted straight away. Our family doctor assured Mum that he would be in the operating room to assist the surgeon as well.

Just before the operation, the nursing staff suggested that Mum should go home, advising her that they would contact her after the surgery and when I had come out of recovery. Then, there were final checks on my identity, date of birth, blood type and allergies. I saw my doctor in the operating theatre before the anaesthetist came over with final instructions for me to count back from one hundred. The mask went on and, as usual, I didn't get very far before I was out like a light.

I woke up in recovery feeling sore, and there were people checking on me. The first thing I noticed—in my blurry, anaesthetic-affected state—was that there seemed to be some tension in the room. I could feel the anxiety in the air. Eventually, I was wheeled back to my room where the tension continued. People kept coming in to take my temperature all the time while a few doctors meandered in and out. I could hear whispered conversations, and I wondered what they were talking about. The multitude of temperature checks and whispering from the team of doctors had me concerned. Was I hallucinating? I could feel my mind drifting in and out of sleep.

The other thing I became aware of was that I was cold, freezing cold. In my stupor, I asked for blankets, but the answer was no. The nurses kept taking my temperature, and I felt like a block of ice; I started to shiver. The nurses undressed me, and I began shaking, my teeth chattering, and all I wanted was warmth. I asked, 'Where are the blankets?' But no one seemed to listen. Instead, they brought ice packs. Soon, I was wearing nothing but my underwear, and I was surrounded by ice. I wanted to scream at them, 'Can't you hear me?' Confusion reigned in my head because I was so cold, and they were making it worse. Why weren't they listening to me?

'Jason,' a doctor finally said, 'we have spoken to your parents because we are very concerned about your temperature. It is not under control, and it is far too high. An ambulance has been called, and you are being transferred to the QEII hospital's intensive care unit. Your mum and dad are going straight over and will meet you there'.

This wasn't making sense to me.

'I am feeling so cold. Why am I covered with ice and not getting the blankets I want?'

'When your body temperature is very high, the mind is tricked, and you can sometimes feel very cold instead. We have to keep you with basically no clothes on and in ice to try to get your temperature down'.

The ambulance arrived, and the paramedics entered my room. Hand-over instructions were provided by the hospital medical team, and I could see confusion on the other patients' faces. I felt like I'd entered the twilight zone. My ice packs and I were very carefully put on the gurney, and I was wheeled to the ambulance. Heavy duty pain killers were administered via the IV drip to manage my discomfort for the journey. I was never aware as to why I was sent to QEII, which was further away than the nearest tertiary hospital with an intensive care unit (ICU), but I assume the medical staff had a clear rationale.

Eventually, we arrived, and I was taken straight through to the ICU, where there was a dedicated nurse for each patient. Mum and Dad were there with concerned looks on their faces as I was carefully moved onto a bed and the drips transferred. While being hooked up to a heart monitor, something was inserted rectally into me. I felt violated, poked, prodded and like I was having an out-of-body experience. Although the staff was kind, courteous and professional in all of their undertakings, I just kept wondering, *What the hell is going on?*

Mum and Dad stayed with me in the ICU all night. By late morning the next day, my temperature—which had peaked at 41.5 °C (106.7 °F)—was now stable and generally within the 'normal range'. The crisis seemed to be over. After listening to the doctor talk to my parents and the rundown on the prognosis, I thought I was home free and would be out of hospital within a couple of days. Back then, appendix operations normally meant about a four-day stay in hospital, but I spent well over a week in the QEII recovering. My body had been through a lot.

Over the next few days, I had a stream of visitors, including a lot of my friends, which helped to keep my spirits up. On my hospital registration form under the 'religion' section, I had entered Uniting Church even though I hadn't attended church for a number of years. The next day, the Uniting Church chaplain came and met me. We chatted and, by this stage, I was starting to realise that something serious had happened. He invited me to attend the chapel service the following day, to which I expressed interest, and he said he would make arrangements to get me there as well as visiting me later on. He never made the arrangements, and he never came and checked in on me again. That hurt me a lot. In my time of personal life crisis, the very person I wanted to connect with to help me reconnect to my struggling faith let me down. That played negatively on my mind for

91

many years to come. Weren't these times of crisis meant to be a point of faith reconnection? Where was God, or the representative of God, when I needed him? Did the chaplain sense something about me that made him feel uncomfortable? The childhood days of my life sprung back into my mind as I envisioned myself wandering down the beach with the Bible in my hand, searching for answers from a Christian God.

When the surgeon came to visit and check up on me, he explained what they knew of the events and what had happened, but there was still considerable uncertainty. I was grateful to learn more of my plight and that the doctors had saved my life. When they had put me under the anaesthetic and started the operation, my temperature had rapidly increased, and they couldn't control it. With appendix operations being relatively uncomplicated and fairly quick, the doctors could physically see the impact of my rising body temperature on my insides, so they moved as quickly as they could to get my inflamed appendix out and then sew me up without damaging any other organs.

In recovery, my temperature was unstable but then seemed to steady, so they had thought I could go back to the ward. However, once back on the ward, my temperature had again become unstable and continued to dangerously rise. Concerned and worried, the doctors on call decided that urgent intervention was required at a specialist intensive care unit. At that stage, they still hadn't any idea of the cause for the spike in my temperature, and it was getting close to being fatal.

A few days later, there were three doctors at the bottom of my bed having a discussion that turned into a bit of an argument between the surgeon, the anaesthetist and an intensive care specialist. They were talking about a medical condition that they seemed to think might have been caused by an infection. What I was hearing was a 'public versus private hospital' debate. One of the doctors was arguing that it was really not acceptable to use reusable cannulas due to the risk of cross-infection in the public hospital system. This raised the possibility that I had picked up a severe infection from an incorrectly sterilised cannula in the private hospital, which was why the public hospital had moved to single use items. This didn't fill me with a lot of confidence. I felt rather grossed out, considering that I may have picked up someone else's infection from a re-used medical instrument. I was not the least bit impressed.

I eventually started to recover over the coming days but was still in hospital for New Year's Eve. Just over a week after the operation, I was finally considered medically recovered from the trauma—as well as the operation—and I was discharged and sent home for further recovery.

A few weeks later, I went back to the surgeon for my follow-up appointment. The surgeon's office was closer to Dad's place of work, so he joined me, which was rather unusual. I felt like we had connected on some level around this event, and by him coming to the doctor with me, he was actually showing some concern. After a full, physical examination, the doctor began speaking. 'We have had several conversations and discussions with other specialists about what we believed happened. We are unsure, but the most likely cause is a condition called malignant—'

I froze, and I think my dad did too. 'Malignant' is the word often associated with cancer, but how would cancer cause such an event?

I am only eighteen, so how can I have cancer? repeated the voice in my head.

The doctor droned on, but I heard no further words beyond 'malignant'. I think he finally realised that we were not hearing anything. No doubt our faces were displaying a combination of shock and numbness. He paused. The silence seemed to refocus us. 'Let me start again,' he said. 'The word malignant is used in medical terms for conditions that are permanent, and we are not talking about cancer.' Seeing our bodies relax, the doctor continued. 'So, we have been talking with a number of specialists, and we think you may have a condition called malignant hyperpyrexia due to anaesthesia. Do you know of any history in your family of problems with anaesthetics?'

'No,' my father said.

'Unfortunately, and fortunately, this is a rare condition, and we don't know if you have it or not. There are only three places in the world where you can be tested for this. One is in Canberra, which, as you know, is a few hours south of Sydney. Basically, this condition creates a reaction or an allergy, for want of better words, to certain types of anaesthetics. It is surprising that this has come up now, given the number of operations you have had as a child. What we want to do is refer you to a professor at the Royal Canberra Hospital. He is a global expert in this field. When can you arrange to go over to see him? He will arrange for you to have another operation and take some muscle out of your leg—'

I stopped listening again. *Did he just say go under an anaesthetic again? Plus, take some muscle out of my leg?* I opened my mouth to finally speak. 'What? I apparently have almost died because of an operation, and you are sending me interstate to see a professor to have another operation?' Even though I could hear myself asking these questions, my brain didn't compute the severity of what I was asking; it was not coping very well at all. The doctor noticed that, once again, I was not following what he was saying. It was surely the classic case of a doctor knowing the information, which seemed normal—given all the research he had undertaken about this rare case—and blurting it out without thinking about how the recipient of that information might respond.

'Okay,' he said. 'Let's go over this again.' He was trying to be as patient as he possibly could be. 'What we know of this condition is that it usually leads to a fatal outcome, so you are extremely lucky. There are safer anaesthetics for operations that last up to around three hours. The operation to take the muscle out of your leg will be relatively quick with the safe drugs, so you really aren't at risk. The professor can then test the muscle in the laboratory and give you a result while you are recovering in the hospital.' I was still dumbfounded, but the doctor had no more to say, and Dad and I were handed an article about this particular condition, some referral documentation and then sent on our way—the doctor's job was done.

Dad and I were inevitably baffled and didn't talk much on the way home. Later that day, we updated Mum, who had lots of questions and, of course, we didn't know the answers, which just seemed to frustrate her. Fortunately, with her job at another major public hospital, she was able to speak to the specialists she knew and obtain some more information. Most importantly, she discovered that I had been referred to the leading professor in the field, not only in Australia, but globally.

The whole incident and the holiday season had left everyone in my family numb. I was left hoping that university the following year would be less complicated and not 'fatal'—a word that would now resonate in my ears for years to come.

Expanding University Life and Life with Doctors

I started back at Flinders University in 1981 for my second year, and I was not feeling excited or happy to be there—I felt drained and depleted from having to spend a holiday going through another operation. I tried to explain about the Christmas holidays to some of my Rotaract club friends and the university faculty, and I said, 'I am very lucky that I didn't die, and I may have to have another operation in Canberra, which will be incredibly stressful.' Everyone I told was horrified as well as compassionate about my story and my feelings.

Communications were established with the professor at the hospital in Canberra, and bookings for my next operation were made for over the Easter break to minimise lost time with my university studies. I learned that I would have to be on crutches for a number of weeks after the operation, so my relationship with the student services came in handy again. They set up communications with all my lecturers and organised a disability car park pass. I would need as much assistance as I could get, and they were going to see that I received as much support as they could arrange.

Mum, Dad and I flew to Canberra for my second operation even though Mum was a terrible flyer. Our first flight was on a DC9 jet to Melbourne, and then we boarded a small Fokker F27 propeller plane to Canberra, which she barely survived. I could see she that was anxious and couldn't wait to put her feet on land. It had been a challenge to actually get her onto the plane in the first place, so I sat next to her because I knew she needed some comfort. Rather than my parents supporting me, I was the support person, and Mum almost crushed and broke my hand because she was gripping on to it with such force on the second flight.

As soon as we landed, Dad collected the hire car, and I was driven immediately to the hospital. That night I slept quite well, which was good because the next day there were lots of interviews initially with my parents and then later with me. The doctors checked my medical background, history of operations and any medications I had been given as a child. The poking and prodding was endless, and this part of the process seemed to take all day, but I assumed it was important to build up knowledge for their research.

After all the testing was complete, they advised me that I also had a heart murmur, which normally would have been of some concern. However, until this diagnosis, the heart murmur had never caused any issue, and I was told it would always be incidental to my life. But, to be honest, it was still a little disconcerting to be told that my heart was a little abnormal—perhaps it was a metaphor for my *other* heart, which sometimes I didn't really understand at all.

The next day, as I was wheeled into surgery, I felt tense. The doctor's knowledge and interest in the field of my condition, coupled with oozing confidence from his overly garish explanations, still didn't put me at ease. I wondered if the anaesthetics would be fatal this time around. I heard the voice in my head, and I tried not to think about my death; instead, I worked hard to listen to everyone around me who was telling me that everything would be okay. I tried to force the word 'fatal' out of my thoughts as I was wheeled from the outer preparation room into the operating theatre. The doctor was there with other medical personnel waiting for me, and I felt like I was about to be cast in a movie. The usual practise started with a cannula in my arm, and then a mask was placed over my mouth as I was asked to count back from one hundred. Before I knew it, I was in another room, which I assumed was the recovery room.

After that operation, I was definitely groggier than usual, and soon after I woke up, something happened which had never happened to me after surgery: I started throwing up. Eventually it passed, and I was returned to the ward. I was thankful to be awake, but I felt worse for wear with a sore, upper-left leg.

After a day, the results came back, and it was confirmed that I had malignant hyperpyrexia due to anaesthesia. As it was a dominant gene, it was definite that one of my parents had the same condition, and I was also told that three out of five children in a family were likely to inherit the gene. The professor went on to tell us that I was the first person to survive such an attack when there was no known family history in Australia, and we were only the thirteenth family unit to be identified in Australia with this condition.

I got to visit the laboratory and see my muscle under the microscope, and I was given some pictures, which regrettably I have lost in various house relocations over the years. However, I observed an interesting fact: my muscle cells are much larger than the comparative standard, which provided insights to the markings that had become visible on my legs at different times.

The doctors requested that I remained in hospital for several more days because they didn't recommend me flying immediately after surgery. Mum and Dad discussed our family history, and although there might have been signs of the issue on Mum's side, it was decided that Dad would go first for the next operation to test for the condition. If Dad was positive, then Mum didn't need to be tested.

My flight back to Adelaide via Melbourne was even more traumatic for Mum, and neither Dad nor I coped with her very well. Dad's impatience was mounting, and he finally lashed out at her, telling her to stop complaining. The look on his face was not pleasant; he looked like he could burst at any second. I tried to console Mum as much as I could, but my leg was hurting, and all I could think about was going home and getting into bed.

When we arrived back in Adelaide, I needed assistance with my wheelchair at the airport, as they didn't have aerobridges connecting planes to terminals back then, so a special lifting machine was brought to the plane to get me down. When we eventually got home, there were a few sour faces as we entered our house.

I had to learn how to walk with crutches. It was difficult for me considering my height, and getting around meant I had to depend on others much of the time. I ended up borrowing my parent's car, which was an automatic. It made driving much easier, as I didn't have to use my left leg as much. The scar had dissolvable stitches and, as the days wore on, I began to see the length of the scar I would be left with. It still surprises me today just how long it is.

The disabled pass for the car was extremely useful, and I was able to drive from building to building while learning where all the lifts were, which I had never used in the past, so the labyrinth of all the buildings became a mystery once again as I manoeuvred my way across campus with my crutches.

Finally, in the middle of the year, Dad headed off by himself to Canberra to have the same tests carried out that I'd had during Easter. He went alone, which was not ideal, especially from Mum's perspective. She was not particularly happy with him flying back alone because we had heard that an international patient had died on their return back from the same surgery and tests. But, his mind was set.

It turned out that Dad was confirmed as the genetic carrier. The probability that Mum also had the gene was so remote that it was not worth the effort or expense for her to get tested as well. Moreover, the trip alone on the plane might have been her death!

After my surgery, my Rotaract friends continued to be supportive, and by the middle of the year, I was appointed vice president. However, academically, I did not cope with one of my second-year maths courses, and I ended up leaving it for a long time to sit the exam before only just scraping through. Computer science was proving to be enjoyable, but my two economics courses were taking a toll on me, and the pressure was mounting.

At the end of the year, we completed our exams, and I was actually feeling quite confident about most of them. When the results came out in late November 1981, I had passed everything; however, my core economics subjects were compensatory passes, which meant they were around the minimum pass mark. This was devastating news, as it meant that I would have to spend another year at university. Fortunately, Dad took the news surprisingly well. I think he had heard about the rates of student struggles in the second year, but I think he also understood the pressures I was put under following my near-death experience and the medical interventions that went on for over half of the year. It was a very unsettling year, so maybe this was the time for some sympathy, especially from Dad.

During the summer holidays the following year, I headed to Darwin, the most northern capital city in Australia. I stayed with the eldest daughter of our next door neighbour and her family for several weeks. One of the best memories of that holiday was the family having a Mini Moke car, which they allowed me to borrow to drive around and explore Darwin. It was a very enjoyable and relaxing time. I was able to take advantage of a post-school holiday travel special to fly from Darwin to Kununurra in Western Australia, which was only possible once I'd urgently had my student ID sent to Darwin so I could benefit from cheap student pricing that was available. There, I was allowed to rent a car when I was still only nineteen years old, but this allowed me to explore the Ord River Irrigation Scheme, which is a man-made system multiple times larger than Sydney Harbour. I drove around some of the Kimberly region, saw the amazing baobab trees and travelled to Wyndham—a very isolated part of Australia on the northern coastline of Western Australia. Having grown up regularly visiting Broken Hill in the desert, I felt at home in this isolated part of Australia, and perhaps this was another metaphor for my life; isolated, and in the desert.

The family I was staying with had connections to a person who owned a light aircraft, and for a very small fee—just enough to cover fuel costs—we flew for three hours over the Kakadu National Park with its amazing and wondrous escarpments. They were so large that our light aircraft could actually fly into and around the extraordinary rock face structures.

One weekend, we travelled to an island resort by boat from Darwin, but unfortunately, I can't remember the exact location now. What I do know is that the family had friends staying at an old-fashioned waterfront resort on the island. There was a lad called Daniel working there, who was perhaps a year younger than me. I assumed he was there for a holiday job, but I can't remember if he was connected to the family or the resort owners. When he finished his jobs for the morning, Daniel joined me in the pool. We mucked around for a while, having a great time. There was something about him that drew my attention.

After a while, it was lunch time, and Daniel suggested that I go and shower in his room before we ate. Daniel's room was one of the motel-style rooms away from the main area used by the resort guests. It was rather trashy, just like a teen boy's room, with clothes on the floor and rubbish everywhere. This was not like mine, where there was a place for everything—even with a specially designed hidden place for my dirty clothes—so that my room always looked presentable. Presentation was key for my acceptability at home.

We sat around in his room and chatted for a bit. But there was an unexplainable tension; something I really didn't quite understand. And in return, Daniel offered the same strain back to me. The pressure must have stemmed from the fact that I didn't know what his intensions were with me. As he showered, I began to snoop around his room and found he had some porn ... straight porn. I felt somewhat disappointed and now even more confused. He came out in his towel, and then it was my turn to shower.

I felt like we were dancing around the room; dancing around something piercingly unspoken. Words and feelings conjured up in my brain as I heard the voices in my head again.

Where is this heading?
He is very cute.
What on earth does this mean?
Is anyone going to make a move?

Was this just a misunderstood tension between two young men, or was Daniel waiting for me to bring out the metaphorical knife and slice through the tension ... the sexual tension? And, if I made advances towards him, would this be a mistake?

Then, we heard a voice from the lunch area. 'Jason and Daniel, the barbeque is ready.' Summoned by the family, we left the room to go and eat. Daniel and I kept talking, and he looked so handsome in the sun, but it was back to the safe small talk.

Lunch was over, and the last ferry was about to leave. When we departed, there was some idle chat about me coming back to visit. But, as much as I wanted to, and as much as I wanted to see Daniel again, it never happened. In hindsight, I realised that it had been too much of a risk for me, and for years, I kept hearing the voices in my head.

Did I avoid going back for fear of the tension in the room and the feelings I was having?

Am I really gay?

I was still struggling with the language.

The next week, my holiday was over, and I commenced the forty-eight hour coach trip back to Adelaide, which had a changeover in Alice Springs.

After the holidays, I felt relaxed although somewhat confused about my encounter with Daniel, and then university recommenced. I had a few decisions to make: I could either slow down and focus on the subjects I needed to repeat—but, that would make me part time—or, I could pick up some more subjects. I was intrigued with computer science, so I took more subjects in that area and began to do exceptionally well. I also discovered that studying economics was much better for me the second time around even though I was with a new cohort of students with whom I obviously had no connection. I still didn't really have any friends at university, but I hung out with some groups. There was a girl I found interesting—she was a science major—but nothing really started there. It could have been my lack of longing for a woman's touch because I still wasn't sure how I was feeling. There was another guy who smoked pot. I knew if I wanted some, I could get some, but I was far too scared to even try some. Dad's huge fear of drugs was so ingrained in me, and his lectures about the evils of pot and smoking would resonate in my mind for a long time. Another university rite of passage missed.

I became a computer room supervisor, overseeing one of the labs when mainly first-year students were booked in to work on their programs. This was another small source of income, which gave me the freedom to travel. I started to make plans for a trip to Fiji for the next summer holidays.

During the middle of the year, I became president of my Rotaract club, which was a great learning experience and it expanded my friendship circle. A Rotary exchange fellow arrived from the USA with his family, and I started to learn about history from him. I took it upon myself to look after him as he undertook research studies at my university, and we became good friends. I looked after his kids when he and his wife went away on Rotary events around the state, and I would visit him and his family many times in the USA years later.

A pattern emerged between Dad and me because we just didn't seem to agree on many frontiers or see eye to eye on a lot of subjects. Nevertheless, I would make sure that I saw him as much as I could to update him on what was going on in my life. We usually chose public venues so I would feel safe. We continued going to Football Park, which back then was the major SANFL and AFL stadium in Adelaide's West Lakes area. We usually talked about football and other stuff that was not a risk to either of us. University would come up, but since I was doing reasonably well and my grades so far that year were making him proud, it became a safe topic. Furthermore, he understood nothing about computing, so I was on top of the conversations because of my knowledge. In a strange way, as this was our safe space, this became the only time and place where I felt I could be relaxed around my father. He had been supportive with my Rotaract activities too, as he knew members from our sponsoring Rotary club. Indeed, the Marion Rotary Club eventually asked him to join because they were seeking a member who had a rail management role.

Later in the year, there were rumours that one of the other members of the Rotaract club was gay. This made me feel very uncomfortable and unsettled, but it seemed to die down as quickly as it started. I didn't want to ask anything, as that would risk perhaps identifying myself as being too interested, which could cause the closet door to open a little more—I wasn't willing to face that possibility yet. I made sure to show I was avoiding every possible notion of wanting to know more because I was so afraid. Thankfully, when the rumours died down, so did my concerns ... those for the person I was trying to be and for the person I really was.

Over the summer, during the penultimate year of university, two school friends and I went to Fiji. It was my first overseas trip, and it was a great week away learning about Fiji Time (or Pacific Time). The one thing I learned from the Fijians was that 'things happen when they happen'; something I should have learned and incorporated into my life but still haven't managed to do. My desire and need for control and managing situations has always been innate in me, but I am slowly beginning to realise that the path towards success can also be driven by a force we cannot actually control.

Coming to and End: Final Year at University

My final year at university was a big ending with a lot going on. I continued with my final elective topics for economics, which offered me a great variety of study. The other enjoyable factor was that I was asked if I would like to be a computer science tutor for the first-year course, as I was doing so well with my own computer science studies and because there were limited numbers of staff in this relatively new faculty. I knew that I had somehow made it because being offered a job during my university studies and teaching other students felt like an accomplishment.

I passed International Economics, The Economics of Labour, Industrial Organisation and Public Finance with credit or pass grades. Overall, I was working at what seemed to be my potential for the first time and gaining some respect from Dad, which was important to me; I was trying to change the narrative of our family. However, with this side making headway and ultimately leading me towards becoming a CEO of two companies at a later date, there was still something missing. Something felt disjointed inside me. I knew I was smart—my professors said so—but what about the 'feelings' part of me?

So, I started to experiment with the other side of me as I tried to unveil who I really was. I discovered adult shops although I never bought anything. Some days, I would travel to the opposite side of the city, to Port Adelaide, just to look at magazines in the adult shops there, and I found myself always looking at the gay magazines.

For my twenty-first birthday, I wanted a signet ring, which I designed with a local jeweller who the family knew. Mum and Dad liked the idea, and while Mum agreed to provide the three diamonds from her grandmother's engagement ring, Dad provided the gold. I was quite surprised that they had agreed to be on board with me about this gift because I wondered if Dad thought I was being effeminate with the idea of jewellery, but I had always been partial to it. Back in high school, we'd had casual dress days where we were out of uniform to raise money for charities. One casual day, I was one of a number of people identified by the teaching staff as wearing too much jewellery. However, Dad never said anything directly to me, so I continued to try and be who I was.

Dad and I went to the jeweller a couple of times for the fitting of the ring. One time as we walked down Jetty Road, we passed an adult shop. Strangely, Dad asked if I wanted to go in. This was very odd and a bolt out of the blue. As we didn't have a great relationship, I didn't want to go in because I was sure that I would naturally gravitate to the gay section, thereby exposing myself. So, I just upped the walking pace to get past the shop as quickly as possible. I still wonder to this day if he was trying to test me or maybe provide me with an entry point to a discussion. Maybe I missed an opportunity?

My twenty-first birthday celebration was a marvellous weekend. One thing that my family valued was commemorating major events and milestones. We'd had a monumental celebration party when my parents each turned fifty some years earlier, and funnily enough, Dad received a signet ring with an opal stone and his initials, which has now been passed on to my son.

I ended up having two parties. One was on the Saturday night at the relatively new Hilton Hotel in Adelaide, which was the first major international hotel in town. Dad liked it there, and we took over two function rooms with access to a balcony overlooking Victoria Square. It was a sit-down dinner for about thirty people, which my closest mates from school, some relatives and significant family friends attended. Mum had arranged for the glass-blowing team at her hospital to blow a twenty-one rung ladder that sat on top of my birthday cake. The following day was a much broader open house with a wide range of family and friends dropping in until the late evening.

I must admit, my twenty-first is still the most memorable of my birthdays.

Since my second year at university, I had been actively researching employment opportunities in the transport sector, having again considered and rejected a career in the Navy that was really about pandering to my father.

During this time, my connection with the student services at university once again came to the fore, as they had programs dedicated to writing resumes and interview techniques. In 1983, Australia was in an economic downturn, but I was fortunate that I was probably in the top 10% of my economics class, and I was the top computer science student. From my economics peers, I understood that I was the only student to receive more than one job offer. At one stage, I was juggling multiple offers at the same time, and I received over six offers in total.

The offer I finally accepted was a role I effectively

created. In my second year of university, I had met the local human resource (HR) manager for a major Australian airline company, who had indicated that there wouldn't be any suitable roles for me in Adelaide. However, he suggested that when I was in my final year, I should write to their head office in Melbourne. So, after some convincing from the HR department, off I went to Melbourne for several interviews at the airline's head office. Internal Audit (IA) agreed to offer me a graduate trainee role, and IA and HR then both agreed that I would not be rotated out of IA for two years.

If truth be told, I had absolutely no idea what internal audits were about, but I managed to do some quick research before I had the interviews. This was the job I was holding out for, but would the offer come? Should I accept one of the other offers in case it didn't? If I took another offer and this one came in, was it professional to then reject the accepted offer? Calls were starting to come in from the other organisations as they sought a decision from me.

I wanted this airline role so much because it was in the transport industry, and it built on the foundation of my computer science courses. I had really only undertaken this course as an adjunct to my economics studies, but computer science was definitely hands down one of my better subjects, and I really enjoyed it. After all, it looked like it had already helped me to land an internal job at the university, but the airline role was the one I was keen to pursue. Eventually the job offer came.

However, a last-minute confusion occurred when Flinders University offered me a position in their honours program in Economics. It wasn't a hard decision to knock back the invitation because I now had the role I wanted, and after four years at university, I was ready to move into the workforce. The honours degree offer pleased my dad, but he also felt it was time to earn my way in society and be employed. What I hadn't realised at that time was that, subconsciously, I needed to move out of home, and the only way to achieve that easily was to move interstate.

My last year at Rotaract continued well, and it was the time of year where I had to hand over my duties to another president. Reflecting back on those years, I can safely say that my time in that role was successful, and it taught me some of the foundations I needed to be a leader for my future business and executive life. During this last year in Adelaide, there was a girl in the club who was keen on me. I enjoyed her company, but suddenly I found myself with a girlfriend, which I hadn't decided upon or anticipated. We tended to only go out together around Rotaract functions, so, to me, she was more of a companion than a girlfriend. We had some good times together, but there was still something that just wasn't quite right in my inner world. The good part about the relationship was that her parents seemed to like me. On the one hand, it seemed nice to be 'normal'—just like you see in the movies—but on the other hand, there was something deeply missing.

My 'good boy' training and my internalised Christian upbringing meant that I didn't want to have sex before I got married, so it seemed to be quite a while before we even kissed. The first time, I felt indifferent, and as time went on, she wanted more hugging and kissing, which made me feel uncomfortable. Maybe Christianity was a crutch that I wasn't yet aware I was using. My innocence and rejection of myself meant that I really didn't understand what was happening in my head. Fortunately for me, with all my uncertainty and lack of understanding or awareness of myself, the relationship couldn't last because I was moving to Melbourne in the new year to start my first professional position.

After four years of study, I'd had enough. The exams were over. The results were very good, and now I had to take a leap of faith and start discovering who I really was without the watchful eye of my parents; particularly my father's. It was time to exercise some freedom and courage.

New City, New Life: My Melbourne and Accepting Freedom

It was a beautiful morning in early December, 1983, with the smell of a different suburbia permeating my senses. The smell of cut grass and the softness of the air were liberating. I was in another city away from home: Melbourne, the capital of Victoria.

I woke up in the morning knowing that Mum and I were on a mission, and I was happy to have Mum with me on this part of the journey. Hopping into our rental car, off we went to look for apartments as we scoped the eastern suburbs of Kew, Hawthorn, Armadale and basically everywhere else in between. This was rapid learning for me, so Mum gently started the education on rental fees and other potentially hidden costs. She knew that my starting income was equal to what my father was currently earning as he neared his retirement the following year. I'm not sure how that made Dad feel—I never asked him.

I was learning how to develop a balance with rental, transport and living costs while being able to just enjoy life. I might have been an economist and computer scientist, but that didn't mean I had sufficient life skills. Some of the apartments—even those that were more expensive— were in very poor condition. Carpets were torn, and there was a musty smell of old, reupholstered curtains covering

115

windows, which also often had tinges of rust around them. The upkeep was terrible.

After a day of searching, we saw an apartment in Armadale. It was on the ground floor, at the rear of a nice block and about seven minutes' walk to the train station with quick access to the city. There were also two tram lines into the city nearby, and restaurants and local shops were within walking distance. Surprisingly, the rental price was reasonable, and Mum and I agreed that, since I liked the apartment as well as the area, I should apply right away. With Mum's encouragement and support, I made the application, and it was accepted pretty much straight away. Taking a deep breath when the six-month lease was signed, I felt free; having my own space was liberating. I could be my own person, or so I thought, and create a home or a living space that was all mine. The days of being under my father's roof were over. Yet, liberation is exalting and painful at the same time when you think about it. My childhood days of living at home were stressful because the closet door kept squeezing in on me. All I could think was, *When am I going to be free?* So, it made me sad to feel that I needed to escape my past, but I would then remember how Dad would control everything in my life, including my bedroom, which he decorated to his own liking.

Although Dad was a railway clerk for most of his life, and finally a manager in the later part of his career, he was an amazing builder. Working with tools and using his hands to build things was his passion. When I was about ten years old, my father took it upon himself to rebuild my bedroom. Yes, he did a fantastic job, but, once again, it wasn't all to my liking; it had no personality although it was perfectly functional. The first thing he did was construct built-in wardrobes on two of the four walls. He then made a desk with four drawers on each side, and he built a bookshelf, which was designed to hold my entire set of World Book Encyclopaedias, with additional space for year books for a reasonably long future. He also constructed a bookstand where I could place my books while I was doing research at eye height at the back of the desk. The bookstand fascinated me; it had wires across the wood, so I could open my book, place it on the stand and the wire would hold it open, leaving my hands free for writing.

Before ordering my bed, Dad measured my height because I would need a much larger one than standard size. When it arrived, it had large drawers underneath for storage, and it was finished off by a set of drawers that acted as my bedside table on one side. Above my bed was another set of shelves for my reading library. The next wall had the window, and the final wall had a major pin board that took up nearly two thirds of the space.

When the room was finished, I was amazed. Like I said, my father did a brilliant job, and it was so well organised. Everything had its place. The room was designed so there would be no mess, just complete order, and that was another reminder for how my life was to be planned and managed. However, there were several, severe arguments at times in this room, which eventually made me feel claustrophobic in there. Also, Dad's design of the bedroom started to creep up on me like a monster I had no control over. I remember during high school, when everyone else was putting posters up on the walls, I asked Dad if I could stick some posters on the remaining part of the wall with the window and on the parts of the wall that had the humongous pin board. Dad was not happy and grumbled that the pin board was sufficient for all posters and other stuff. I had collected many pennants from lots of the cities I'd visited, which already took up most of the space on the pin board, but his argument was that sticking up posters elsewhere would damage the walls. I tried to reason with him, but he replied, 'That's the exact reason for having the pin board, Jason.' He was speaking like a general from the war, and his stubbornness was stifling.

Before that, when the framework of the room was complete and it was about to be painted, we'd had an argument about the colour of the room. Dad had envisioned everything in the room being neutral. His preferred colour was called 'Driftwood' and that was the colour of most of the walls in the house except where there was wallpaper. It was a staid colour and bland, which was definitely not my personality.

Our neighbour's son, who was quite a few years older than me, had been allowed to decorate his own room. Such freedom to be able to just throw paint on your bedroom wall fascinated me, and when I saw his room, the feeling of liberation was stirred. His walls had a lime-green base, and then he had used a darker green and splashed it at the top of the wall, allowing the paint to run down. It created a visual, stalactite effect.

After seeing our neighbour's son's creativity, there was no way I was going to settle for boring Driftwood. Dad and I argued for days, and once again, Mum had to intervene. She sided with me and asked that there be compromise between my father and me. Finally, after more arguing and stomping around, a compromise was reached. The walls and the supportive frames of the built-ins would be painted in Driftwood. However, every door and visible drawer—twenty-four of them in one room—were to be painted 'Burnt Orange'. Additionally, every door handle would be painted black. Allowing Dad to win on the walls and frames ended up making the rest of the colour scheme very dramatic—a compromise win in my mind.

After I had signed the lease for six months at the Armadale flat, Mum and I had to make arrangements for furniture. We ordered a bed to be delivered and assembled as soon as I arrived, along with a trundle and also a chest of drawers for my bedroom.

Back home, there was a small table in our family rumpus room—Aussie slang for a living room—that would fit in my small kitchen and be a mini dining table. My parents also had a futon that converted into a bed, which they said I could take. Dad, who was overly frugal sometimes, wanted me to have an old fridge that he had stored in the back shed. However, I didn't take it because rust was starting to surface on the corners, and it looked like it had had its fair share of explosions from home-made beer. So, I ended up buying a new one. Friends and family donated spare, small items, and for Christmas, they bought me cooking utensils, knife sets, pots, pans and other knick-knacks. I also invested in a small television. I was set!

There are times in your life that you land in the right place and, for one part of me, this professional place was the best; yet on the other hand, it turned out to be a surprising challenge. The internal audit manager, who was the head of internal audits for the company, was an older gentleman from the UK and a chartered accountant. In the UK, chartered accountants didn't normally have accounting degrees because the firms employed graduates with a wide variety of qualifications and then taught them the vocation of accounting, auditing and business advisory. This was also the approach they used at the airline, so I had absolutely no accounting qualifications, nor training in any auditing techniques. In fact, I had never heard the term until I heard about the job and asked the post-graduate lecturers at university what it was about. One of them had heard of the term EDP Audit, which was when I was able to do my quick research in the library to try and work out what I was heading into before the interview.

But my lack of training in this area wasn't a problem.

The internal audit manager, along with his IT audit manager, had a plan to teach me the skills I needed. As the trainee, I was part of a small team, and around these higher-ranking men and women, my professional development started. I began with a combination of undertaking technical IT audits and then developing or updating computer programs to provide reports for the financial internal audit team. I was definitely learning a whole lot.

About a year into my life in Melbourne, during one of my parents' regular trips to visit, we were on a weekend drive when a discussion about university dropouts started to brew. It began because the radio news program was reporting how students at university were dropping out and not attending all of their lectures and tutorials. It was some person, perhaps a right-winged politician, speaking, who clearly wanted to have a go at young, brash university students. My dad took the opportunity to address the subject, hook, line and sinker. He started to go off about university students wasting their time and the fantastic opportunities they were given. He shouted about how students were lazy and ungrateful, commenting, 'If they didn't want to do all the work, then they should leave and get a real job.'

His comments hit a nerve with me having recently graduated from university, and I was taking offence at his rampage on students as a collective. We bantered for a bit, back and forth, with Mum and me trying to knock some reason into him, but I was not making any headway. I had been a very studious person at university, somewhat out of fear of my father, so in the end, I said, 'Dad, I did extremely well at university, and even I missed the occasional lecture or the occasional tutorial.'

He was definitely not happy with me sticking up for myself and my peers, and he shouted, 'But how much better could you have done if you had attended all the lectures and tutorials?' His tone took Mum and me by surprise because it seemed he was now verbally attacking me.

I was shocked and could barely say much more than, 'Well, I did really well at university, and attending those few more wouldn't have made any difference.' The conversation stopped, and there was sudden silence in the car. Dad tried to pick up the conversation, but I was too pissed off to engage with him. When we got home, I went straight to my bedroom. I was the top computer science student as well as being in the top group of economics students, invited to undertake the honours program in what was then the number two economics facility in the country. Furthermore, I had received more job offers than any other of my university peers. What the fuck more did he want from me? There in my room, I started to make a mental list of my achievements, which at my young age was already growing fast.

Some months later, I was called into the internal audit manager's office; it seemed serious. My insecurities and a lifetime lack of acceptance meant that at the end of every internal audit and six-monthly review, I anxiously sought feedback on my work and performance. Much of this was about me trying to find ways of validating myself; trying to find ways of being accepted or acceptable. The down side of this was also the fact that I always developed a 'worst case scenario' in my brain when anything seemed likely to cause me risk, and some days ... just because.

The meeting started with one of my superiors saying, 'You're not being suspended, but ...' My heart sank—had I done something unacceptable? Had I failed? He continued, 'There has been an issue with a recent internal audit, and it would be best if you worked from home for a couple of days while we commence a review. I'm afraid we can't say much more than that at this stage.' So, with fear in my very heavy and burdened heart, I collected my gear, some activities to work on for a couple of days and then headed home. As I drove, the hammer in my head was pounding.

Is my career about to be over?

Over and over again.

Is my career about to be over before it even takes off?

The days seemed to take a long time to pass, and paranoia began to sink in. The hours felt like months. Fortunately, after a couple of days, I received a call at home. I was told that everything I had done regarding this internal enquiry had been handled appropriately, that it was all okay and that I could return to the office.

When I returned, I met with my two senior executives again and was brought into an amazing story—elements of which I still use in my training of company directors and internal auditors today. My work program and working papers were of the requisite standard. They assured me that my conclusions were appropriate, and my element of the report clearly identified the issues and recommendations. I knew that I was sometimes sloppy with my working papers' cross referencing, so that was a relief. I was told that the issue related to the Western Australian Accounts Payable audit because I had identified that some of the debts were very much past their due dates, which then started this dramatic and terrible chain of events. It turned out that a sales representative had taken control of a friend's dormant account and used it to flush through highly discounted travel.

My experiences with people who commit frauds as well as research carried out on the subject show that fraudsters can become irrational when they are identified or their scheme comes unstuck. Some commit suicide, as they can see no other way out. Some even go to extreme measures and try to go above the law with the intention to create severe harm or death. In this case, in an attempt to have the business write off the debt, the sales representative took an axe from home, drove to his friend's office and attempted to chop his head off. Fortunately, his friend wasn't killed, but now I was involved in a major fraud and attempted murder enquiry.

I was then allocated to the investigation team. My role was to use my IT skills to search for all paper and electronic records and then build a database to assist the police and the subsequent court case. What a journey, and what a first fraud!

But, even at this early point in my career, I found myself asking, 'Who is the real fraudster?' In many ways, I still felt that it was me.

All the while, life continued to move on. The only thing that was familiar to me when I arrived in Melbourne, and that happened to be located around the corner from my apartment, was a Uniting Church. As the third largest Christian denomination in Australia, the Uniting Church had been created from the merger in 1977 of virtually all the Methodist and Congregational Churches and around seventy-five per cent of the Presbyterian Churches.

I had stopped going to church through the latter parts of high school and throughout university. Basically, I hadn't attended church for the last four years, but, after a few weeks in Melbourne, I walked around the corner one morning and entered the Denbigh Road Uniting Church. As happens in many churches, I was one of the youngest in attendance, but I was made to feel very welcome. That afternoon, the minister, a Dutch gentleman, visited my home to welcome me.

About a week before schools were to return for the year, I received another visit. This time there was a request. They were in need of a Sunday school teacher, who would be based at the parish's other church on Kooyong Road. My immediate reaction was, 'No way! I haven't been to church for four or more years, so what could I teach in Sunday school?' Nevertheless, my new minister was very persuasive, and I found myself agreeing. This started a phenomenal journey during my seven and a half years in Melbourne, and teaching Sunday school turned out to be a good thing for my own journey of faith. In many ways, it took me back to the basics, as I had to communicate Christianity's message to a group of primary school students. On reflection, this was perhaps where my own faith had regressed to.

As time went on, I found myself connecting with young adults in other congregations around Melbourne, and on occasion, I would attend their churches in the evening. I undertook my confirmation studies and became a confirmed member of the Uniting Church, and sometime later, I even became an elder in my parish. We also developed a youth group which started to expand nicely. During this increasingly active time, I managed to attend the National Christian Youth Convention (NCYC)—a week-long, youth-focused Christian event that is run every second year by the Uniting Church on rotation around Australia. In 1987, in Ballarat, I managed to shake the hand of, and briefly talk on two occasions with, the Nobel Peace Prize-winning Archbishop Desmond Tutu from South Africa, who was the daily speaker. It was captivating to hear him preach, and he had the 2,500 delegates in the palm of his hand as he spoke. I remember that, one night, in a massive tent, core worship was held alongside his speeches, and they brought in an additional five hundred visitors. His aura was enchanting, and wisdom oozed from every breath and word he spoke. He had a beautiful way of delving into, defining and delivering his message of God's love.

By the time NCYC came along in 1991, the young adults group at my local church was very active, and we ran monthly contemporary services and sometimes coffee-shop-style services in the hall. Many of us had also completed the social justice leader's training offered through the youth ministry unit of the synod—the state level of the Uniting Church. Personally, this involved me visiting a soup kitchen and supporting organisations in St Kilda. We helped homeless people, who would knock on our door in desperation when trying to find emergency accommodation. Often, if they couldn't find a place to rest their heads, they became violent. Along with all other sorts of people from this eclectic seaside suburb, prostitutes came in for supplies of condoms. Drug addicts, homeless mothers, homeless fathers, old people, young people, poor men and even up-and-coming businessmen, who were seeking syringes for their high-flying, drug-taking activities, would visit us. Part of the service was to limit the transmission of HIV through the sharing of syringes and unprotected sex.

I became a youth representative on the Nepean Presbytery—the regional structure to which my parish was attached—and I became involved in a committee that provided financial oversight and property management across parishes. It was in this role that I first heard of gay ministers in the Uniting Church, but everything I heard was negative. One of the ministers had a very large manse, which is the house a minister and their family live in that is attached to a parish. He was single and gay, and he used his expansive two-story home to provide emergency accommodation for homeless young men. The suggestion was made that he must have been a paedophile, and I found this connection between his service to help the homeless, him being gay and the connection to being a child abuser very distressing. Although I was appalled by the rumours surrounding this poor man, I didn't understand enough to engage in the discussion. If truth be told, I was perhaps frightened of what people would think about me if I ventured into the conversation and provided the gay minister support.

The Uniting Church had also started the process of including lesbian and gay people in its congregation, but there was a vocal group who were very disappointed by this. Again, I never engaged in this matter, as no one in my parish seemed to be very concerned with the broader conversation.

As I became more engaged as a volunteer with the synod's youth ministry unit, I assisted with the quarterly youth services at a large church in the city, and I helped to run city events, such as the dance parties. However, despite the efforts to remain busy, there was still something that felt hidden within me; something that I still was not willing to fully accept. So, I stayed in my cocoon, pretending and moving along with life without causing any ripples around me.

Was it really my life, or was it a life constructed for the perception of acceptability?

A First Attempt at Sex and the HIV Crisis

During my time in Melbourne, the AIDS crisis seemed to be on the rise. I didn't live far from St Kilda, which was the bohemian area of Melbourne—at least, back then it was. It was a mixture of poor people and alternative people, such as hippies and prostitutes. I would often stroll down the streets watching people and studying their differences. Other times, I would go into the adult bookshops, where I would find myself once again in the gay section. I would purchase magazines to take home, keeping them stashed under my mattress.

There was an evening where I almost plucked up the courage to speak to another man at the Malvern swimming pool where I had started exercising. He was a very handsome guy around my age, and on many occasions, I tried to time my arrival at the pool with his so I could have a chat with him. But, it never happened, and he seemed to stop coming. I felt rejected again. My insecurities were flaring up even when I considered following through, and the awkwardness was not getting any easier.

On a later visit to a St Kilda bookshop, there was another young man, this time of an Asian background, in the gay section. He was so good looking and attractive to me, but once again, I didn't know how to start a conversation. I was so desperate to say hello but was

127

verbally frozen. When he left, I didn't know what to do. I was so enamoured by his looks that I eventually moved quickly out of the bookshop to follow him. However, the dusk of evening had turned to the darkness of night while I was inside, and the shop was on the corner of an off-angled T intersection. I looked both ways along the main street and then down the side street, but he had gone. This handsome man, who had practically stood next to me moments earlier, had now disappeared. Once again, my fear of myself had stopped me from talking or acting. A real opportunity had been presented, but now it had gone, like a star burning out in the night sky.

I was beginning to wonder if there was an angel on my shoulder, who might have been protecting me from meeting someone because of the mounting global AIDS crisis. Fortunately, unlike in the USA, our government decided that this was a health epidemic, and this was a time for bipartisan politics. The then federal minister for health and his shadow minister—his equal from the opposition party in Parliament—agreed to work collectively on action. Australia was seen as a global leader with the HIV response as governments and community groups worked together. An outcome was one of the most effective advertisements aired across Australia even though the *Grim Reaper* television campaign about the spread of HIV literally scared the shit out of me. The advertisement had multiple 'grim reapers' bowling large balls down bowling lanes with people of all ages—including a baby—and genders being the pins to be bowled over while the voiceover provided a HIV and AIDS safety message.

Unfortunately, it was also a damaging campaign, as an unintended consequence was that it created more hostility towards the gay community; a community with which I had not yet connected or identified. The conservative religious leaders were hitting the airwaves on radio and on television, suggesting that HIV and AIDS were God's response and punishment for gay people's lives.

How can this be?

I couldn't talk to anyone about what I was feeling or thinking; it all seemed too dangerous. Would I be rejected and not be seen as an acceptable person? Would my job be at risk if I was seen as a gay person? I just had these thoughts about men, but surely I couldn't be gay? What did this all mean?

As the *Grim Reaper* campaign was being broadcast, there was a complex two-week period between me and my parents. You see, every Sunday night, Mum and Dad would call on a three-way line so we could all speak to each other at the same time. Occasionally, I would make other plans, and if Dad wasn't informed and I wasn't at home when he called, he would often leave a harsh message on the answering machine. Anyway, one particular Sunday, at the height of the *Grim Reaper* campaign and on one of our calls, my father blurted out, 'If you're having sex, I hope you are using condoms!'

'It is not an issue for me,' I said. A true response, so I wasn't lying. I then tried to explain to Dad that using condoms was not something I had to worry about because I was still very much a virgin, but he didn't seem to want to listen. The strong message from the *Grim Reaper* campaign had already sunk deep into his mind.

The following week, I was in a dark spot. I knew what I was really feeling, and I knew what I wanted to say, but I refused to own it. Was this Dad seeking out information? Could it be that he was actually reaching out? Was this the second time that I missed the subtle cue? There was no one in Melbourne that I could talk to, and I didn't feel safe. While I had purchased gay pornography and magazines, I had not connected at all with any of the LGBTIQA+ community in Melbourne—that would have been a step too far for me. Indeed, my mind raced every time I thought about it. And even though it was probably in the magazines I bought, I never picked up any of the local gay community magazines, so I didn't see any of the support options that may have been available in my area. What was I going to say to Dad the following Sunday? I didn't think I could say, 'Dad, the reason I haven't had sex is because I think I like guys, but I haven't found anyone, and I would be scared as hell if I actually did find someone.'

The hammer in my head started pounding again.

Will I say something?

Should I say something?

Will the disappointment of my teen years be restated and reinforced?

Will the unacceptable feeling I have grow to another level?

It was torment, going around in my head. But there was no one to help take it out of my head or to talk with about it. So, round and round in my head it spiralled. Sunday arrived, but I still had no resolution, so I didn't say anything at all, and it was never spoken of again. But it did stir up internal confusion.

In the magazines I purchased, I could see the number for male brothels. I looked at them. For days, I looked at them. Was this me? Were these feelings connected to me? Were they separate? Could they be kept that way? I kept looking at the list of options in the magazines, and I narrowed it down to one. Yet, more days went by.

Why am I looking at these ads and the telephone numbers?

What do I need to know?

Who am I really, deep down?

One Friday night, I decided to call. I couldn't eat dinner; the stress levels were too high. I looked at the ad as I sat on the lounge next to the telephone. I got up and moved around, and then I sat down again.

I'm 25 and never had sex apart from masturbating

regularly.

I'm 25, and I am confused about sex.

I'm 25, and I am so confused about myself.

Can I call?

Should I call?

I paced again, and my heart started beating faster; I could feel the thumping in my chest. I sat down and dialled before I could change my mind, and a female voice answered the phone. She sounded surprisingly nice and comforting. 'Hi, how can I help?'

'I-I really don't know,' I feebly answered.

'Do you want to spend some time with someone?'

'I-I think I do, b-but I'm really not sure.'

'We have some very caring and gentle girls here.'

I paused again.

'Hi, are you still there?' she asked. 'Can you tell me your name?'

I think she must have had many of these calls from young and confused men over the years. 'I'm Jason,' I whispered.

'Hi, Jason. Is this all new for you?' Her tone was gentle and soothing.

'Yes.'

'You don't need to rush,' she reassured me. 'Our girls here are gentle and kind. I can help you out.'

Another pause, and then I said, 'I'm not sure it is the girls I want.'

I could sense the change in tact and that the woman had knowledge of how to handle these reactions as she replied, 'We have some very nice and caring boys here too.' She didn't drop a beat, and she retained her calm and modulated voice. There was a pause yet again as I struggled to work out what I wanted. 'Would you like to come in? You can meet some of the boys and decide where to go from there.'

'I don't know.' More silence.

'The easiest thing is to come down here,' she said, 'and we can chat more and find out what you are needing and wanting.' More silence.

In the end, and after what seemed like minutes, I finally said, 'I don't think I can.'

'It's okay. There is nothing wrong in coming down.'

'Really, I don't think I can,' I said as I wondered what the hell I was doing.

'Okay, I understand. Whenever you're ready, we will be here for you.'

I put the receiver down, but part of me was torn. Apart from my regular masturbation, I had never had any form of sex. I had only ever kissed two girls: my girlfriend in Adelaide and my current girlfriend, Alison, who was a school teacher I had been dating for a while. Alison and I would go out sometimes on Friday evenings, and I would call her from the office, which was an open-plan layout. The admin staff at her school got to know me and the regularity of the time I would call. We would go to see a movie, see a play or have a meal. I would often pick her up from her apartment and drop her home afterwards. Sometimes, I would go in for a nightcap, but we were never physical and, in fact, we never passionately kissed at all. I think this frustrated Alison because I could see she liked me a lot. But, as time went on, I became fully aware that I didn't really want anything physical with a female at all.

My abstinence also stemmed from the messages I had received as a young boy. The message of the Church was also convenient for me: one shall not have sex before marriage. Furthermore, one should minimise physical activity to reduce the risk of any sexual activity occurring. Alison was a teacher in a Catholic primary school, so doing nothing sexual seemed proper to her, too, despite her mounting frustration. She also unwittingly provided a good level of subterfuge, as people heard me talk to my 'girlfriend' each Friday afternoon in the office. On Monday mornings, I could then have the normal conversations that others around me were having. It felt like my acting skills were working, and the actor in me was presenting very well.

Yet, what I wasn't fully aware of was that Christianity was becoming a mask for what I felt but didn't understand. However, for now, and for my convenience, it was a useful cover.

The next years of work were productive and successful, and they helped the public-facing side of my self-esteem soar. I was doing very well in the corporate world, yet my longing to come out still resurfaced at times. Heading into my late twenties, I still had the strong urge to explore who I was. I still purchased the magazines, and I saw there were saunas where gay men met. One Friday night, I thought that I would go to one of them. I saw that there was one in Richmond, which was not that far from home. However, I still had no real idea what happened at these places. Were they even for me?

I very nervously drove out to discover if I could unmask the fraudster in me. It took me a while to find the sauna, as it wasn't as though they could have large signs out front. Eventually, I found a place to park my car, and I walked in. There was a waiting area, but no one was at reception. I sat and waited ... and waited. I seemed to be waiting an eternity.

Is there a bell somewhere?

I looked but couldn't find any, so I carried on waiting. Eventually, a burly guy came through a door, and he stared at me, up and down. I later learned the language that one would use to describe this person: a 'bear'. I must have looked rather weak because he came closer and growled, 'This is not the place for you. Go away!' I was shocked and stammered something that was inaudible, but he stood his ground and didn't move. I really didn't want to take him on; although I was taller than him, he had much more bulk. He also had a bad attitude, so I got up and left. Demoralised, I realised that I had an empty feeling; I had tried something and failed.

Who am I?

I don't seem to fit in anywhere.

This other part of me might put my acceptability at significant risk.

The fear of failure started to creep up again.

Jason, what's wrong with you? You can't even take yourself to a gay sauna.

Some months later, I decided to try again. There was a gay sauna in the city, somewhat dangerously close to the office. So, I went one Saturday night when no one from work would be around. I drove into the city, parked the car and checked the place out. Looking around to ensure there was no one I knew, I went up the ramp to the entrance. There was a group of three younger guys ahead of me, but the man at the reception was not convinced they were over eighteen and didn't believe that their IDs were legitimate, so he wouldn't let them in.

Is this what it is like in these places?

I made my way to the counter, provided a name and paid the entrance fee. I didn't provide my real name because caution whispered in my ear to play it cool in case I knew anyone inside. Funnily enough, the man didn't ask for my ID. It must have been my height.

It seemed very surreal but, in one sense, I felt relieved to be inside. I had already decided that I didn't expect to do much other than wander around, explore and basically to see what these gay venues were about. It was obvious that sex was part of the purpose, but there seemed to be more than met the eye. There were pools and masseurs for muscle relaxation, a restaurant, a café and a spa. I decided to pluck up the courage and learn by experience, and I was almost undressed when ... *Shit!* I recognised one of my colleagues who worked at the check-in in Melbourne Airport. I had recently completed an internal audit there, which involved having a few discussions with him. I knew he lived in a small township on the opposite side of the airport. He had a towel around him, so I prayed that maybe he was going to change and leave. *Shit! Shit! Shit!* I quickly got dressed, hoping like hell he hadn't seen me, and left.

As I walked back down the street to my car, I realised that this was the third time I had tried to explore my sexuality but had ended up running away. The only way I could process this was by imagining God saying to me, 'Jason, this is not you, wake up.'

I ran into that colleague once or twice after the sauna incident. Thankfully, there were no comments about our chance meeting. Like many people in the airline, he transferred to become a flight attendant. Once, I ended up on one of his flights, but yet again, there was no comment. Thank God! It was years later that I realised, just like the Exclusive Businessmen's Clubs in major cities around the world, what is discussed there stays inside. There is a code of secrecy in those clubs that is similar to what I have noticed about some gay venues I have since visited.

Often since that day, I wonder what might have happened if I had not turned and run away. Sometimes, in my dreams at night, I play out scenarios of what might have transpired had I remained, had we had recognised each other there and if I had spoken to that fellow employee. Years later, my psychologist still frequently brings up the question of facing up to what I need to do rather than running away. So, this incident rings familiar.

Much later, an important learning from my doctor and psychologist is that you can't relive your life through a series of 'what ifs'. I keep coming back to the fact that I have been able to do some phenomenal and amazing things in my life. Yet, for a while, it seemed that every time it came to trying to explore who I was, I was thwarted, and this behaviour pattern became a crutch in my life for many years to come. Looking back at scenario re-runs in your head only makes you tired and doesn't achieve anything to enable forwards movement. This, along with my skill in catastrophizing any perceived threat, was absolutely exhausting. Constantly, I would try to assure myself that somehow God's guiding hand was in this— that he was telling me I could not be gay. So, maybe I wasn't a fraud after all?

There was generally a good atmosphere in the office. I soon progressed to IT audit senior, with someone under me, and eventually IT audit supervisor. We would regularly have drinks at the hotel bar next to our office after work on a Friday, which was always a welcome relief as I enjoyed some human connection amid these social gatherings.

Sometimes, we would end up at a disco. I love music, and I remember my odd CD collection, which consisted of both Christian and secular pop, jazz and rock, with some classical music to round out the assemblage. However, although I loved listening to my own music and cranking up the volume whenever I needed some relief, I always found discos a difficult place because I was awkward on the dance floor. I reassured myself that it was my lack of coordination and that I didn't really understand disco dancing even though I had enjoyed ballroom and Latin dancing during my high school days. Really, though, it was the public space of a disco that overwhelmed me. I enjoyed discos at school and a wide variety of dances from bush dancing—which is a country style of dancing like line dancing—to dances hosted by the Rotaract clubs in Adelaide for the four years I was a member there. I guess it was the comfort factor that was missing at a public disco: I didn't know anyone there and felt intimidated. I kept thinking that I must have grown two left feet as I grew through my twenties, but I think the reality of dancing with a woman wasn't really for me, and two left feet seemed to be a good excuse.

In 1987, the internal audit manager decided that it was time for his retirement. It seemed many in the office were involved in organising a major party to celebrate him and his vocation at a restaurant on the edge of the city. We had an internal auditor and internal check officer in Brisbane, who was a conservative Christian man and much older than me. I think I may have been the only other active Christian in the office, at least publicly, so he asked if he could stay at my home in Melbourne because he blatantly explained to me that he didn't really respect many of the other people in the office. I reluctantly agreed because I wanted to attend the retirement party and wasn't sure if he would stay the entire night as I was certainly planning on doing.

Our internal audit manager had been kind to me, taking me on in the first place and working on my development. However, heading towards his retirement, he had imposed a level of conservatism and resistance to change that had become frustrating for the team in his final years. So, the party was a dual celebration to recognise his amazing service to the profession and our company and a release, perhaps, to allow for renewal and fresh ideas in the office. There was great food, great drinks and wonderful company. My boss was a wine buff, which meant there was a great collection of wine, excellent speeches and much frivolity, but my colleague from Brisbane did not enjoy what I think he saw as the 'excesses' because they contradicted his Christian faith and ideals of what was right and wrong. Drinking and having a good time were obviously not part of his religious scope. Fortunately, I had given him a key to get back into my apartment, and when he left early, I bid him farewell for the evening so I could party on. We kept drinking and chatting and, obviously with the consumption of alcohol, we became more and more boisterous and perhaps less inhibited.

Apart from my Brisbane colleague, I was probably seen as the most socially conservative, but I was having a good night and had already drunk way too much, as had everyone. The conversations at the party were good and fun. Then, my peer from the financial side of the office came up, put his arm around me and said, 'P'fer, you need to unwind and relax more, and I think what you need is a good fuck!' We all laughed.

My nickname in the office was *P'fer* because I always insisted that my middle initial 'P' was used in my signature block, and I would reject a letter if it was missing, so the typing staff would have to fix it, much to their annoyance. My father always signed PE Masters, so I think in one of those minor efforts to find acceptability, I copied him. Later in life, I dropped the middle initial from most of my writing.

Anyway, my colleague was right. I was past the midpoint of my twenties and still a virgin, and I had never gone beyond kissing anyone. Well, actually nothing more than a peck and, as I had only been with women, the kissing wasn't that inspiring and certainly never passionate. Yes, I did need a good fuck, but it probably wasn't the fuck he was thinking about.

The Birth of New Roles: The Emerging Business Executive

At Copelen Street Family Services, which I had begun working for when I was nominated by the Nepean Presbytery as their nominated director, I was starting to learn about the important work of being on the board of not-for-profit agencies and the delivery of very important social services to the community. We were a multi-faceted agency that was willing to work on the edge of society. At one end, we were a large foster care agency and the only provider of adoption services for disabled children, and we provided many services for families. At the other end, and on the edges, we were one of the first agencies in Australia to provide services for adoptees looking to find their birth parents. We also took on innovative risks when we founded the first violent men's program in Australia— similar to the twelve step AA program—but for violent behaviour. I accepted the treasurer role on the board, which expanded my commercial accounting knowledge as a non-accountant.

Years later, I completed the Company Directors Course, which was run by the Australian Institute of Company Directors, and came to realise how naïve I had been as a director back in the day—particularly with the important and significant risks we were undertaking in running these leading-edge, social welfare programs. Having done the course, I wouldn't have changed my involvement, but I may have changed some of my discussions in the boardroom on strategy and risk.

As my work with the airline continued, my boss and I discovered a significant gap in some of the academic work in the IT audit profession. We spent a year or so with an academic leader from RMIT University, undertaking a major ground-breaking study of the level of computer security at a national level. After researching and writing with many bottles of red wine involved, we published *Computer Security in Australia* in 1986, which generated much media and academic interest across Australia and the world.

After the publication, I started undertaking more and more speaking and media engagements across Australia as well as in the USA, Hong Kong, New Zealand and Malaysia. My work at the airline also continued with some high-profile and pioneering internal audits, and my colleagues became like family members. My IT boss and I had become great friends, enhanced through those years of working very closely with our research project and the resulting book, and we would regularly leave the office together at lunchtime to pick up something to eat.

One day, as we went for our usual walk, he said, 'I have been headhunted for a role at a chartered accounting firm to head up their IT audit.' I was shocked; my mentor, friend and research partner was going to abandon me. Neither of us held the IT audit areas of chartered accounting firms in high regard, so why abandon me for a business area with such a poor reputation?

Another block further along our walk, I found out there was a condition precedent on him taking the role. It was then that he revealed a role and salary had been negotiated to include me joining their firm as well. 'I've done a deal. They were after me, but I stated that it was both or neither. If you're not keen, then the deal is off.

What do you say, Jase?' As he spoke, I could hear the excitement in his voice. To say that I was in a state of shock was an understatement.

Are we really going over to the dark side?

Clearly, I had already decided in my mind that I was on board with the idea; I wasn't going to be abandoned. The airline had been very slow in working out who would replace the head of internal audit. No one had been confirmed for the role, and neither had my role of acting IT audit manager been formalised. So, maybe we could actually have some positive input into the chartered accounting profession on the IT audit side.

We continued walking along to the next block. 'Well,' my friend went on, 'if you think it is something worthwhile, the salary is excellent, and your role would be as audit manager. You will be treated as a senior manager. How can you pass up an opportunity like that, Jase?' Again, his excitement was intriguing me. A manager at my age, let alone a senior manager? I couldn't have asked for anything more. In those days, a senior manager was considered one level below a partner, so I agreed to meet the person responsible for an interview. This turned out to be an odd experience, as I think the partner was more nervous than me; it was really me interviewing them because, ultimately, if they failed to impress me, then the whole deal was off.

In the end, I agreed to join the new firm, and shortly afterwards, my friend and I left the airline and started work with a major international accounting firm. Some of the other managers were surprised I was given a senior manager's office and that I was invited to the Friday evening drinks with the partners, which was an exclusive get together.

I also had to contend with Dad, who was a bit annoyed I had left the airline. He had worked for the railway his entire life, and his philosophy was to stick to the same place because that was the way he believed it should be. I tried to explain to him that, in my profession, there were limited roles within a company, so changing companies was needed in order to progress. Yet, he just couldn't understand why I didn't change professions and stay within the one company like he had. He had been a conductor, a station master, a train planner and a freight controller, and he had worked in HR and then passenger marketing. So, he believed that you could have your entire career in the one company. The concept of a professional career like the one I was working on was completely foreign to him, and he wasn't happy.

Dad was also getting increasingly frustrated that I hadn't purchased an apartment yet. I had taken out a loan with a credit union to develop a credit rating, and that was supposed to be building a deposit. When he'd grown up with his alcoholic father, they had moved from rental to rental because they kept being thrown out for not paying the rent on time. As soon as Dad could, he had purchased a home. Many of our conversations were about the importance of me buying a home, and my lack of action on this was becoming a mounting frustration for him. So, I thought the news about me being in a position to purchase a nice new car would be a good counterpoint— for the time being. I wanted to demonstrate the value my profession held, which helped me to afford to replace the car I had bought from my parents in my first year of university.

However, the argument between us went horribly wrong. He used words like *waste, wrong* and *uneducated,* and trying to reason with him just made him fume even more. 'Firstly, Jason,' he said, 'you should have purchased a family station wagon, and secondly, it is a waste to buy a luxury car. You should be putting money into buying an apartment or a house. Not being frivolous and uneducated. What did you go to university for?' The verbal abuse never seemed to stop. No matter how hard I tried, Dad was never happy. There was anger and spite as I tried again to explain myself.

'Dad, I don't have a family, so a large family station wagon would be a waste.'

Through gritted teeth, my father tried to force home his point. 'No! Because a car should last for a long time, and when you do get married and have a family, Jason, you would have a ready-made and appropriate vehicle.'

Once again, Mum had to diffuse the situation and partake in another intervention to calm both of us down. Our Sunday calls stopped for a short time, as the same conversation kept coming up, and I was getting bored and agitated with the same mundane fights all the time. Taking a break from Dad helped me to get my head in order for starting my new job.

My work at the accounting firm had some exciting components, and we focused on establishing an IT audit consulting business. My part would involve training the IT audit chartered accountants, getting the IT elements of external audits back on track and recruiting clients.

Shortly after our arrival, it became obvious why we were so desperately needed. Other partners in America were putting a lot of pressure on the Australian firm to get their act together, as our part of the external audits for clients was putting global relationships at risk. The team and I succeeded in turning those clients around and stabilising them, working through the issues and redeveloping the training of our team members. I introduced a gamut of modern techniques that we had been using at the airline, such as the Computer Assisted Audit Techniques (CAATs).

My friend and I became increasingly more respected for our work efforts. We started to bring in new clients from mainly airlines and financial institutions, and we ended up with a very interesting portfolio of work. The global consolidation of the chartered accounting firms was about to commence, and our firm announced a global merger with a similar-sized firm, which was one of the first of the new wave of mergers. I was put on the national team to draft a new training course for the Chartered Accountants Professional Year IT Audit module. Finally that year, I was awarded the formal title of senior manager with the responsibilities that I was already exercising.

My faith never waned during this period in my life, and as time progressed, I took on more preaching in my local parish and sometimes at other churches through my youth leaders' network. This was something that I really enjoyed, and people said I had good communication skills and the ability to reach an audience.

Eventually, I visited the Theological School open day at Melbourne University, where the Uniting Church had a partnership with two other Christian denominations. After discussions with many people, there were conversations around whether or not I should apply as a candidate for the ministry in the Church. This can be a lengthy process of discussions with the elders and the minister at local parish level before then going to the next level up at Presbytery. Following this, there would then be testing and interviews at the synod and college level. This was a big deal.

My preliminary discussions with my minister and the elders were encouraging, and I got support from my friends. However, before I took it any further, I thought I would go over to Adelaide and see my parents to talk it over with them. I usually drove over; it took me about eight hours from Melbourne, and I was very comfortable with the drive. However, something about this trip and this conversation made me think it would be best to travel via bus; I could think about what I wanted to say without having to focus on the road. So, I boarded the express bus, which took a little longer than if I'd gone by car due to the stops. I had planned a long weekend of visiting my parents and was very nervous about how this would go.

I was not at ease at any stage over the weekend because I had a feeling that Dad wouldn't react well. Eventually over dinner one night, I—with some reluctance—outlined what I was thinking of doing. There was an immediate and negative reaction from Dad. Again, I was accused of throwing my life away, and I was accused of disrespecting everything that he and Mum had done to get me to where I was, especially with my career. The feeling in the room that night was as if someone had died, and that someone was me. I was very disheartened. What made it even worse was that on this trip back home to Adelaide, I didn't even get to sleep in my own room. Mum and Dad had slept in separate rooms since I was about ten because, as I had learned on my trip to Mildura and the Grand Hotel, Dad snored exceptionally badly—in hindsight, he probably had undiagnosed sleep apnoea. The extension to the house had been made in the mid 1970s, with the extra bedroom that had originally become Dad's, a bathroom and a family room, but Dad took over my bedroom in the main part of the house as his soon after I moved out.

The family room in the extension was designed to fit a three-quarter-sized snooker table, and there was sufficient space for a large lounge and dining area, which had its own sliding door to access the back yard. The concept of this design was so that, when I finished university, I would move into the extension. Then, when I got married, a wall could be inserted between the main house and the extension to allow privacy for my wife and me. After that, when kids arrived, Mum and Dad would be retiring, so my family would move into the original house while Mum and Dad would move into the extension. My family life had been predetermined, but, with me leaving, Dad's grand plan for my life was now destroyed. His plan for the family living arrangements had been destroyed.

Was Dad missing me ... or controlling me? He had moved into my old bedroom, and now I was staying in what was his old room and not mine. Later, I found out from Mum that Dad really hadn't coped with me moving out of the house and was trying to get Mum to agree to them moving to Melbourne. Fortunately for me, Mum hadn't wanted to make the move at that time and persuaded Dad to stay in Adelaide.

After the dinner conversation, I was devastated. It seemed that my whole existence was for Dad's gratification, and being a minister was not good enough for his son. Mum tried to console me, but I didn't want to talk.

The next morning, as we were heading to town for me to board the Greyhound bus back to Melbourne, there was complete silence. Then, at the bus station before the bus arrived, I received another talking to. Dad shouted, 'Get all of these flighty ideas out of your head. Especially concerning the Church. You have a responsible position, and you will not proceed with such foolery! Do you hear me, Jason?'

Of course I heard him! He was so loud. I tried to say goodbye, but I couldn't even look him in the face. He was still talking as I boarded, but I didn't hear the rest of what he was saying; I was looking for my upgraded seat on the bus. This was going to be a very long and lonely trip back home, as I was so sad and shocked by the realisation that my whole existence in life was to satisfy Dad's expectations.

Looking back, I have often wondered if, like some gay people, I was seeking to enter the ministry as a way of managing or denying my sexual orientation. I have carried on in many leadership roles within the Church, and I also have many years of preaching behind me. So, do I really need to resolve that question now? I think I am learning that these questions of the past really don't need to be resolved right away or, in fact, ever. It was what it was, and I need to simply accept those parts and move on without rerunning stories of optional endings in my head; I have to stop playing the same tune of 'what if?' because it doesn't serve me any purpose now, nor will it in the future. I have realised that this type of thinking just gets me stuck in the past.

From that point in my life, when I boarded the Greyhound bus back to Melbourne, and for around the next thirty years, my aim was to pray for the gay thoughts and actions to go away. Once a month, we would have communion in my local church, and during this most sacred Christian service, the hammer in my head asked God to help me.

Make me normal.

Take the queer out of me.

Shortly after the firm's merger, we were the first group in the Australian practice to win an important new client: the National Power Corporation of the Philippines. It was a major body of work over a two-year period, with teams going to the Philippines on a four-to-five-week cycle. Because I was single and no longer had a girlfriend, I was asked to do two cycles per trip to provide continuity between teams. While I had spoken at conferences overseas, this was my first big opportunity to work in an international context.

There were improvements in democracy, but it was still a turbulent time in the Philippines. We were briefed on some security protocols and potential emergency plans from the Australian Embassy, and we soon discovered that there were significant security problems with our apartment. We backed onto a police academy, and there were military barracks across the main road. In any coup attempt, the soldiers loyal to the former president would fight for control of the shopping centre across the road from our apartment for supplies.

My initial role was to organise the purchase of computer equipment for the team to undertake their Computer Assisted Audit Technique training program. The initial audit progressed very well, and we then debriefed with the responsible manager. It was then that I discovered I hadn't invested any time in learning about the culture in which I was working. The vice president wanted to talk about what had happened the day before, regarding the audit exit meeting with an executive, and I received my first lesson of 'face' in the art of delivering a negative message without directly attacking a person's reputation—I had learned a lot about how an IT audit report could be seen as an attack on an individual's reputation. On this day, rather than being the teacher, I was the student, and that became the start of learning about cultures in the business world, which became very important in my later career.

My father had been very concerned about my security when travelling to the Philippines, given the ongoing coup attempts. During my second trip—another two-month stint and again supervising two one-month teams—a bomb went off in the Greater Manila area every day, and I was able to work out the pattern. One day, after some local intelligence had raised my concerns, I rang the Australian Embassy and spoke to my usual contact, who was reasonably high up in rank.

'Hi, John, I've just received intelligence from two sources that there is a plan for a coup this evening. Have you any information and recommendations?'

'Well, Jason, the official Australian position is that the Philippines is a safe and stable country. However, I was talking to my wife this morning over breakfast, and she indicated how good the sales are in Hong Kong this weekend.' This was code for, 'It would be good to get out if you can.' So, I managed to get a Cathay Pacific flight that evening. However, as the flight time came nearer, it looked like I would miss my escape because a typhoon hit, and the storm was so bad that it caused buses to overturn on the main roads. When we eventually got to the airport, my flight was delayed, but fortunately the coup still hadn't happened by the time I did manage to leave the country.

When I arrived in Hong Kong, I spoke with my project's lead partner in Melbourne, and he indicated that he would send the next team member to the Philippines on Monday even though I wouldn't get back there until Monday myself. I asked him to wait until I was able to return and connect personally back into the information network that I had developed.

I arrived back late Monday morning and went to the client's office. I touched base again with Melbourne, only to find out that the partner had made his own remote enquiries and decided to send the next team member up to arrive that very day. She would arrive later in the evening, but I was very annoyed and also saw it as a breach of trust. It also happened to be my birthday—not exactly what I needed!

Later that afternoon, our client's vice president came to find me. 'What happened to the coup?' I asked.

'The storm was so bad they couldn't proceed, but word is that they are going to try again tonight.'

It was too late to evacuate to Hong Kong again, and I now had a staff member arriving early evening, so I booked two rooms at a major hotel in the city. Then, I went back to the apartment to collect some things and hopped in the car with the driver to collect the new team member. When she saw me at the airport, she wanted to know what was happening because she knew I didn't want her to come as yet. I said, 'I got back on the ground this morning and the vice president has indicated there may be a coup attempt this evening, so we are evacuating to a hotel in the city.'

When we arrived at the hotel, we checked in and then met at the restaurant on the top floor. We agreed that, because it was my birthday, the partner could pay for a splash-up dinner in the circumstances.

Anyway, we got over this incident, and, apart from the ongoing daily bombings, the rest of my work in the Philippines was relatively uneventful. Every week, I would get questions from Dad regarding my safety and security in Manila, and no amount of explanation would reduce his level of tension. On one hand, it was nice to know that he was concerned—as we were—but I was on the ground and could see the reality of the situation, while they were responding to distant and perhaps sensational media reporting. Soon, it became frustrating to know that the weekly calls were just a repetition from Dad about my safety, so I stopped looking forward to our weekly chats.

Frequently, I considered my future with the accounting firm and saw the struggles that my friend was having in becoming a partner. The firm had just introduced the concept of a principal, which was a new level between a senior manager and a partner. Eventually, my friend was made a principal after what seemed like a lot of delay, in my mind, and I realised that it would be a long time before I had my chance. So, I contemplated which industry would be the area I could possibly continue to learn in and take my skills to the next level. The one that stood out was in the banking sector, but I would need to wait. I needed the right opportunity.

In January, 1991, the next NCYC was held in Toowoomba

in Queensland, an hour southwest of Brisbane, across the ranges. My youth and young adults group had continued to grow and had renamed itself the People's Front of Armadale (PFA). There was a serious discussion with the parish elders around the new name; some said it was too close to the Palestinian Liberation Organisation (PLO), which was very active around this time, and others saw the connection to the Monty Python film *The Life of Brian* and its People's Front of Judea and all the other variants in that famous skit. However, enough of the elders thought it was clever and that it would resonate with younger people as part of our evangelism and outreach. So, those who went to the NCYC as part of my group organised some specially made polo shirts with the PFA logo and our names on the back, which I was able to have made in the Philippines.

Some, but not all of our group, went on the synod coaches that took a couple of days getting from Melbourne to Toowoomba and likewise coming back. We usually camped in school halls for our overnight stops. When we arrived, the guest preacher that year was the famous Tony Campolo from the USA, and the theme was 'Breaking New Ground'. During one of his talks, he commented that, sometimes, there would be a few people who would need prayer around them—those internally breaking new ground within themselves—but he reiterated that the prayer was not for everyone. It was supposed to resonate with the broken; those who felt they needed to be remoulded. It certainly resonated with me, so I talked about it with my close friends at the conference. We agreed that it did seem to apply to me, and so we had a time of prayer. I did feel broken, but I assumed it resulted from the abuse that I'd had from my father and his rejection of me exploring a call to ordained ministry. I did not yet know that there was more to come, as I had not yet understood or comprehended the level of abuse

151

he was capable of.

On the trip back, as we were approaching Canberra, the Australian Prime Minister, Bob Hawke, responded favourably to the request from the American President, George Bush Snr to participate in the invasion of Iraq. This led to two busloads of young adults becoming very concerned about the justification for another war in the Middle East. We arranged a protest in the major mall in Canberra, and this was to be one of my early political protests. Soon after arriving home, we continued with our fortnightly young adults Bible study home group at my place.

One of the things I did after the NCYC conference was to enrol in a Bachelor of Theology at one of the divinity schools on campus at Melbourne University. The level of the conversations was of the highest order, and I found the work academically challenging—I hadn't done any study for a number of years, and certainly not in this field. Soon afterwards, and rather unexpectedly, a job was advertised for an IT audit manager in one of the major banks, but it was based in Sydney. I spent time talking with my home group friends about this and asked them for their advice, as the core of this group had been part of the prayer time we'd had at the NCYC in Toowoomba. After a week, we agreed that I should have a go at the new job offer, so I submitted my application. Shortly afterwards, I had a telephone interview, and I was then asked for a face-to-face meeting in Sydney.

The interview went well and, a few days later, I received a job offer. We negotiated a bit on the salary, removal costs and temporary accommodation, and soon the final written offer was received. I then went to see my reporting partner to resign, and he was shocked. I liked that he felt that way and that he'd had no indication that I wanted to leave. He said he usually knew when a member of staff was thinking about resigning because their work effort dropped off, but he stated that mine had actually increased. In my mind, though, the improvement in work effort was because, as a perfectionist, I wanted to ensure that all my assignments would be finished to a high, professional standard before I left. The partner wanted to know if there was anything he could offer that would keep me, but I told him no although I appreciated the consideration.

The one thing I had already learned as a senior manager was that when a person was ready to leave, you might be able to keep them for a while, but they generally do end up going. I had decided to leave for a wide variety of reasons, and it was something that I had prayed about and spent time with my friends discussing at length before making a final decision.

Planning for my departure was then underway, and there were many friends and colleagues who were surprised with my decision to move to Sydney. It was the right thing for me to do professionally even though there was sadness in leaving so many of my friends behind—many of whom I would stay in contact with, but that contact would come and go over time. I also felt sad leaving my theological studies, and I knew that it would probably be a while before I would start them again ... if ever.

I thought about the reasons why Sydney was a good place for me to relocate to. While Melbourne had helped me to get closer to discovering who I was, it was still too close to Adelaide, where Dad continued to try and have influence over my life. Ultimately, it was a bit too close for comfort, so I knew that it was time to move further away and try and start again.

A Move to Sydney: Unspoken Words

Towards the end of the first quarter in 1991, there were bittersweet celebrations surrounding my departure from Melbourne and a new spring in my step for what Sydney would hold for me as a young, senior executive. One of the main benefits in my move to Sydney was that the bank provided me with a temporary apartment for several months. Basically, all I needed was my clothing, while everything else was to be put in storage until I found a permanent place of my own.

The transition from Melbourne to Sydney was smooth, and I quickly adapted to my temporary apartment in Artarmon, which was close to the train station. This was a very convenient way to get into the city rather than battling Sydney's congested traffic. A special bonus was that, every morning and evening, my train crossed the iconic Sydney Harbour Bridge—something special that I don't think I will ever forget.

Work was starting to settle, and I had a major project that I had to focus on with my team of about six people. I was disappointed, though, because part of my personal objective in joining one of the four big banks in Australia was to further my own learning, but I found myself more the teacher rather than being taught more technical IT audit skills. However, this unexpected turn continued to add to my future skills bank. The major project I was working on involved replacing the core retail banking systems, which was a mammoth activity, and it wasn't going well. Every time I asked questions, there seemed to be another issue that led to even more questions. I was also surprised by the politics in the internal audit department: I wanted to raise some very serious concerns that I'd identified in the short period of time I'd been there, but the message from the top indicated that they wanted to stop me from reporting on my findings. I felt boxed in personally and professionally.

How can we be Internal Audit and exercise our ethical responsibilities if we acquiesce to some executives' view that we can't criticise this project?

We also acquired a small bank and, again, I was involved in the integrity of the amalgamation processes whereby we kept recommending to the bank that we were not ready to bring the value—the customer account balances—in. Back in my earliest vocational training in the airlines, I had been taught to be methodical. However, against our advice, the bank proceeded with the acquisition. I was the designated internal auditor to monitor the process and undertake independent reconciliation between the amount showing in the other bank's records of their customer balances and what our system had created for these new customers. I checked my work because there was a disparity, and I knew that my reconciliation work was right. I also knew that it wasn't my fault; we had clearly told the bank's leadership that the import program wasn't working correctly, and now I had to certify the funds received into our system. To my horror, but not to my surprise, hundreds of millions of dollars went into suspense accounts and not into our new customers' accounts.

I had my job to do, which was to attend to what was to be the post-conversion meeting—now a crisis meeting—

on how to manage customers, media and the financial regulators. As people came to withdraw money when the bank opened at ten o'clock in the morning soon after the acquisition, it seemed highly possible that there would not be money in their accounts.

There were other ethical issues emerging during that time, and I actually decided to leave after only eighteen months. It was a good learning experience in having to deal with a financial institution that was in crisis and going through a period of being unprofitable; however, I was definitely not in a good position with this major bank, particularly as a newly brought in non-banker.

Throughout these transitions, I remained committed to my church community albeit at a different parish: Chatswood Central. One of the people I had met at the NCYC suggested I might want to consider looking into this one, and it turned out to be the start of a fulfilling journey. The first Sunday I attended the service, I introduced myself to some people and had a feeling this was a different, but good, place to be. One woman was really pleased to meet me, particularly when she found out that I had been doing youth work at the Uniting Church in Melbourne. She said, 'Well, this is an answer to our prayers. We've been looking for somebody to help work with our youth and teenagers for quite a while.' I felt an immediate sense of belonging. The comment that perhaps I was 'an answer to their prayers', was gratifying. I eventually found a great apartment up in Lindfield to rent and, again, not too far from a train station, which was well within walking distance.

While I now felt secure and was having some fun, I couldn't shake a niggling feeling I had. As time went on, I kept having issues with my dad. It was, however, seemingly all in my head, or so I believed. My thoughts were starting to frustrate and worry me, and I got to the point where I decided that I needed to stand up to my father. These thoughts reached a critical point just before my parents were due to visit me in Sydney around my birthday in late August. This would be the first time I had seen them since moving to this part of Australia in May.

I started preparing myself for what I was going to say to my dad: that I really didn't like the pressure and that I didn't appreciate him always making me feel like I wasn't good enough. I kept playing these conversations around in my head. It was like a movie in my mind, and releasing my feelings towards my father was giving me a massive sense of internal grief. But was I brave enough to stand up to him? This would be my twenty-ninth birthday, yet I still felt like an oppressed child.

Before their visit with me, Mum and Dad were in Hunter Valley and in Maitland, which is about a two hours' drive north of Sydney. They were catching up with some old Navy people, and Dad was being interviewed for the first time about his war experiences on *HMAS Australia* from World War II.

Meanwhile, I had gotten to know a couple of people in my apartment block and had been invited down one night for dinner; it was nice to meet some neighbours. I had a late night, and when I got home there was a message on my answering machine asking me to call a number that I didn't recognise. I called it anyway, but I only got as far as saying, 'My name is Jason—' before they told me I had to call Maitland Hospital urgently. So, I called straight away and asked for Mum. I could already feel something was horribly wrong, and when Mum came on the line, those feelings were confirmed: I found out Dad had died that evening. It was a shock, and it was unexpected.

I told Mum that I would drive up to Maitland straight away. She insisted that I ask her friend Lorna, who lived in Sydney, to come up as well. When I called Lorna, Mick, who was Dad's mate from his Navy days, answered the phone. He was devastated, but I asked if I could speak to his wife and passed on Mum's request. Lorna immediately said she'd come with me, so I went and picked her up, and we started to drive. It seemed to be a slow journey with not a lot of conversation. I actually had to stop halfway for a bathroom break, which was very unusual for me, but obviously my body was already reacting.

Eventually, we got to Maitland and found the hospital, and in the emergency ward, we found Mum. I spent a little bit of time alone with Dad, who still had tubes coming out of various parts of his body. He'd been cleaned up as best as the hospital staff could manage, but there was only so much they could do. There had to be an autopsy because he'd died out of his home state, and everything had to be left in situ for the medical examiner.

A sense of frustration and anger rose within. Only days earlier, I had decided I was going to confront Dad about our relationship, but now, I had lost my chance to find some closure.

Are these unreasonable thoughts and feelings?

Is it reasonable to focus on my needs when my dad has just died?

Will having these, what some might consider selfish, thoughts add to my shame later in life?

He'd died before I could actually say anything, so instead, I gave him a bittersweet kiss and then went and found Mum again. I got a bit of the story from her about what had happened. They were finishing up dinner, and Dad had complained about stomach pains. He thought it must have been his appendix. They had actually argued, as Mum believed that where his pain was couldn't be appendicitis. An ambulance was called, and they managed to get him to the hospital alive, but he died soon after he'd arrived.

For the next few days, we stayed with the family they had stopped with for the interviews, and they were just so generous. They treated us like their own family while we sorted out a whole raft of things. There were stories, and there were tears, but actually not a lot of tears from me. It was a surreal time. Then we had the issue of their car, the caravan, Dad's body; we were two hours away from Sydney, and a long way from Adelaide. Fortunately, Dad always over-engineered most things, including insurances, but on this occasion, it was our lifesaver. I rang the motor vehicle insurance company, and they said, 'This is not a problem … it is all covered by the insurance. We'll work with the hospital and a local funeral parlour, and the insurance will cover the cost of getting your father's body, the car and the caravan back to Adelaide. We will also pay your mum's airfares.'

The next day, we received an update from the medical examiner about his report, which was to be submitted to the coroner. 'There probably is no need for a coronial inquiry,' he said. 'It's very obvious, and I was wrong to think there needed to be any further investigation. I was blown away because I've actually never seen such good surgery for a triple heart bypass. But unfortunately, your husband, your father, died of a ruptured aortic aneurysm. His kidney problems, and the enzymes they were producing, weakened that major artery through the middle of the body. It gave way, and he bled to death.'

The way the doctor described my father's last moments actually brought a tear to my eye. I couldn't imagine anyone bleeding to death … and on the inside too. Dad's death was affecting me even though I didn't want to admit it.

It was a difficult drive back to Sydney, and then we stayed the night at my place. The next day, my mum and I had to face the several-hours flight back home to Adelaide. I didn't have a birthday; instead, we started the funeral arrangements. We already had a funeral director in Adelaide, so we called them in and then tried to work out how to celebrate my father's life. The only thing we knew he really liked was my school, so we contacted them to see if we could hold a service in the school chapel. Without any question, the response was, 'Of course.' The school chaplain came around and visited with us, and he helped us through part of that process.

Quite frankly, I thought it would be a relatively small funeral. We knew that the final part of the process would be held at the Centennial Park crematorium. After the funeral director asked questions about which clubs and associations Dad had been involved with, he said, 'I think, just to be on the safe side, we'll book the larger chapel.'

The day of the funeral came, and the service at the school chapel went well. I don't think I mourned very well that day, as I think I took the role of being the support and carer for my mother. The funeral procession then headed to Centennial Park, where more people were waiting to pay their last respects. The funeral director was right; he obviously knew his business very well, and it was fairly full, including the mezzanine level. I just hadn't made the connections between the Rotary Club and the Probus Club, the HMAS Australia Association and the HMAS Burdekin Association or the connections across the Navy and his work there. There were a lot of people in attendance.

I think the hardest part at the cremation interment service for me was when the returned servicemen came forward to put their poppies on the coffin. You expect these sorts of things, but you're never prepared. You never know how these old war veterans actually want to do things—no doubt the right things. There were many who obviously had injuries, and there were even more who were just struggling with old age. Others had many different disabilities. I don't think I will ever forget the image of the man with his walking frame, who came up to the platform where the coffin lay. He got to the ledge and refused to have his frame up on the higher platform. He also refused to have any help. It was a mark of honour and respect, but I still struggle with that image. Why did he want to struggle so much to put a poppy on the coffin? His pain and discomfort as he shuffled ever so slowly up and around made me uncomfortable. Was it bravery? Was it stubbornness? Was it pride? Was it respect? I didn't understand then, and in a sense now, I still don't understand. That was the moment I found most depressing.

The coffin was then interred for the cremation. So, we returned to have our morning tea at the reflection rooms, and then we went home. We were lucky that a number of our closer friends came home too, but I felt empty, and I felt cheated. I'd had something I needed to do, yet I'd never felt strong enough or brave enough to say what I had set out to say to my father. And then, when I had finally decided to confront the person who had made my life very difficult, the tables had turned on me, and I didn't get to have my closure. I felt so angry. But now, I had to ignore that, as I needed to support Mum.

A few days later, I headed back to Sydney, and away we went again with work and life and church. However, a few months later, when my mother was visiting a neighbour, she fell off their front steps and badly broke her ankle. She spent quite a few months in hospital, so every other weekend, I'd fly back to Adelaide to see how she was doing and to provide whatever support I could through this secondary trauma that was happening for her. She was hurting, and it presented as this injury, which you often see when a family member passes on. I could sense her loneliness.

Around this time, I was in a good Bible study group, and I was starting to build some friendships and networks in Sydney. The youth ministry unit in Melbourne were saddened that I had left so had contacted their counterpart in Sydney. I was invited to join the board of the next NCYC, which was to be held in Canberra, in 1993. It was actually good to join, and although I hadn't anticipated being on the board of such a big conference and event, it was yet another good learning experience and a way to meet more people. They only had one free board position to offer me, and that was covering three areas: delegates from other churches—who were our ecumenical partners— our international delegates and our differently abled or disabled delegates. I had small sub-teams working on each of those, which I oversaw, and then I disseminated back to the main board.

In hindsight, I never really grieved properly for Dad, and here I was, back in Sydney without family. However, my network of church friends was amazing and supportive in whatever ways they could be. But I was hurting: I was twenty-nine, I had buried my first parent, and I didn't know how to grieve. Furthermore, I was still angry about not being able to confront my dad. Sexual confusion also continued to rage within, and the sexual rage and the rage around my father collided with a destructive force.

I headed out one night to see a male prostitute. It was as if this was some way that I was going to hurt my now-dead father, but in the end, the hurt in my head would only hurt me. I arrived, and when I got undressed, we lay next to each other. But nothing happened; not even a kiss. I wasn't there for me. I was there to hurt someone else. And that person had died.

After driving home in tears, I ran into my en suite bathroom and found the bleach and other household cleaning products, which I then used to wash my body— chemicals that shouldn't have ever touched my skin. I cried myself to sleep that night in distress, which stemmed from my fear, after praying angrily to God.

Where the hell are you?

I felt my time at the bank had been testing, so when an opportunity presented itself for me to be the head of audit for a new rail freight operator, I made a move. At the end of the day, the ethics within the banking system were a very challenging phase in my life, and they became one of the major factors in me deciding to leave.

It did feel somewhat ironic that I would end up working in the same industry as Dad had done for his entire working life. I never disclosed this to my peers, but it meant that I had some knowledge of the sector, which was particularly useful when some tried to pull the 'you don't understand rail operations' wool over my eyes.

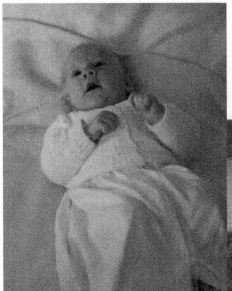

Below: Jason, 1 year old, walking in the front yard of his home in Adelaide, South Australia.

Above: Jason, 6 months old, Adelaide, South Australia.

Below: Jason, 4 years old, starting school in a mid-year intake of school-based kindergarten, Mitchell Park Primary School. May, 1967.

Above: Jason, 4 years old, always had a love for teddies.

Below: Jason, 11 years old, travelling by train on a family trip from Adelaide to Perth. Cook station in the Nullabor.

Above: Jason, 8 years old and already playing U12 basketball.

Below: Jason's 21st birthday party at the Hilton Hotel, Adelaide. 1983.

Above: Fortunately, Westminster School were not strict with haircuts in the 1970s.

Above: Jason's Bachelor of Economics graduation from Flinders University of South Australia in 1984.

Below: Jason at a function for his departure from Australian Airlines Internal Audit in 1987

Above: Attending the Sydney Gay and Lesbian Mardi Gras parade in 2019, after coming out.

Below: Jason at a look out overlooking Broken Hill, NSW (but in the South Australian time zone!)

Above: Mother (Joan), Jason, Father (Peter). Mother's Day lunch in the Adelaide Hills. This may have been the first time Jason had a little too much to drink!

Below: Kate Masters (Jason's daughter), 2 years old.

Above: Joshua Masters (Jason's son), 4 years old.

Above: The wedding of Jason's mother and father, Joan Beatrice (nee Smith) and Peter Eric Masters, 1961.

Above: The house Jason grew up in. This is an external drawing prepared for the sale of the house when Jason's mother moved to Sydney.

Below: The foundation stone in the centre of Westminster School. Overlooked by the magnificent school chapel.

Above: Jason's confirmation into the UCA, with the Rev Peterschlingmann, then minister of at Armadale Uniting Church, Victoria, 1985.

Left: The grounds of Westminster School. The trees under which Jason could not talk about how he felt with another boy.

Above: Westminster Preparatory School entrance. Jason moved here from Mitchell Park Primary School at the beginning of year 5, when he was 9 years old.

Above: Senior School Changing Shed, with privacy partitians than were not in existance when Jason was at school. Private shower rooms have become the norm in updating school facilities.

Above: Jason attended Flinders University of South Australia. The building to the front has been significantly remodeled since his attendance, however the buildings in the background include Mathematics where Jason studied Maths and Computer Science.

Above: The courtyard of the Social Science building where Jason studied Economics and Geography at Flinders University of South Australia.

My Evolution in Sydney

Through this period, my association with the Church in Sydney continued to evolve. I was working with an emerging youth group and occasionally helping with Sunday school. I was very involved with a Bible study group and starting to meet a number of people around my own age. As the youth group started to expand and grow, I got to know more of those families. One of the techniques I used was to visit each of the teenagers, probably about once a term, just to talk about life, the Bible, God—or whatever they wanted to talk about. It seemed to be a really useful relationship-building strategy. I started to run a youth camp every year, with each year having a different theme, and we'd go away for perhaps three days, often around Easter.

One year, one of the boys involved in the group wanted to get his mates from high school entered in the local basketball competition. He asked if I'd be willing to coach their team, and I agreed. In fact, I ended up coaching them for three or four years, and it was a wonderful experience and another part of my own growth. My youth groups and my basketball team were a safe place where they could talk with me about life, the universe and everything. It was because of running that basketball team that an idea—one that's come back to me much later in life—

started to emerge. When a boy or young man made an error on the basketball court, they'd often get distressed or annoyed with themselves, and they would stop trying or, at best, be sluggish as they moved into the next play. This often meant that the team—in a sport that is meant to have five people on the court focusing on the game— would ultimately only have four focused team members on the next active play.

What emerged was a mantra, a saying, which became something that they could anchor themselves to in that instant of the game. It was to reflect the fact that, sometimes, stuff just happens. You can wallow in it, or you can acknowledge it and move on. As the mantra emerged, it became a very clear statement.

You can't change the past, but you can influence the future.

This became one of the sayings I used regularly with the basketball teams I coached. It was about the fact that mistakes happen—or, for a more increasingly real take on it, 'shit happens'. We would talk about them in a time-out, in a half-time break or during their next training, but in the game, if you made a mistake, you couldn't change it. You could, however, influence what happened in the next movement of that game.

Looking back on some old files and notes in preparation for writing this book, I rediscovered some letters I received on my Emmaus Walk—a Christian retreat where your sponsor asks your family and friends to write you some letters of encouragement. I found one from the boys in the basketball team, and the line one of them wrote really struck a chord with me.

To Jason,
Thanks for teaching me that although I can't change the past, I can influence the future ...

And there was also one from a mother.

I'm sure you know we all appreciate the obvious things you do for the boys in the team, and I'm sure most of the parents can see what a difference it has made in their son's lives—certainly for [son's name], it has provided direction, structure and focus. It came at a time when he was floundering, and he could have really gone off the rails or, at best, continued floating in unhappiness ... You have given him and the others a very positive male role model—not just the example of a male giving up time and lots of effort to help develop them ... but the positive example of a male with a demanding job, a good education, varied interests, a spiritual life—a rare and very special example for them—and your awareness, sensitivity and caring. Qualities we mothers would love our sons to develop. Those qualities have undoubtedly come from your personal pain, but as you well know, they are the jewels one receives from those experiences and will ultimately be the source of the greatest blessing in your life. When you have completed your journey into wholeness, I am sure they will enable you to have a much richer feeling and spiritual life than those who have not had such experiences or the courage to work through them.

Rereading these from 1994, and having been through my first mental health crisis, I still had no idea where the personal journey would go.

Parallel to these experiences, I started my executive role at the railways as one of the first heads of internal audit or chief audit executive of a major corporation that was not an accountant. Mid-morning on my first day, the general manager of HR turned up in my office. He said to me, 'Jason, we need to have a brief talk. One of the key things we need to do in turning this industry around is to be very different in how we engage with our workforce. As part of that process, we're in negotiation with the Australian Council of Trade Unions (ACTU) about an enterprise bargaining agreement that will be very different from any that have gone before. One of the key elements of this is that we're going to have a very flat structure, and we're going to have teams. So, it will be teams rather than individuals who are going to be held accountable. Therefore, I need you to think about how internal controls will work in that structure, that environment, and how internal audit will work in an organisation that does not have individual accountability but has team-based accountability.' He went to leave my office, but then he stopped. 'Oh, by the way, I'm out of the office for the rest of the week. I'll be back in the office for a short period of time on Friday, and you need to present your thesis then on how, as an organisation, we should approach this key critical issue to the secretary of the ACTU and their executives on Monday morning. I'm sure you can do it. Good luck.'

I was stunned, but then again, there was also an air of excitement—this would be the first time I would be part of the executive team. Today, I still remember the first executive committee meeting I attended there, when the CEO said, 'This is the last appointment to our executive team; I've asked Jason to join. We are flexing this business as we work out how to do it, and I think it's important, from an internal audit point of view, for Jason to understand where we're going. I think it's important for him to comment and to add value to our discussions on our strategy and what might be some of the internal control implications of what we're thinking.' There were nods around the room and welcomes, but then the CEO turned to me and said, 'But, Jason, when we're in this executive room, we don't limit ourselves to our area or our domain of responsibility. You need to bring all of who you are and all of your knowledge to the discussions as is appropriate.'

Years later, I would ponder this point once again: to bring all of myself into the room. I *was* bringing all my knowledge and all my expertise into the room, but I was forever, it seemed, the actor. What did it even mean to bring all of yourself into the room?

Looking back now, I can ascertain that it would take over twenty-five years for me to finally bring all of myself into the executive room.

In January, 1993, we held the NCYC in Canberra. We constructed an educational model that encouraged the young people who came to this convention to start thinking independently about their journey and their relationship with God and Jesus Christ; we didn't necessarily want it to be filtered by their youth leaders. However, we learned the hard way, as we didn't manage to prepare the youth leaders or convention chaplains for that direct learning model very well.

Two things caused us grief in the middle of the week: a skit and a speech. The speech, given by the gay student minister, was probably the first time I heard discussions about how one might consider the biblical interpretations of some of the texts that are often used to oppress gay people in Christian churches. There was certainly some pushback from that. But surprisingly, it was the skit that actually caused the most problems in many ways. It was a short play about a youth group and how a heterosexual teen couple in the group had sex. The skit then focused on how those young people were treated when they were found out: they were ostracised.

With these two sessions, some youth leaders went berserk. My hypothesis—unproven, but I like it—is that, potentially, a lot of the youth leaders had yet to properly work through their theology around sexuality in all its forms: what did sexual theology mean, and what was appropriate sexual activity? It helped being religious for them to use the strict, sexual construct to manage their own sexual thoughts, desires and activities. Also, I wonder if a number had not actually worked through their own sexuality, so the conversations were potentially a personal, internal threat.

The backlash was pretty vigorous from a number of people, and I became involved in many crisis talks with the leadership around how to respond and manage anger— particularly with some who were using their anger in a fierce way.

One of my responsibilities was the international delegate contingent, with many of the members coming from Papua New Guinea (PNG) and the Pacific Islands. After the skit and the speech, there was significant threat of a walk-out from the convention, with potentially over a hundred of the international delegates leaving. I clearly remember standing with a significant number of these leaders on the grass hill outside the main sporting stadiums in Canberra, where we were holding the big rallies, and negotiating with the delegates to stay in the conference. It was a hard conversation, and it was hard listening. Yet, it was a really interesting cultural conversation for me because, in many ways, I was naïve, underprepared, unskilled and had a lack of knowledge of the different cultures from Fiji, Tonga, Samoa, PNG and Indonesia. Some of them held a more conservative position on many issues and biblical interpretations than I held then and currently hold now, and there was a lot of listening and reflection. There was encouragement from me to explore with them where the conference was going to go from that point on, how they could respond with their communities of youth at the conference and how difficult conversations might end up being rewarding for all. Thankfully, they did not walk out, which came down to reciprocal listening, respect, perseverance and patience.

When I returned from the convention, I was exhausted. I suspect I was also totally unaware that one of those topics was speaking directly to me. My minister, whom I had a phenomenally good relationship with, suggested that I needed to take some time to recover and recuperate from the event; I readily agreed. But, as the days turned into a week, I felt worse, not better, and as weeks turned into months, I continued to feel like I was disappearing into a darkness that I had never experienced before.

My mental health was deteriorating, and I felt like I was in a very long train tunnel; one that was very familiar but that I hadn't registered before. In the tunnel, there was a train—imagine a steam train—coming up behind me. With my business and all my activities, I had somehow been able to keep in front of the train following me through the tunnel, but now, I was doing less. I had taken a leave of absence from my church leadership roles and a break from my youth group. Yet, rather than feeling refreshed from this downtime, I felt more sluggish. As I slowed, not knowing what to do, the train seemed to pick up speed, and I no longer had the energy or the mental capacity to keep in front of it. I could hear the noises behind me as the train came closer: the hissing and screeching of the engine, the sound of the bell and horn and the rattle of the locomotive on the tracks. Darkness grew and enveloped my brain and my life; helplessness overcame me.

A friend thought it might be worthwhile for me to see a counsellor, and they recommended somebody local.

Very graciously, they then said, 'You know what? Seeing a counsellor can be hard work, and you live by yourself. Why don't you stop by, if you see him on Saturday morning, and have breakfast with us after your session?' So, I started a journey; a pattern. That journey took over three years. And it was fucking hard.

This counsellor and I started to explore a variety of things, and then my dad came up. But, what I struggled with as we talked was how he likened my relationship with my father to emotional abuse. I'd heard of sexual abuse, and I could understand the psychological consequences of being sexually abused at any stage in one's life. I could also understand the concept of physical abuse and being beaten and hit or denied food or whatever. I could understand that. I could see that was real. However, I really struggled with this concept of emotional abuse.

You see, there was no sign; nothing outward. You couldn't see any bruising, bleeding or any other physical marks, and for me, being a victim of emotional abuse seemed to highlight a weakness in me as a person. I struggled, and I struggled, and I struggled even though the counsellor kept telling me, and trying to explain to me, that the emotional abuse from my father *was* real.

I wrote a poem around ANZAC Day and how I hated it because of what it did to my father. It spoke about the memory of the war and what it had done to our family. Moreover, it shared the way my dad had developed as a man, with nobody helping or supporting him with his mental and post-traumatic stress disorder. I wrote about the impact it had on my mother and more so on me. And the writing—in that poem—was like a waterfall of emotions that had been suppressed within me, just waiting to be released.

While I have since lost the poem, and I can't recreate it, it was a piece of text written for that point in time. Just writing this brings tears to my eyes, and I'm helpless to stop them from running down my face. I remember sitting in that room, my counsellor's room, as I handed him my poem. He cried as he said that he hated the poem because ANZAC Day was the most sacred of all days in Australia, yet he could see how much pain it brought me.

Americans talk of their Memorial Day, but many Americans I know that have been in Australia or New Zealand on ANZAC Day say this is what they wish they had in America. It is not a joyous day, and it is not a celebration; it is a day of mourning, of commemoration, of reflection and of criticising the implication of war. It is a hard day for those who have been through it and who have suffered the consequence of those wars. Through his tears, my counsellor said he hated my poem not for the poem itself, but for the challenge it gave him about ANZAC Day and for the insight it provided into my psyche; this was the first time I had really bared my soul. He could see that the grief in this poem was a proverbial key for the locked door of my history, my struggles, my fears.

As time went on, I made good progress in acknowledging that there were significant issues between my father and me. However, I still struggled when my counsellor said, 'Of all the emotional abuse patients I have seen in thirty years of counselling, I have never had a patient that has suffered the extraordinary emotional abuse that you have suffered.' I just couldn't accept it, and this was one of the biggest blocks to my healing. Acceptance and recovery were stalling.

My counsellor put me in touch with a program that ran over ten to twelve weeks, where you attended with the same group of people and then, towards the end, there was a weekend away. In one of the weekend sessions, I remember I was encouraged to do an exercise with a rolled up newspaper—I had to use it to beat a table, and I couldn't do it. There was so much fear in me that if I let my anger loose—that which I had controlled and oppressed and suppressed over the years—the violence within me could be extraordinary and uncontained, and I couldn't let it escape. Simply put, I was scared shitless to actually take a heavily rolled piece of newspaper and hit a table for fear of what it might release in me in the long run.

People had the opportunity to put their name in a hat, and if their name was brought out, they could do some Gestalt therapy—trying to find and see experiences and issues in their simplest form—in front of the group. As the weekend went on, this became more and more destructive for me, and the darkness began descending further with each session I observed. There was a therapy session with a woman, who had been raped by her father and her uncle; there was a session with a young man, who had been raped by his father and his sister; there was a session with another young man, whose father had beaten the crap out of him regularly. All this did for me over the weekend was feed into my idea of emotional abuse not being a real issue. Clearly, I was just a weakling. Indeed, it showed that I was weak as piss. I mean, I could hear and understand their abuse, their pain, and I could imagine the scars and the physical and emotional consequences. Theirs was real; mine wasn't.

On the last day of the retreat, my name came out of the hat. I went up onto the elevated platform with the therapist, and we started to explore one of my issues. God, it was tough. It was so, so tough. He wanted me to do some movements in response to my father, but I was stuck. I couldn't budge. And in the forty, long minutes of that session, there was continued stiffness in me and the inability to move. The tightening of my body, the clenching of my fists, the screwing up of my face ... oh, it was painful. It was hard. It was exhausting, and I was ready to collapse.

When the session finished, though, it became one of the doorways to my recovery. The woman who'd been raped, the man who'd been raped and the man who'd had the crap beaten out of him as a kid all came up to me. They all started hugging me; I didn't understand or comprehend why. To me, I had failed once again. Even in the safety of a therapy session, I could not seem to progress. I could not take the action that would have been helpful for me. Once again, in front of everyone, I was as weak as piss.

But then, the lady said, 'None of us wanted any of what's happened to us to happen. But if I had a choice, I would not want to have had what you had, Jason. I'd stay with mine.' The other two grabbed me and held me— these two men whose scars I could imagine justified their struggles, while I rejected my own. For years, I had been continuing to reject me. However, there in that moment and holding me were family rape victims and people of physical domestic violence who saw the emotional abuse I had experienced as being so real, raw and dangerous that it was, in their own minds, far worse than what they had experienced. They could see something on the outside that reflected the depth of internal pain and anguish that I would not, or could not, accept. That was the tipping point for me, and the start of recovery, but I still had an awfully long way to go.

Through this time in counselling, I also struggled with something else on top of having to deal with this emotional crisis: I had not yet been diagnosed with sleep apnoea, which I'll talk about a bit more later, and I often struggled to stay awake in the afternoons of the railway's executive committee meetings. Although I think my peers would have said that I performed well, I believe that my performance was absolutely restricted by the crisis I was going through.

Years later, when I caught up with the female executive who had been the organisation's second to the head of human resources, we talked about some of our life journey, our business and the other stuff, as you do when catching up. She said, 'Why didn't you talk to me about it? We had an employee assistant program provider, which may not have been that helpful for you, but we might have been able to put some support around you.'

At the time, though, I had been too frightened to tell anybody about my significant mental health issue. Would my position in the organisation be unacceptable if they knew I was struggling with mental health issues? This was the challenge I faced at the time, and my internal answer was that it would have been deemed as such. Unfortunately, this is the sad reality for many men. Even if they do seek help for their mental health issues, they are too frightened to discuss it with anyone other than their doctor out of fear for their employment, friendships and manliness.

It took three different counsellors to support me over the three-and-a-half-year period of this process, but when the topic of sexuality came up, I was still able to convince them that no, it wasn't an issue. It wasn't hard because I had already convinced myself the events that had occurred when I was fourteen and the event that had happened when my dad died—when I went to the male prostitute—were aberrations.

A couple of years later when Mum came to Sydney, I started to open up about my life with Dad from my perspective. She was sad. I think the sadness for her was that she'd had some inkling that something really bad had been going on, but she didn't know how to do anything about it. I don't blame my mum; that's often how these things work out, especially during the times my parents were alive. Familial abuse, whatever the form, can be hidden.

Mum wrote a letter for me to read at an Emmaus Walk retreat I went on. It was an acknowledgement of what may have been missed.

Jason,

I would like to think that, as well as your mother, I am a friend.

Your life has not been easy, but then, whose has?

I am very aware that during some of the decisions you have had to make, I have not always been there for you because, at the time, I didn't want to interfere—we all learn from our mistakes, and you can't put an old head on young shoulders. All I ever wanted was for you to be happy.

If I had known about a lot of things that you were worried about in your younger days, I may have intervened—too late for that now.

I look back over the years and think of all the joy you have given me. When you were very small and relied on me for so much, I loved you. Then came the teen years, where you were so grown up and didn't need me, but I still loved you. When university came along, you left for Melbourne. How I missed you! But the choice was yours, and I now understand.

I wish I had done a lot of things in the past … but then, that was yesterday, and I think the best thing to do now is to live each day looking forwards, not backwards.

Dear Jason, I still love you as much as, if not more than, the day you arrived into this world—please be strong, and take each day as it comes. Try not to worry too much about things you can do nothing about.

Love,
Mum

I knew that the next step was to continue to find myself. My faith and being a Christian had helped me through this period in my life because it offered me support and encouragement. However, it did not dissolve all of my problems, as I was still in denial of who I was. In fact, through the three years of counselling, I continued to deny who I was regularly, as I thought it would help with my acceptance and acceptability.

Marriage and Family: Classical Suburban Life

One year, in the middle of all the counselling, I became so distressed that I went as far as working out how I would commit suicide. The pain of the process was so severe, and at times, I didn't know if there was actually a pathway through it. Partly, it remained hard for me to identify if emotional abuse was still real. The doorway was opening up, but I kept doubting myself. I wasn't on any antidepressant medication through all of this, so I navigated these bad times as best as I could.

One Saturday, I planned to go out with a group of friends to the local motorised kart racing centre; however, I was really struggling, and I was convinced that I needed to end it all. I had reached the detailed planning stage of my chosen method to end my life. When all was said and done, I didn't really want anybody else to be harmed or to grieve and pity me, so it seemed like a car crash was the best way to do it. I decided that I would head out onto a country road and drive around, make sure there was nobody else around, work out where the trees or the power poles were and then drive at speed into one of them, hoping like hell the crash would be bad enough to kill me.

Yet, as I got up to leave, I thought about the group from my church community that I had organised to meet.

It promised to be a fun night, ideal for bonding and for continuing to get to know each other. I think it was just the mere fact that I thought I had a responsibility to this group that I got in my car and headed to the karting venue rather than heading to the country road. Whatever it was, something stopped me from entering the dark side of my psyche again. Was it God? Was He protecting me and helping me to see a different perspective of life through the eyes of this group?

When I got home later that evening, I was utterly exhausted. I cried. There had been so much joy shining on everyone's faces when driving those karts and lots of laughter and chatter. Somehow, it had got me through the night. Yet, I still felt as though I was going backwards. Yet again, it seemed like I needed to focus on one day at a time because, every night as I went to bed, I had doubts about who I was.

Every first Sunday of the month, we would have communion in church, which was an important part of any Christian's faith cycle. Usually during communion, we would sit in stillness; a time for contemplation. But month after month, year after year, it would be the same. I'd be praying for these feelings to go away; these feelings towards men that my little internal voice told me were so unacceptable. Surely with all this praying, God would take away these feelings. Month after month, year after year … wouldn't He hear me at some stage? What I thought about in the isolation of my bed at night as I went to sleep, though, meant that I was not acceptable. Communion after communion, with the bread and the wine to link me through time and history to Jesus, I said my prayers, begging in silence so that no one knew. But the answers never emerged. These thoughts were supposed to be able to be taken away through prayer, weren't they?

God, for fuck's sake, why aren't they going away?

In the Church, we had home groups and Bible studies,

and there were excellent resources provided from within the Church and from outside. I was surprised that around this time there was a new resource on sexuality—something we often didn't talk about at all or, if we did, it was in a very negative context. When I reviewed this new resource, the material actually seemed to be quite good. But boy, did I find it confronting! I still hadn't had sexual intercourse; I was thirty-one years of age and still a virgin. Yet, I was about to lead a home-group discussion on sex and sexuality. Was I a fraud?

In the group, we had good conversations about respecting ourselves and respecting other people as we embarked on traversing the topics in the series and the associated conversations. We were all very nervous about these topics and what might unravel, but I'm proud we pushed through it even with my own lack of experience and trying to keep it open. I had the famous book *The Joy of Sex* to help me understand the physical basics, and as I prepared the study material, I found myself cross-referencing the book for the more physical sides of the discussions—which I found very disconcerting. Yet, despite knowing my own confusion, and trying to ignore what might be my own sexuality, I had to be present as the heterosexual with the heteronormative view of sexuality. In other words, I had to reflect the 'good' Christian view of what it was to be accepted while I completely avoided who I really was.

There were many awkward moments through these conversations, and I tried very hard not to be cumbersome with my guidance of the discussions. I became the actor in action again. The actor, the fraud, and their coexistence, once again, worked tirelessly in my life.

189

On one occasion, friends from Melbourne looked after my apartment in Sydney while I was on holiday in Alice Springs. When I returned, they mentioned that there was a message from a girl from my church. Apparently, there was a group going to go and see *The Phantom of the Opera*, and the girl asked if I would like to go along. I got excited and said yes. Before I knew it, she and I became more familiar and started doing more activities together, such as travelling away on the odd weekend. Eventually, we became a bit of an item. I was chasing her, but by now, this is what I thought I was meant to do; this was who I was supposed to be. My chasing seemed to be noticed by others at church because I acted like a puppy dog around her, and soon I wore her down and we began dating.

Our minister, whom I loved dearly, was part of a group within our denomination, which was then called the Evangelical Member of the Uniting Church (EMU, for short, which is really just a large and unusual flightless Australian bird similar to an ostrich). This group was unhappy with the movement towards accepting homosexual members and ministers within the Uniting Church. Our minister never really pushed his point in our parish, but for me, there was the subtle comment here and there that bothered me on occasions. It fed into my anxiety about what was in my head. I had failed to progress relationships with two women before, and I had failed to progress anything with a man even when I'd paid for it. I just ended up distressed. So based on my minister's leanings, I decided that, despite what was in my head, if I headed into marriage, then maybe I would finally be acceptable to everyone around me.

As a result, the girl and I became more serious. People began noticing, and I enjoyed the attention and love. In September, 1994, Mum came to visit me, but part of me was frustrated because she quite rightly expected time with, and attention from, me, but now I was in a relationship. Then she told me the news that she wanted to move to the outskirts of Sydney because she knew that one day, when I got married and had kids, it would be too much for me to fly back to Adelaide regularly—as I had been doing—to keep an eye on her. In the end, her timing seemed impeccable, and we soon found a retirement village close by. Within a few months, she had made the move to Sydney.

My new relationship kept developing, and it felt right. Life, it seemed, was settling into a new routine that felt good; it felt like what 'normal' was supposed to feel like. I felt acceptable and accepted. Towards the end of the year, we moved towards discussions about marriage. Was it a possibility? How many kids did we want? It was an intriguing topic of conversation, and as an only child, I was thinking six. She said two would be fine.

Later, I caught up with a trusted friend of mine. I needed an older male to talk through what I was proposing to do that particular Saturday night. We talked in his study, and it was a good conversation. All seemed to go fine, but then there was an odd question. Did I feel sexually attracted to her? I was confused by this question, and I remember how it made me recoil. Of course, I felt something, didn't I? As a couple, we were consistent with our faith around how far we would go physically. There was a level of intimacy, which was appropriate but not too much. But still, the question sat uncomfortably as my friend waited for my answer. Then, I realised that to allow the question to linger and the response to be slow might highlight an issue, so I responded, 'Of course I feel sexually attracted to her.' But was this the actor or the fraudster speaking?

In December, 1994, my girlfriend and I announced our engagement, and in January, we attended the NCYC in Adelaide, where we were both chaplains. It was here that God also threw his little spanners in the works. One night at an outdoor concert, we were talking, and I reflected on my two experiences—as a fourteen-year-old and then as a twenty-nine-year-old—with guys. I was very tearful when I told her about those two incidents and, as I had managed in my counselling sessions with myself and others, I convinced her, too, that it was just one of those things that happened in life.

We came back from Adelaide, and we started to plan our wedding. Given our respective family situations, we were funding our wedding ourselves, so it was just as well that we both worked. For me, I started falling back into what I had always seen my father doing, which confused me. For the most part, I had been working hard to move away from the patterns of my father's life, and yet, in planning my wedding, I adopted some of his tools and techniques, which perhaps was a good thing—finally there was something helpful from him. I began documenting lots of items and making lists, planning things to the tiniest details, down to the minutes required. I built spreadsheet lists and timetables for the day with contingency plans attached. To top it off, I was so excited that my best friend, who had moved to the USA, agreed to come to Sydney to be my best man. I had been the best man at his wedding some years earlier.

Like many couples, my fiancée and I were encouraged to complete a pre-marital program for a number of weeks, but nothing untoward came up.

Just before the big day, everyone arrived for the wedding rehearsal, which was a happy time, and it was followed by dinner at a local fast food outlet.

And then our wedding day dawned. There are always hiccups on the day, but fortunately ours were few. The weather turned dreary, and as I took our luggage to the hotel where we would end up for the night, they indicated that because the weather was so poor, they would expect us at the hotel for our wedding photos. We had hoped for the beach, but the other option was the hotel's magnificent grand staircase, which ended up being a beautiful backdrop for our photos.

We had a wonderful wedding. The service was great, and we had friends—some who had been in my youth and young adults groups—playing music and sharing readings. When our marriage was announced, my new wife turned around with a great smile and put both thumbs up to the congregation. We took some traditional photographs and then some goofy ones. All of my groomsmen were in Snoopy socks, and I had Snoopy boxers on, which was unusual for me.

Our reception was held in an old church that had been converted into a restaurant and function centre. The speeches were great, and my wife talked about how, while I was a very conservative person, there was something about me that made me a slight radical. She equated that part of me to my odd socks, my different socks, the Snoopy socks and the cartoon socks. It was an inkling, for her, that there was something more than met the eye to the conservative front I portrayed to most people.

There was only one thing that jarred me during the reception, and it was when I danced with my mum. She commented on how proud Dad would have been to have witnessed this. The comment caught me off guard, but I soon recovered and moved on with the dance.

After our wedding night in a Sydney hotel, the next morning we flew off to Cairns. We were going to go slightly further north to a resort in Palm Cove for a week or so. For the first few days, all went well. Then, I started to find our intimate life a challenge. I remember being so distressed that I ran off to the bathroom to have a shower, where I just cried my eyes out. What the fuck was wrong with me? I was following God's calling, so why was I feeling so bad? Why couldn't I commit? Masturbation was something I could complete multiple times a day, even in my thirties, so why couldn't I have sex that day, no matter what I tried. Fear gripped my body, and it turned into a very long shower, but I told myself that I'd made a commitment. I had made a faithful commitment, and that was what I was going to uphold. I was an acceptable, married Christian man.

Initially, we decided to move into my flat, as I owned it—and the bank owned me—and then a few months later we decided to purchase a house. We found one ten minutes away, in a quiet street, close to schools and with reasonable public transport.

Soon after we were married, my wife became concerned that I repeatedly stopped breathing at night, and this was somewhat disconcerting. So, I received a quick referral from my doctor to see a specialist, underwent some tests and was diagnosed with sleep apnoea. And so, within six months of getting married, I had a continuous positive airway pressure (CPAP) machine and a mask to wear at night while I was sleeping so that I could breathe properly. But, no matter what I did with the machine—like putting it in a container with egg cartons and other things around it to try and dampen the sound—for her, it was too noisy. So, very early in our marriage, we ended up in different rooms. Was this family history repeating? I began to wonder if my father had sleep apnoea too, and that had been the cause of his appalling snoring.

A short time after this, I was also diagnosed with multiple food allergies and intolerances. Some nights, the indigestion was so bad that my doctors thought I might have a heart condition. More tests were carried out, and when we knew what the food issues were and adjusted my diet accordingly, my symptoms dramatically improved.

Eighteen months after our wedding, our first child arrived. Our son. He was a wonderful joy, but with this beautiful bundle came a number of challenges. He was born overdue but was suspected to have an immature respiratory system, which is normally associated with premature babies. At three weeks of age, he spent the night in hospital with a breathing monitor, and the next day the paediatrician confirmed the diagnosis.

Once the diagnosis came through, we were trained in baby resuscitation techniques, and we had to learn how to use the breathing monitor that would be attached to his abdomen twenty-four hours a day. We then had to learn the other management activities of this condition. Basically, one of us had to be within roughly three metres of him at all times. Every time he stopped breathing, there would be a little beep, the alarm would go off and one of us had to be prepared to resuscitate him. Eventually, he started to settle into a rhythm with the machine, and so did we as we focused on a newborn baby and what life would now look like.

At about three months old, our son had his check-up with the community nurse. She said, 'There's something wrong with his skull. It's flat, and it shouldn't be flat like that; you need to see your general practitioner now.'

So, off to the GP my wife and son went. 'She's right,' said the doctor. 'I hadn't picked it up. His head is flattening out. It could be a thing called craniosynostosis, which is premature fusing of the skull. We need to send you urgently to a neurosurgeon.'

When I heard the news, I became anxious because I had almost died from having anaesthetic—a condition caused by a dominant gene that could have been passed on to my son. And now we were talking about skull surgery near the brain of our three-month old boy. We really had to consider whether or not to go ahead with the operation. While craniosynostosis is not life-threatening, our son's head could develop completely out of shape. So, in the end, it was an easy decision, and we made the choice to proceed with the surgery. This meant opening the skin on the back of his head and carefully cutting the skull open to make sure nothing was breached underneath to cause any damage to the brain.

This became a good teaching opportunity for me to

explain to my wife about the issue of the anaesthetic allergy. Being a dominant gene, we needed to assume that our kids would have this until proved otherwise, and I had learned that you needed to be proactive with the medical system around the unusual. So, I rang the hospital and said, 'I'd like to speak to the director of anaesthesiology please. My infant son is coming in for neurosurgery, and I've got malignant hyperpyrexia due to anaesthesia.'

Another complication was that we had to have the surgery before he turned six months old, but given his immature respiratory system problem, they wanted to defer the surgery for as long as they could to maximise the probability of his respiratory system working properly. However, our respiratory paediatrician said, 'At the end of the day, yes ideally we'd like to keep him on the monitor longer, but here's the problem: has your child actually developed a strong enough respiratory system yet versus Mum and Dad going absolutely crazy and their own mental health significantly deteriorating because they're being called every two or three minutes?' You see, we learned very early on that kids are smart. My son had discovered that he had a cord coming out of his nappy, and if he pulled the cord, there was a great sound and his parents would come running. He would laugh and giggle because he had created his own game from his cot. So, we made the decision to take off the respiratory alarm before his scheduled surgery.

Thankfully, the surgery went well, but it was hard being in the neurological ward of a children's hospital. I was grateful that our son didn't have any complications or severe ailments similar to other children in there, some of whom had major brain issues.

I remember sitting on the balcony of the room we shared with another family. Our son had no idea what he'd been through. His head was bandaged, but it seemed that he knew that he was safe and secure in either of our arms. When he was awake, we just kept caressing him and holding him. I remember him sitting on my lap and gently rubbing the back of his head on my chest as a way of stroking the stitches under the bandages. It was such a relief that our boy was going to be fine.

Some months later, I wanted to get an earring. My wife's response was, 'Yeah, why not?' I had discovered that you needed to leave a new earring in for a few weeks to let the hole form, and being a straight Christian male, I would have my left ear pierced because having the right ear done was a symbol to others that you were gay. I found a place near work where I could pierce my ear just before my summer holidays. I walked into the hairdresser, and the lady talked me through the process. I selected the stud that I wanted, and the lady asked, 'So, we're piercing the right ear, are we?'

'No, no, no. The left ear!' was my immediate reply, but in my head I was saying, *What are you talking about?*

Returning to work, I needed to remember to take the earring out before arriving. This was about me trying to remember what was personal time—earring in—and professional time—earring out.

Nineteen months later, we were back in hospital. This time, it was early in the morning when our equally beautiful daughter was born. Because of our son's immature respiratory problems, she was automatically tested at three weeks of age and passed with flying colours. Our son was delighted about having a sister and was forever cuddling her. But, unsurprisingly, it didn't take too long for her independent streak to appear, given her two grandmothers.

After a number of years working at the railway, I thought that maybe it was time to move on. As I contemplated this, an advertisement came up for a new head of the internal audit department for an international IT company's operation in the South Pacific, which was based not far from home. This was the first time this organisation had

had a head of internal audit, and unfortunately, it was eighteen months of battle. They undersized the role, but I was able to negotiate a significant funding increase. However, our New Zealand subsidiary ended up in financial trouble, so I saw more of New Zealand's airports, hotels and offices than I had wished for—and not much of New Zealand, which is the curse of the travelling executive.

There were also major issues in finance, manufacturing and service management systems, and then I undertook an internal audit, which was quite complex around a historical tender. As the results came back, the managing director challenged my ethics, so I knew it was time to go. Fortunately, a head hunter called just as I was deciding on whether or not to take the risk of quitting my job without a role already lined up for me to support my family. The interviews were arranged quickly and, before I knew it, I was able to resign and move to a new career away from internal audit and into an executive management role, where I had to manage facilities and procurement for a major insurance company. Once again, however, I was stepping into an organisation that had gone through a messy restructure, and the results weren't that encouraging. My assignment was to recover the situation once more and to try and get this area of the business operating properly again.

The more I worked in business, the more I realised that doing the right thing wasn't necessarily what was wanted by the powers-that-be—those even higher up in executive management. My downfall came when we undertook a major property leasing transaction and, as the Sydney office we occupied was only half-owned by the investment arm of our insurance company, this required the establishment of a lot of independence and integrity protocols to manage the market engagement risks. I spent considerable effort and my own credibility to convince the property market that we were serious about moving to a new location and that we wanted to create a competitive tension in the marketplace. It was therefore important to follow the protocols I had created to ensure transparency and to manage the risk of some less than scrupulous players in the Sydney property market.

Midway through this transaction, my third chief general manager didn't want to follow those controls because he saw himself as an expert 'wheeler and dealer'. We were getting close to a deal, but I pushed back on what he was trying to do, as I wanted to protect the integrity of our market engagement. Then, out of the blue, I was called to the human resources department. To my shock and horror, I was made redundant. I was escorted out of the office within a couple of hours with my box of possessions. A lot of people across a number of departments were more than surprised.

My wife was also astonished to hear me coming in before lunch and then stunned as I told her what had happened, and I had no idea what I was going to do next. The insurance company provided an outplacement service, and with their assistance, I started looking for full-time employment while also looking for short-term consultancies to keep money flowing in to pay the mortgage and to put food on the table. I was lucky: a former executive at my IT company had moved to another company where he had identified some significant problems with their procurement processes. So, he asked me to come and consult with him and to do some problem solving in order to work out the process.

By that time, I'd interviewed for a few jobs, but nothing was really coming up. Although not wanting to return to internal audit, I'd even applied for a job in that field, yet nothing had happened. So, unexpectedly, several months later, that firm came back to me and said, 'We'd like to talk to you about heading up our internal audit practice in Sydney.'

Even though I still didn't feel acceptable internally—that struggle was starting to rear its head once again—the years of counselling allowed me to finally stand up for myself. 'Thanks,' I stated, 'but I have decided to move on from internal audit and move into other roles.' Their response surprised me, not only with its swiftness but also with its directness.

'We have a procurement and sourcing practice in our Canberra office, and we'd like to establish that field of consulting service in Sydney. Maybe you can head that and launch it for us there?' It seemed to be a good fit, and so I returned to consulting. The firm had been so successful in Canberra, they thought they could rapidly replicate it in Sydney, but it wasn't that easy. We struggled, but we kept going.

In 2003, much to the nervousness of my wife, Chris—a partner in the company who was also on the music team at the NCYC in Canberra in 1993—and I decided to leave and set up our own consulting firm: Masters Le Mesurier. We started to build a client base and managed to get some early and very supportive clients. We started to grow and employ staff, and it seemed to be going very well. We added an office in Canberra, and we also added a human resource consulting practice.

But in the end, I think we grew too fast, adding considerable costs, and the revenue growth wasn't increasing by at least the same rate. Cash flow became a major issue. I remember being at a board meeting in Canberra when we were so close to being insolvent. I'd been driving back and forth to that city for a long time, so I knew the road very well, but I was so exhausted. I now had about five people dependent on our business for their families—for their food, water and shelter—and our business was so close to going under. The solution was for me to borrow more money against our home to provide some more liquidity and cash for the business to get us through this time. These were very difficult and challenging conversations with my wife, but she was so generous, and she trusted my judgment that this was the thing to do. We used the cash to help close the Canberra practice, and we refocused the business on the Sydney market. After a while, we were able to repay the money, and I was relieved that my judgement had been justified.

As time went on, I began to realise that both my business partner and the head of our human resources consulting practice were gay. My business partner was really struggling with his sexuality, and it came to the forefront when he was doing his first year at the theological college. It was too confronting for him and so, unfortunately, he withdrew from the college.

We decided to advertise our business on a Christian radio station in Sydney and actually managed to receive some enquiries and, ultimately, a client. My partner also suggested that we advertise in a gay magazine, but this made me feel nervous. If our business was advertised in a gay magazine, what might people think or infer about me? I quietly suggested that it wasn't our market, but I later learned that this was not necessarily a great business decision of mine.

For a while, my business partner embraced his gayness and joined an organisation that hosted a monthly function called 'Fruits in Suits'. He suggested that it was good networking. Sadly, though, in the end, he seemed highly conflicted between his Christianity and his sexuality, which may have contributed to alcohol issues and his early and untimely death some years later, but I will never really know for sure.

For four and a half years, I did a lot of international travel. As much as that was very hard for my wife, it meant that we had a steady income. But it also meant I didn't have to have sex. I was legitimately tired because I was working so hard and travelling so much, so this gave me a very good excuse to avoid intercourse.

Our kids started school, and they had different challenges in their own unique ways. Over time, my wife wanted to go back to work but realised that she couldn't work full time. We agreed it would be to her advantage to undertake some retraining, and she found some part-time work that suited her needs.

Before long, the continuing stress I was putting myself under by not accepting who I was as a person—of ultimately not confronting my own identity—led to my mental health breaking down once again. With the support of my wife and encouragement from my business partner, despite them not knowing the true cause, I saw my doctor to discuss the blackness that was once again enveloping my head. He wanted to put me on medication, but these didn't agree with me, and I stopped them after a week. He also thought I needed to see a specialist. So, he referred me to the husband of one of the other doctors in the clinic, and I met with him for a period of time. He was a gentle soul, and he was happy just to focus on my busyness, my business and how to manage my work stress, and I was easily able to deflect going anywhere else. Furthermore, it seemed to help, at least for a while, when I was more disciplined with my food intake, my sleep and getting out into the sunshine.

Eventually, we merged our practice with one of the leading international second-tier accounting firms. We'd been approached by another firm on and off for quite a while, and we thought we should test the market by talking to two of the interested firms. Maybe, in hindsight, we selected the wrong one; they didn't really want our staff because they had their own, including a partner in our area of risk and internal audit. So, we gradually let go of our staff, and just the two of us merged in. It was hard; they really wanted us for our government business understanding, but they didn't want to invest in our business—it was all about instant returns.

I continued travelling a lot to Canberra to take the strain at work because my business partner had family issues and needed to be with them; his sister was unwell. We continued struggling with our profitability within this new form while we questioned the firm's commitment and support. I applied to get onto various New South Wales government panels that made it easier to be selected to deliver consulting assignments, and we were just starting to make some headway when the Global Financial Crisis (GFC) hit.

It was also around this time that I was asked to be a rugby touch judge for my son's junior rugby union club. As I left after the last game one Saturday lunchtime, I crossed the footpath, but the manhole cover over a telecommunication pit collapsed as I walked on it. I fell down the manhole, injuring myself very badly. I was in so much pain, but fortunately, there were still a couple of people nearby packing up who heard my cries for help. An ambulance was called, and I was sent to the local hospital. Many X-rays and a lot of morphine later, the diagnosis was that I probably had a fractured hip. I went to see a top orthopaedic surgeon in Sydney, only to find out I didn't have a broken hip, but I had severe bruising from the episode. I would be off work for a couple of weeks.

Soon afterwards, I was released from hospital, and while I was home in bed recovering, the CEO and my senior partner from the firm came to see me. He said, 'Sorry, Jason, I know you've potentially got a broken hip, but we need to shut down your division, so we're going to let go of you, the other remaining partner and all the staff.' To me, it was just another example of how bad business ethics can be, and I had another fight on my hands just to get what was owed to me.

By now, the GFC was well and truly underway but, yet

again, I was lucky. I had just finished up a contract with a major federal government agency in Canberra when another part of that organisation, now knowing that my engagement with their internal audit unit had finished, asked if I was available to do a major consultancy for them, and away I went. The project was ultimately helping them to implement a number of the internal audit recommendations I had made in my prior role. Because of the relatively short length of time I'd been in this chartered accounting firm, I was able to take my business back. I started to rebuild my life and my career. Again, it meant lots of time on the road with three months in Canberra, where I would drive the three-and-a-half hours down on Monday morning and come back Thursday or Friday night.

The years seemed to slip by, with our kids going through various ups and downs at their school. My son had some challenges with school and needed significant support, and we ended up moving him to a private school where he was able to thrive. My daughter was—and still is—an amazing sportswoman and continued to perform incredibly well academically at school even with her major sporting commitments. Looking back, I think that's what kept me going: every weekend was taken up with sports.

We seemed to have a happy life. We had moved into a double-storey house and extended the back deck for a large, outdoor entertainment area and a swimming pool. My wife and I took turns on medical issues or regional sporting competitions with our children, and my work was now stabilising. Church was going reasonably well—I had pulled back from all leadership roles to focus on the family—but, as time went on, the darkness from deep within started to creep up once again.

The timing couldn't have been worse, as the issue of marriage equality for LGBTIQA+ people was surfacing as a major issue in Australia once more. I remember my wife saying, 'Oh, you'd be very much supportive of this.'

But I felt like I had to say, 'No, no, well ...' In some sense, I was almost becoming just a tiny bit homophobic because I was trying to avoid dealing with who I was.

As our children grew up, my wife and I had so little time with each other that we decided we needed to reconnect and re-bond somehow. After a while, we agreed to watch one TV show every week that we could enjoy together. I was led by her, and we watched a British series called *Halifax*. As it went on, though, I started to find it more difficult and uncomfortable, as one of the lead characters was a lesbian who'd left her husband and entered into a same-gender relationship. It was getting harder and harder to watch. Not driven by this, but perhaps it was one of the sparks, I started to spiral into depression and its accompanying negative coil of shame, hatred and feeling like I was outside of myself again. And then, an unexpected outburst at the end of a church service led to lots of concerns, and this time I recognised some of it myself.

Probably an overreaction ... no ... definitely an overreaction but an early indicator of the rapid decline in my mental health!

Stresses in my life had been building up, and this became a boiling point. At the end of this particular service, I stormed out, yelling and making a scene; not the usual, relatively passive, pleasant Jason. When my wife came home, she asked what was happening and was obviously very worried about my state of mind. Once again, she was so concerned that she insisted I saw my doctor about my mental health. The darkness was so much more than last time, and for my wife and my doctor, the cause was still unknown. But I was not in a good state, and they could see it. Not only was the darkness in my head present that we had all seen before, but this time it had led to an outburst in a very public way, and that didn't resonate with the issue at the time. So, my doctor insisted that I started medication and that I began seeing a psychologist quickly, this time from a different practice.

A very dark period was once again encroaching on my life as the cloud of unacceptability loomed like a hawk. This black cloud sat with the infamous black dog in my head, and nothing I was doing was getting them to move.

Some Dark Days

As much as we always wanted to go to church together, my wife understood that part of the issues I was having was with the local parish. However, because we had spent a long time going there, she had finally made some good friends and didn't want to move parishes. In contrast, I had made connections but no real friends although I had made a significant effort to do so. Wondering if I should have a break from the Church or go somewhere else, I called a mate of mine for recommendations of some churches to go and check out. So, on a Sunday soon after my outburst, I went to Eastwood Uniting Church, which was the first on my mate's list for me, and I sat in the back row to observe but not engage.

I soon became a regular at Eastwood Uniting Church, but I very much kept a low profile and didn't particularly get involved. One of the older ladies did comment that she liked my colourful jumpers, though, which had been lovingly knitted by my late mother.

There was something else notable too. One Sunday morning, a single woman got up to talk about a conference she had attended called *Daring* that had been run by the Uniting Network. It all seemed to be discussed very quickly, and LGBTIQA+ people were mentioned. Was this conference actually for the LGBTIQA+ community?

I wasn't sure. I also became aware of two women who seemed to have a large group of kids with them every week. Were they a lesbian couple? As time went by, I learned who they were. They had one child of their own, and they were fighting for the adoption of one of the boys in the large group. I discovered that part of their ministry was to provide foster and respite care for young kids.

My wife also strongly encouraged me to see my doctor again. As much as I didn't want to go onto anti-depressants, my doctor felt they were now more targeted, and as the initial prescriptions would be relatively low level, he thought they would take the edge off how I was feeling, making it easier to deal with my day-to-day activities. This time, I stayed on them past the initial two weeks, which meant a minimum period of six months, and it seemed to work. The black cloud and black dog were still very much in my head, but they were balanced out by a little bit of sunlight at the edges.

My doctor also provided a referral to a local psychologist, Valerie, whose practice was located relatively close by in the neighbouring suburb of Macquarie Park. It was very convenient for me to get to my appointments from either home or the office, and the sessions progressed well. I had forgotten some important basics of getting out of my office and getting sunlight, and Valerie encouraged me to join a gym, where I decided to seek the services of a personal trainer.

Over time, Valerie must have had some issues at the centre where her practice was based because she mentioned she was moving to new rooms at West Thornleigh, which was much further for me to travel for appointments. As we had covered a lot of ground, but still with a way to go, I didn't want to start again with a different therapist. I also thought that I wouldn't mind the additional car travel to the new location, as it would give me time to think and mentally prepare for my sessions with her. Traffic from North Ryde to West Thornleigh can be a little bit challenging, given the Sydney traffic, so I always gave myself plenty of time to get there. If I got there too early, I would have a coffee at the small shopping centre opposite. There I would reflect on what had been happening and any issues that were bothering me to optimise my time in the therapy session.

As these consultations went on, I kept thinking about whether I would raise the unthinkable. Every time I sat in my car waiting for my therapy session, there was so much head talk.

Shall I tell her that I think I might be gay?

Shall I tell her today?

I don't know if I am, but these thoughts never go away!

What is the definition of being gay anyway?

Then I would repeatedly stop and decide that I wouldn't, really just to ignore my thinking.

After a while, I found the sessions became more limiting because I hindered where they could go; I was now starting to damage the purpose of therapy as I became an actor once again. Of course, I knew there was one area they needed to go, but with Valerie, I couldn't take us there. Was it because I hadn't worked out where she stood on the intersection of psychology and Christianity? I had heard stories of Christian psychologists, who placed an evangelical Christianity perspective ahead of therapy. Was she one of them? I didn't know, and I couldn't tell. The unthinkable was too much of a risk for me to raise in this climate of uncertainty within my own head. The little I'd heard was enough of a safeguard—I had been searching on the Internet, especially on YouTube, about the unthinkable, where I had watched stories of Christians being sent to camps and abused by 'therapists'. I didn't know where Valerie stood with regards to my situation, but I was hurting, hurting so much, and I didn't want to be hurt further in another way. Valerie might have been perfectly fine, but something in the back of my head told me to shut down, and so I just simply stopped seeing her.

At the end of my last session with her, I indicated that I had a few things to juggle over the next month and would call back for an appointment rather than make it at the end of the sessions, which was my usual practise. This sounded perfectly plausible given our discussions about my work, but it was dishonest on my part because I knew I wouldn't be coming back. Therefore, in November, 2014, I just disappeared from Valerie's patient list.

What was I frightened of? Was it the fear of being rejected as a patient because many Christians thought you couldn't be gay *and* a Christian? My life had been a struggle to find acceptance from other people, and I had never inwardly accepted who I actually was to myself either. The fear of being rejected by my therapist, as irrational as it might seem, was a real fear, and a fear that was too great to allow me to continue in therapy with her.

I found myself secretly looking at porn, and I also became a clandestine, regular watcher of 'coming out' videos. There were so many of these videos on YouTube; however, they were predominately younger people, who were typically from fourteen to around twenty-five years of age. Nonetheless, their stories resonated, so I kept watching them. It was as if I was watching others from my past and seeing, in my youth, when I went deeper and deeper into the closet. Each of them had a nuance; every one of them was unique. Some had supportive families, reflecting the twenty-first century and a modern understanding of LGBTIQA+ people, and others were rejected by their family, often for religious concepts, becoming homeless as a result.

My YouTube searches expanded. Watching partly to understand how male to male sexuality worked, I was also seeking to confirm that a part of this was me. Then, unexpectedly, I stumbled across videos discussing a new concept for me: they explained how people could be both LGBTIQA+ and Christian. Slowly, as summer progressed, a message appeared clearly at the forefront of my mind.

I'm gay.

I had to be careful when I was in my study watching these videos that no one came in, and I made sure I knew all of the short cuts on my computer to hide the screen. There were some close calls when my kids suddenly barged into the study wanting help with their schoolwork or my wife came in to work at her desk. Usually, I would hear them coming through the kitchen, but not always, and as they opened the door, there was just enough time to change the screen before they saw anything.

The questioning message 'Am I gay?' or sometimes an exploratory comment, 'I am gay,' crept into my head, but I didn't own it. However, it kept coming. I kept looking at all the material. And it kept coming.

There was a young Australian YouTuber and vlogger called Troy Sivan who caught my eye. It was as if I was still stuck in his age group with my own lack of acceptance regarding my sexuality. Eventually, I found his coming out video, which had over 8.5 million views. This was seminal: most of the videos were American, but this was an Australian youth. Even in 2014, there was still a sense that he had some struggles to deal with himself, but it was so much easier and better than when I was fourteen. When he'd told his parents, rather than being discovered at my age, with all the pain and shame that came with that, he had been accepted. The thoughts about the unthinkable kept coming, but still I lived with denial.

I am married!

I assumed all this would have gone away, but it never has!

I honestly can't remember why, but one day in 2015, I was sick of the questioning message going around and around in my head all the time.

Am I gay?

It seemed like the inevitable was about to crash through my stubborn head. I was home alone, so I stood in front of the mirror in my bedroom and spoke out loud to my reflection. 'I'm gay.' The vocalisation seemed unreal, so I said it again. Hearing the words really made a difference … this somehow seemed to make it real. I repeated myself. Something was changing. Every time I said it out loud, it was as if I was taking ownership of who I was. I was getting one step closer. Then suddenly, I didn't need to say it anymore. Somehow, this seemed to integrate my sexual orientation into my very being. Somehow, I seemed to accept this part of myself. Then …

Shit! What the hell does this mean?

My wife and I were now heading towards our twenty-first wedding anniversary. What did this mean for our marriage? What could I do? What options did I have?

At this point in time, my mental health started to deteriorate significantly once again. The conflict in my head had now moved from a black cloud to a full-blown dark thunderstorm, and rather than a small, black dog, there was a pack of black hounds that were roaming around in my head and taking control. My wife was becoming more and more concerned, and she suggested that I should go back and see Valerie. It was then I mentioned to her that I had stopped seeing Valerie the previous November because I hadn't been getting that far with her. 'So, I don't see the point of going back to see her,' I said.

'Jason,' my worried wife replied, 'then I think you should go back to our doctor and find someone new to see.' I told her that I would think about it. The challenge I faced was that all of the doctors at the medical centre our family visited were Christians, and I had no idea how my doctor would react to this. So, I spent a week or so pondering the approach I would make. *How* would I approach it? How would he react? Eventually, recognising this in itself was making matters worse, I decided to make an appointment. I actually decided to book a double appointment because it had become a practise of mine to write up a list of things I needed to talk to my doctor about on my iPad.

So, on a Thursday in June, 2015, at 4.30 p.m., I had my appointment. Nervous and sweaty, I wondered what I would say ... and how my doctor would respond. As usual, with it being an afternoon appointment, my doctor was running late, but it was good because it delayed the unthinkable from being voiced. However, I knew in my head that I really couldn't afford to delay the conversation for much longer—I wanted, no needed, to get the confession over and done with. The waiting, the wanting to wait or the not wanting to wait ...

Oh shit ... what is happening?

The internal stressors were on high alert, and I could feel beads of sweat running down my back.

Eventually, the doctor walked into the reception area and called my name. I walked to his office—a walk that I knew very well. It was the second doctor's room on the left and not really a long walk, but on that day, it seemed like an eternity.

I sat down.

'Jason, what can I do for you today?' my doctor asked in his usual manner. So, I started with my list, hoping that the items on there would allow him to talk for at least the first fifteen minutes, or maybe even most of the double appointment, and then I wouldn't have to say much. But, those early medical points seemed to be addressed incredibly quickly. He, as usual, was professional and quick to the point when answering the items I'd listed, and all of my queries were ticked off in just over five minutes.

Shit. What now?

Silence.

Shit.

More silence.

'Jason,' my doctor finally said, 'I noticed you booked a double appointment, so is there something else?'

Silence.

Shit, it's now or never.

Silence. My doctor was so patient with me.

Deep breath … keep it together. 'Well …' I fumbled as I looked at my hands. 'Well … I've been struggling for a while.' *Can I even remember to breathe?* 'I've come to realise …' *Remember to breathe! Shit, why are there tears?*

This was the point of no return. This was the point of acknowledging the feelings I'd had since I was around ten years of age but never understood. I had spent years knowing about gay people and years of walking on the very edge of the gay community but never really crossing the line. This was about the internal core of who I was, the person I was and the sexual being I was that I had oppressed, rejected, hated and tried to pray away, and it was about to be blown away in the next few words. The line was now about to be crossed. Once crossed, it was likely impossible to cross back.

'I've come to realise that I am gay.'

Fuck, it's out there! I've actually told someone.

Silence.

As this conversation was going on in my head, I was not able to see anything; I might as well have been blind, and the focus on the words had sucked away all my mental and physical energy. And whilst this transpired, my doctor had been quietly and slowly rolling his chair away from his desk to be more open and more in front of me, but with good space between us.

Silence. He seemed to be waiting until I was able to look up and focus.

'Well then,' he said, 'that makes an awful lot of sense.'

What? Wait … this makes sense? I'm hardly making any sense of this or anything at the moment, so how does this make any fucking sense?

'How?' I managed to ask, so my doctor began the discussion as we considered the mental health issues I had been struggling with for a long time—those he knew of in detail and had managed me through. This type of internal conflict, the secrets that go with it and living in an opposite marriage all seemed plausible as the reason for my black cloud. This was going better than I could have ever imagined, as I felt an immediate acceptance that I had been really struggling and that being gay and married could be a significant contributor to my mental health.

The next part of our conversation was also unexpected, and it actually made our patient-doctor relationship even better for him to help guide me through this challenging period ahead. 'Jason,' he said, 'I need to make an assessment about whether you are in an emergency situation or in a crisis situation. I have a view, but I want to test it with you.'

'Okay,' I responded cautiously.

'My definition of an emergency is that I need to have you see someone in the next forty-eight hours, and a crisis is that we have two weeks. I am thinking that you are in crisis, but what do you think?'

My mind was racing; I hadn't had any suicidal thoughts for a while and none since coming out to myself. Usually, it could take a while to find a new therapist and set up an appointment. *Am I in an emergency situation? Am I likely to do myself any immediate harm? No ... I don't think so.* Yet, I actually hadn't prepared myself for such language as 'crisis' either. *But shit ... this is a crisis on so many levels! I have no idea how to manage any of this, and I have no idea about the road ahead, so yes, the word 'crisis' sounds like the right word to me!* 'Yes', I responded. 'I agree. I don't feel that I am in an emergency situation, but I do feel that I am in crisis.'

So, we had the triaging done.

Now what?

What happened next was one of the best examples of modern medical practise that I have experienced: complete honesty and vulnerability from my doctor when faced with my own vulnerability. 'I have not had a patient in this situation before,' he said. 'You are the first person that has come out to me in practise, and I am not sure to whom I should refer you.'

Where will this go?

'Given that we have two weeks to find you someone,' my doctor said, 'and only if it's okay with you, I would like to consult with other doctors here. No names will be mentioned, and I'd like to connect with our broader medical network to get some suggestions too. Would that be okay with you?'

Wow! 'Yes.'

A plan was agreed that, once my doctor discussed matters with colleagues both in the practice and outside, he would call me with suggestions, which I would review. If I was happy to proceed, a referral would be written, but we agreed it might take a few goes for me to be happy with the preferred psychologist. Importantly, in the meantime, if I was feeling worse or at risk in any way, I was to contact the surgery immediately. If it was after hours, however, I was to head straight to the local hospital emergency department. I settled my account, left the clinic and went home. I was absolutely exhausted, so I kept my distance and really didn't invite any conversations that night about what had just transpired.

A few days later, I received a call from my doctor suggesting a psychologist from the same practice where I had first visited Valerie, and he suggested that I look up her details on the Internet. When I did, my concerns around the practice reared again. While my experience with my Christian doctor was positive, I didn't feel like I could trust, and bare all to, a Christian psychologist because of what

I had seen on the Internet. While a Christian myself, I felt very uncomfortable about talking to a psychologist who advertised themselves as a Christian because it was such a generic term. Which arm of Christianity did they come from? Were they ultra conservative to the point where I would be judged, condemned and told I was making poor or inappropriate lifestyle choices? Would I be told that I could be changed to become straight? Or, would they be more progressive and able to provide real and effective support?

In my mind, without these qualifiers, any psychologist who advertised themselves as a Christian was someone I probably couldn't consult with at this most extremely challenging time in my life. I needed someone to help me survive and not take me down a pathway of further destruction, for that was something I was completely capable of doing myself.

So once again, I was probably doing them a disservice, but I was too fragile to take a chance, and it was not a risk I could afford at this point in time. A day later, I called back and left a message for my doctor to call me when he had a chance between patients. However, it seemed that a request had been left with reception to put me straight through, so I mentioned to him that I really didn't feel that comfortable with the suggestion of the first psychologist. He indicated that he thought that might have been the case, and he would continue with the search.

A few days later, another call came from my doctor with a new name. It was another woman but in the opposite direction of West Ryde. I looked up the website and was stunned; my doctor was taking this very seriously. This person had a lot of experience with transgender people and, specifically, transgender youth. While I was not transgender, the issue of gender identity was pivotal, so this made sense.

I was aware that the clock was ticking, as I was in crisis and needed to be in therapy within two weeks. Even with my dark and cloudy head, I was able to make at least one very useful decision: I would interview the potential therapists on the phone first rather than waiting for an appointment. So, I called and left a message with the new woman.

A few hours later my call was returned. The conversation started well, and she allowed me enough space to explain the situation and my doctor's dilemma. She was grateful that my doctor had considered her, but then the bad news came. Her practise area of dealing with transgender teenagers had grown so much since she had last updated her website that she was no longer taking patients with other sexuality and gender issues.

Shit!

I was only just starting to get my mind around the alphabet of LGBTIQA+ and only recently had become more familiar with the issues confronting transgender people. But, what was more surprising for me was that there seemed to be, in the next suburb over from home, a clinician whose field of work had grown so successfully that it was able to focus on dealing exclusively with transgender kids.

'But ...' she said.

Wait ... there's a 'but'?

She had a suggestion. Her own supervisor—always a good sign when seeing a psychologist—did practise in the area of my need, and she provided me with another name and a telephone number. Another call later, this time to Michael, I left another message and then awaited his call back.

When it came, I followed the same approach: I briefly provided an overview on how I was given his details and number, and I told him I was married but that I had just come out to my doctor as gay. He listened patiently to the brief background. Then, we talked about his work, both as a therapist and an academic, and there seemed to be a level of connection. So, an appointment was made, subject to my doctor agreeing to a referral. However, Michael was a registered psychologist and this was all the confirmation my doctor needed, as he thought the professional referral from his last recommendation was appropriate. He agreed to this development and let me know I could pick up the referral the next day. With that, the next part of the journey commenced.

The Second Time Coming Out

Although I had talked to Michael on the phone, actually meeting a psychologist for the first time is always somewhat scary: would we really connect? Like many psychologists and counsellors, he worked from home. Fortunately, he was in a trendy residential area where I absolutely did not know anyone.

For my first appointment, I managed to arrive rather early, so I doubled back to find a place where I could get a coffee and nervously wait. Eventually, the time came for me to knock on the front door, where I was greeted by Michael, a man younger than me but not youthful, standing and displaying complete professional competence. A friendly greeting ensued, and then I was taken into the first room to the left.

Michael's consultation room was a well-proportioned study, which had a table where he sat, with views out through the bay windows. Perpendicular to the table and against the wall was a nice couch for his patients, where I was invited to sit. There was a coffee table, and then on the opposite wall, there were floor-to-ceiling bookshelves that were full of professional and academic books and journals. It was then that an odd object—a dildo—caught my eye and let me know that sexuality was safe to discuss in his office. Noticeably, on the back wall, there were various certificates and highlighted degrees, diplomas, professional accreditation and some artwork. On the coffee table was a jug of water and a glass, but he asked if I would like a hot drink instead. Black tea with one sugar was my request.

We exchanged some documents, which is to be expected when seeing a health professional for the first time, and I offered the referral from my doctor. Michael offered me a clip board with two documents: one requested the usual personal details, releases and so on, and the second document was the K10 Anxiety and Depression Checklist that would be revisited at the start of every session. And so we began.

'Why are you here, Jason?'

We continued with some general background information, current family situations and arrangements, and I said, 'I'm married and have kids.'

'What do you want to do with these sessions?' Michael asked.

How the hell do I know?

Then, Michael asked what my working arrangements were and how stress played into that.

'Running a small business is stressful,' I said, 'particularly when government agencies have an obligation to pay their bills on time ... and don't. This means that I have to personally fund the operation of my business because I often have a quarter of a million dollars well overdue from New South Wales government departments and agencies, who have no reason or justification for their delays in payments.'

Michael then went on to ask me about my other interests and activities, including basketball and church. We took a little diversion into the latter, with him wanting to know more about which church and my involvement with it.

'I have had a long tradition with the Uniting Church,' I said, 'and both the Presbyterian and Methodist Churches prior to the union of these two denominations, plus the Congregational Church back in 1977.' As I spoke, I realised that my tone was monotonous as though I was reading from a text book, but I briefly carried on to outline my parish and roles in wider activities, such as a synod board.

We seemed to move on suddenly, and thoughts whirled around in my mind.

What am I really talking about?
What am I really thinking?
What am I avoiding?

Later in this first session, I asked him why he had wanted to drill more into my faith initially rather than any other aspect of my life.

'Christianity and being gay,' he said, 'can have significant issues depending on the denomination. With the Uniting Church, it won't be plain sailing, but if you were involved in other denominations, then other actions or discussions might be needed around your safety.'

I suspect the context to this is that the Catholic Church still globally rejects LGBTIQA+ people, as does the Sydney Anglican Diocese, which is notorious for the rejection of this community—the respective archbishops over time being particularly unfriendly. In my opinion, Sydney Anglicanism is very close to being a religious cult that is driven by its rejection of the LGBTIQA+ community. As I am finalising this book, they are updating their 'doctrine' to ensure they have the right to discriminate against LGBTIQA+ people, should new laws permit it, and establishing ways they can get around any future laws to outlaw LGBTIQA+ conversion therapy. As with many conservative Christian groups, there is a particular anti-transgender focus around the world at the moment.

Don't get me wrong, there are *some* LGBTIQA+ friendly priests and people in their communion, but so extreme is their majority's disdain for LGBTIQA+ people that during the Australian postal survey to guide Parliament on marriage equality in 2017, it was disclosed by accident that the Sydney Anglican Church had used one million dollars of their own funds to donate to the 'No' campaign to fight against marriage equality. Much of their money was for supporting advertisements based on mistruth, while at the same time they donated a mere five thousand dollars towards a campaign to eradicate violence against women in their church context. This makes sense when you understand that they despise LGBTIQA+ people and they also refuse to have women in leadership roles. They fund other Anglican churches, often in poorer countries such as North Africa, on the basis of their ideology of oppressing women and rejecting anyone of the LGBTIQA+ community.

Conversely, in the Uniting Church there are basically three factions. At one end, there is a faction that perhaps would be more comfortable being connected to the Sydney Anglican Church. The other end is very progressive and fully supportive of LGBTIQA+ people, and then there is the middle faction, which tends to be progressive and, if pushed, would support LGBTIQA+ people although it's not a higher order issue for them.

If I was a Catholic or an Anglican and coming out as gay, this could have been even more complex and potentially more dangerous to my mental health than the 'usual' extreme dangers of 'just' being a Christian and being gay. Suicide rates among LGBTIQA+ people are four to six times that of their straight or cis-gendered peers. Transgender suicide rates are twelve times that of their peers, and the LGBTIQA+ Christian suicide rate is up there on par with the transgender people's rate. Hence Michael's questions.

From my first meeting with Michael, there were many tears, and he was so generous with his time. There were times when I was so distressed that I stayed for almost twice my allocated time—fortunately, there were no other patients after me—because he wanted me to remain, talking through issues to a point where he felt it was safe for me leave his office and head home. There were so many things interplaying with this: my relationship with my father; the rejection of my sexuality when I was fourteen, primarily by my father, with later reinforcement during my teenage years; my own rejection of myself and who I really was; and my fear over acceptance, perfectionism and acting on my sexuality. Sometimes, we went round in circles, as part of my struggle was trying to fully integrate who I was.

We talked about what I wanted and what options were realistically available given my situation. Having come out to three people now—me, my doctor and now, Michael— my sexuality and sexual needs had been dramatically heightened. I was yearning to experience the pleasure of sex that matched my orientation. I was craving that experience so badly that it was becoming a distraction in many ways. While I looked at options available to me, there was a significantly strong desire to have these thoughts met, but I knew I couldn't act on them until I was out more broadly and until my wife knew what was happening to me and to our marriage. So, in many sessions, we talked about all these options. Some of them seemed to make me uncomfortable, but for some reason, I still wanted to explore them:

1. Reject who I was. Well, that hadn't worked for the last forty years, so I knew that wouldn't work now.
2. Accept who I was and then stay essentially in the closet. I knew pretty much straight away that wasn't going to work either. The door on the metaphorical cupboard was getting fairly rotten, and if I didn't manage to open it and handle the resulting process, it was going to fall off and expose me anyway.
3. Accept who I was, remain in the closet in public and act on my sexual needs in a discrete way. I knew

that, relatively soon, neither my value set nor my mental health would cope with this option.

4. Accept who I was, come out to some family and agree on an open sexual relationship model. Again, my value system wouldn't really cope with this option.

5. Accept who I was, come out, leave the marriage and start again with relationships that were natural to me. After many weeks of knowing this option would hurt me, and even knowing the hurt this would cause my wife, it seemed like the only realistic option that provided any chance of survivability.

So, we eventually started working on a plan. A key driver for me was that my son was in Year 12 and doing his Higher School Certificate (HSC). As it was his final year, it was a stressful year on all sorts of levels. Each subject, with their complexities and his own issues, required a fair amount of school and parental attention and support.

My daughter was working her way through Year 10, which is a very odd year in the New South Wales education system for all sorts of reasons. Additionally, she was an up-and-coming athlete, competing in her final age level in the Netball State Age Championships. Out of approximately eighty associations, her team had come third and fifth in the earlier years, and then first and finally second in the last year of her four-year journey. She subsequently made the state team and then went on to win the National Schools competition. Due to the pressure of playing at this level, she decided to take up volleyball as both a hobby and a sporting relief.

Michael and I continued to plan.

'There is no optimal time to tell your family that you are gay,' he said as he tried to protect me from timings whilst instilling courage in me, 'but there may be less traumatic times.'

It became obvious that it would be best to wait until after my son had completed his final exams. Not knowing nor having any control as to how anyone else would react, I didn't want to add to the already significant stress he was under with Year 12. He was planning to take a gap year in the UK to work in a school boarding house the following year, so it also seemed important to tell the family as soon as possible after his exams, which finished at the end of October, 2015. That way, if there was any fall out, there was a chance I could address it as much as possible before he departed on New Year's Day.

So, we now had the 'CO Day', or the 'Coming Out Day' for the rest of the family, and we had to work out matters around this. When would I talk to my minister at church, and who else did I need to tell?

As sessions continued, there was so much grief and pain. I think I kept the tissue manufacturers in super profit during this period of time. I realised more and more that I could not continue being the actor that I had been all my life, hiding the type of person that I was and the people who I was naturally attracted to. I kept coming back to the concept of the lid on the box—it was obvious after the reaction of my father, the follow-on comments, and my church life and its comments, that this part of my life had been put in a box. I was a good Christian lad, man, father and husband, so the box had been buried deep within me. The issue reared its head every time my wife and I were intimate, and then every Communion Sunday, I would be in pain, praying to God to take away the unacceptable thoughts and feelings. The acting on these fronts was in that box, with its lid so tightly sealed and buried so deeply within me that the box was never meant to see the light of day again—ever.

For several sessions, I kept asking Michael, 'Why has the lid come off the box?' I needed to know. I had never had any affairs while married, and I didn't have any memory of seeing a bloke in recent history and thinking, 'Oh, my gosh, he is beautiful!' This didn't make any sense. Every crisis is supposed to have a trigger, right? So, what the fuck was going on?

In Michael's gently guiding manner, he offered two pathways that we could follow. The first was to not dwell on this and to be forward thinking from here onwards. The second was to spend time trying to find the trigger; to work out why the lid had come off the box. However, he warned, based on his experience with other patients with stories parallel to mine, this could mean spending a long time trying to find this out and, more likely than not, never finding the answer. I had learned to trust Michael and his guidance, and one of the therapeutic strategies was preparing for October.

As I worked through all these extreme anxieties, knowing that significant change in my life and the life of my family was about to come, it was not unsurprising that my moods became wilder and less manageable; something that was obvious to my wife. On a number of occasions, she asked if seeing Michael was actually helping, as, from her perspective, I seemed to be getting worse. But I had a relatively stock answer for her: 'I am working through some tough things, and I know where I am going. Sorry that I seem to be getting worse, but it will get better.' Acting, yet again. Fortunately for me, she knew of my very toxic relationship with my father that had afforded me years of counselling, and I was hoping this 'cover' was going to continue to work.

Yet, the questioning from my wife about whether Michael was helping or harming my healing process became more intensive. It got to the point where I ended up raising it with him because he must have seen something like this before. Michael suggested that, while we had a plan, we needed to prepare for an unexpected coming out earlier than we had scheduled for. We began role playing how the 'coming out disclosure' might go, and this turned out to be very insightful on Michael's behalf. I turned 53 late in August, 2015, and then the following Monday was my therapy session, which was useful but still stressful. When I got home, I headed upstairs to my bedroom to chill out, but my wife came in and wanted to chat.

'What is happening?' she asked. 'Things don't seem to be improving, so is Michael actually helping?'

My response, honed from my role playing with Michael in preparation for this repeated worry of hers, was to bat it away. 'I know where I am at, and I am working through things. Michael is working well for me.' We chatted backwards and forwards on this for a short period of time, and I found myself implementing the next layer of strategies that Michael and I had talked about. But this was not sufficient. So, I attempted another strategy. 'I really don't want to talk about it until after our son has finished his last exams,' I said, but that didn't really help at all, and my wife's next comment left me in a corner with no way of knowing where to take the conversation; it wasn't in the role play Michael and I had practised.

'Oh, so you have a terminal disease?'

I was shocked at the thought, and I had to dig deep into the concepts that Michael had taught me. I know through history that people thought being gay was a mental illness, and for a significant part of the twentieth century, being homosexual was in the American *Classification Manual of Mental Disorders* (DSM) and led to many suicides around the world. No, I didn't have a terminal disease. Was there another deflection technique I could use? What option or pathway did I have?

Shit, this wasn't in the scenarios that Michael and I talked about.

Silence.

Remember to breathe!

My brain was racing at a million miles an hour, but I

229

knew that I was snookered. I couldn't let it stand that I had some terrible medical condition that meant I was going to die soon after my son's final exams. There was only one pathway forwards even though I did not want this to be the time of disclosure.

Fortunately, I had been doing research in preparation for my disclosure, and I had discovered that, in Sydney, there was a government-funded support program for women whose husbands came out as gay or bisexual— it could be found at the Leichardt Women's Community Health Centre. I had those details up my sleeve if I needed them. However, despite all of my research, I really couldn't find any support services for teen kids of a parent who came out.

Trying to remember all the advice that Michael had provided me, I started to think calmly. *How am I actually going to do this?* I opened my mouth. 'No, I don't have a terminal disease.'

My wife then asked another question straight away. 'Are you going to leave me?'

I knew the options that Michael and I had been working through, and I had an idea where this was going to end up; this was going to be the moment that really changed my life. I turned towards her and said, 'No. I don't know.' I realised that I sounded more confused than rational. *Breathe!*

There was absolute silence in the room. I now had no choice but to continue; there was no turning back. Our family life was about to change forever, and I was no longer in control of the trajectory of my life. 'The issue is,' I said as calmly as I could, 'I have come to realise that I am gay. I know this will be disruptive, but I didn't want to talk about this until after our son had finished his exams.'

I waited. What was her reaction going to be? An explosion? Silence? Screams? There was silence, but there was also a gentleness in the response. Definitely there was shock. I knew of the heartache that she'd been through in her early thirties when her parents divorced. No doubt that sense of insecurity was bubbling up and flowing through her mind. 'What does this mean?' she finally managed to ask.

I clumsily talked through the options that Michael and I had been discussing and how it seemed to me that most of them wouldn't work, which left separation as the only viable outcome. The measured way I spoke of this did come back to sting me a little later on, but communication has always been a challenge for me when under extreme stress. I also don't feel like I necessarily expressed myself that well to my wife in that moment and, to a minor extent, she may not have fully heard what I said. But the foundation had been laid.

Thinking of what would have been concerning for her, particularly given her father's behaviour, I thought it would be prudent to tell her that I had never had an affair. The immediate response I received suggested this was a useful thing to say. We gently chatted, but it was clear that we were now entering a very difficult period of time. Interestingly she did say to me, 'I often wondered if you were bi.' Until I began this journey, I really didn't understand much about the different sexual orientations although one of my friends was bi. But, given the level of my sexual interest over the last seven years, bisexuality absolutely didn't fit the bill. I was definitely gay.

It was clear that her comment was a sign or offer of graciousness, and I took it as such without any additional comment. So, now was the time for her to hear the details. Where did I go from here? I mentioned the Leichardt Centre and said I would get her the details that night. Then, I suggested that she call them as soon as she could. We agreed that we would not tell the kids anything until after our son had completed his final exams. With this massive upheaval in our lives, we would try to continue on as much as normal to protect him from any new issues to add to the list of challenges he already had moving towards the end of high school.

We agreed that we needed to have very good communication as we navigated the months ahead. I was sorry. I tried to say that, but I know I probably wasn't very effective in saying it in a meaningful way during that conversation. The room had an overwhelming sense of darkness in it, at least for me; the same darkness I had seen and felt when I was fourteen. I wouldn't have been surprised if it was the same for her. The most critical disclosure had now been made. A significant change in all of our lives was about to commence. But I really didn't understand that this was only the start of lifelong disclosures. Yes, a load had been lifted, but I still wasn't out of the closet because we couldn't do anything until after those final exams.

Next Sunday is Father's Day. How can we go out as a family for lunch to celebrate both my birthday and Father's Day after this?

That would be the next immediate challenge.

Shame, Separation and Preparing to Come Out

I had finally told my wife the truth. As it stood in our family now, only my wife knew my secret, but now we both held the secret. We both knew there was an abundance of information that we needed to process, and I can only imagine what might have been going through her mind: anger, fear, confusion, wondering what had our relationship had meant? What this all meant for her and now her future?

In the kitchen, different and difficult conversations between my wife and me commenced. Now it was more about money and how the finances would work in the event of a separation. I could understand her concern, but it meant financial difficulties for me as well. I, too, feared that I might end up with nothing when I retired. We both wanted to keep lawyers out of the process as much as possible, only using them for the technical material, and for the two of us to work out the key decisions that they would then draft on our behalf.

Sometimes, we would have conversations in the laundry or deep in the backyard—rarely did the kids ever venture that far. Why would they? To them, it was just parents doing the laundry. On one of our 'laundry days', there was a question on my wife's mind; it was a painful question for her and equally tormenting for me. 'Did you ever love me?' she asked. 'If you knew you were gay, why did you chase me?' This was one of her biggest questions. But, these were the most honest and, at the same time, potentially soul-destroying questions because they went beyond the superficial to the core of who we were: friends, parents, lovers and marriage partners. They went to the core of how we each wanted to be understood. 'Did you ever love me, Jason?' she asked me again.

Crap!

Do I really want to respond to this?

How do I respond to this?

The hammer in my head started thumping.

'How do I really know?' was what I wanted to actually say to her, but I knew that it wasn't a useful response in any way, nor a helpful one that she may have been looking for. I don't think I responded well. I stumbled, struggling to answer the question honestly but without causing more pain. *What are the resources that I can draw upon?* Those resources, given to me by my therapists over the years, guided me to be honest where I could be, which might have meant saying that I didn't know was an honest answer. I also remembered that there was a lesson on breathing. This was a lesson that I began to keep at the front of my mind for quite a while. In answer to my wife's question, though, I responded as best I could with my knowledge of me and my understanding of love. 'I did love you when we got married.' However, the challenge was that I was in an opposite orientation marriage, and my understanding of what love was had become disassembled. Still, today, I haven't yet been able to reassemble myself and my understanding of love.

For my wife, I believe my coming out created a sense of betrayal, of hurt, plus more fear and uncertainty in her life. More importantly, from her perspective, I suspected she was now feeling terribly fragile about the future. I tried to be there for her, but I also needed to focus attention on my kids and their well-being. They were young, and this shift in parenthood was something that I wanted them to understand even if there wasn't full acceptance from them. I needed them to know that I still loved and cared about them deeply.

Regardless of our disagreements, I hoped that the crisis program that my wife was attending at the Leichardt Centre was helpful, which it seemed to be. I was pleased that she was also seeing a therapist on a more permanent basis. We continued our meetings in the kitchen when the kids were watching television or studying. We would close the kitchen door, something we had rarely done in the past, hoping that this would not draw too much attention.

Doors closing—but I just pushed open the closet door!

My psychologist, Michael, and the counsellors at the women's support centre had some very useful suggestions for both of us, in particular around the process of telling our kids. Their first suggestion was that we should tell them together, which I thought sounded quite reasonable. Secondly, we were told to reinforce to them that we loved them dearly. I later wrote in my journal that that would be the easy part because my kids were, and still are to this day, my everything.

The next step was interesting, and when I thought it through, it was obvious; however, the comment resonated more strongly and immediately with my wife. 'Don't demand respect from your children,' said Michael. When my wife's parents split up late in life, her father expected her to still respect him. There was no doubt she still cared for him as her father, but respect was a different issue.

My counsellor also said, 'When telling the kids, spend

time listening to any questions and comments, and be prepared for anything. It could be silence, acceptance, anger, confusion, tears or a combination of all these emotions. There may be some or all of these in that short period of explanation. The processing of their feelings might be immediate or may be delayed.'

I tended to be on edge during our kitchen conversations in case either of the kids suddenly came into the room—it was the epicentre of our home and, more importantly, their food supply. We were constantly listening out for them, and we would stop our quiet conversations at the slightest sound. There was this awful tension because of having these difficult conversations whilst also worrying that the kids would overhear when we were mid-sentence.

But for me, there was my own further tension. I was slowly coming out, but it was as if closing the kitchen door was symbolically signalling that the closet door was still firmly shut. Therefore, I felt caught in a place where it was unclear whether I was in or out of the closet. Feeling stuck in this 'halfway house' was creating additional stress on my brain, sapping me of the limited energy that I had, and the black clouds kept sweeping in and around my brain.

One of the early things that my wife and I agreed upon was that we needed to do this process well. We wanted to ensure that we could go to gatherings, events and functions with friends and family and, while not technically being there together, we would be able to coexist. This was also important for our kids as we wanted to be able to be at their birthdays and marriages—if either of them wanted to get married—and be comfortable sharing those spaces.

After one of my wife's early sessions with her new private therapist, our kitchen conversation turned to the question of my therapist, Michael. 'Do you know if Michael is a Christian?' she asked.

'No,' I responded. 'It is not something that I have particularly asked.'

'Well, in talking today with my therapist, she wonders if you would be better off with a Christian psychologist?'

The idea of mixing my therapy and my faith had already caused me concern. As I briefly mentioned before, in my Internet search around the time of my coming out, I had come across 'ex-gay' or 'gay conversion therapy', which was administered by Christian groups and often via so-called therapists. Essentially, this was a product of the fundamental Christian belief that being gay was one of the most deeply sinful acts, and that with appropriate prayer and their style of therapy, you could be 'healed' of your homosexuality. It is based on an archaic belief that LGBTIQA+ people suffer from a disorder. Of course, this is absolute rubbish, but it unfortunately is one of the major forms of abuse by religious organisations against LGBTIQA+ people, often leading to suicide or long-term mental health issues.

'Seeing a Christian psychologist might help you to get a better integrated perspective,' my wife said, looking at me with profound concern. It seemed like she wasn't listening to me, but there must have been so much confusion on her side as well.

'I understand that,' I said, 'but I have a good working relationship with Michael. We have worked through a lot, and there is more to work through, which includes my faith and my Christianity. So, I think I will continue with him.' I contained myself, using all of my skills to remain composed and diligent without letting the kids hear what we were discussing. The actor in me was at work again and coming to life. It just added to the exhaustion.

In the kitchen that night, my wife and I agreed—I think with some reluctance on her side—that I would continue my sessions with Michael as she would with her therapist. I had developed a model in our relationship where I generally gave in on issues, but fortunately in our married life, there weren't that many issues where I felt that I needed to stand my ground. The only other time when I had really stood firm was when my mother died and I had insisted that our kids, who were five and seven years old at the time, came to her funeral. It was probably the only time we'd had a major argument, which led to me storming out of the house and walking around the streets for well over an hour.

Through the journey towards accepting who I was, I was slowly learning to stand up for myself. I had never stood up to my father, but now I had to stand up for myself on so many different fronts; I didn't know how many more fronts there would ultimately be.

I had developed an effective therapeutic relationship with Michael, and that was important to me. If my wife's therapist didn't like it, well, quite frankly, that was just too bad. It really shouldn't have affected my wife one way or the other. How we sought professional help, especially with fragile themes and family matters, had to be a personal choice, and I was steadfast in making her understand that Michael was the right match for me at that moment in time. With the significant mental health issues that abound in the LGBTIQA+ community, and the appalling statistics around our health, which I discovered when I started my advocacy work, there is a need for a strong and effective relationship between a patient with mental health issues and their therapist.

In a later consultation with my doctor, I raised my concern with him over what I believed was the inappropriateness of my wife's therapist's comments. I had been mulling over whether or not to lodge a complaint with the Health Care Complaints Commission. My hesitance in doing this, however, stemmed from my role on a medical health regulatory agency, where I had seen how complaints against health practitioners in the midst of family separations often didn't help the family. My wife and I were struggling, but I thought we were doing far better than many families going through the early stages of a separation.

Since I realised early on that separation would undeniably be the outcome, we wanted to do it as well as we possibly could when we managed to get to that point. So, what did this mean with regards to my frustration and anger towards my wife's therapist? Maybe I needed to let it go. I wanted to ensure that she had good continuity of care with her therapist, and any complaint I lodged could have been detrimental to our ongoing relationship and potentially her therapy. So, in discussing this with my doctor, we agreed that I should let it go. I would leave it to him as a health professional to determine whether or not he had a mandatory reporting obligation to the relevant health authorities.

Michael began teaching me how to operate normally when the world I was actually living in was in a spin. There is no rule book on how to do this stuff, and when I say 'stuff', I mean all of the emotional baggage and revelations that surround the act of coming out. Each of us is a unique individual with different backgrounds, personalities and circumstances in which we are operating. No doubt, there would be questions from my family, but did I really have the answers? Until the questions came, I didn't know if I would actually feel comfortable with answering them. Sometimes, I wondered what would happen if I didn't even know the answers, and that was a struggle. When this happened, I needed to go back to one of the early lessons Michael had taught me when he'd said, 'Sometimes we will never know, and the safest thing is to let the question go.'

The perfectionist in me struggled with this strategy, but I needed to fly now, and I was being promoted to captain my own ship. I had to be the leader in this for me. After all, I was the one who came out, opened the closet door and allowed my family to see who I was. I constantly reminded myself that life goes on. Work goes on even through the uncertainty, and I had to soldier on.

The hammer in my head was drumming its familiar, questioning beat again.

Has this been worthwhile so far? I am not so sure! I barely do enough work to keep a basic income coming in.

When you are a consultant, your mental capacity is about the only thing you have, and my head was just not working anywhere near capacity. The cloud was growing, and the anti-depressant medication was helping me to hold on, but how long for, I wasn't sure.

But, how do I meet people?

This was one of the burning questions that kept appearing in my mind. I needed to be with people who could understand me without question or fear, and there was a part of me whose needs had never been met. I did not know the LGBTIQA+ community or the way into it. In many ways, a different type of loneliness was creeping in, and I sensed a new isolation was coming. I had only ever had a small number of friends, and a lot of them were through the Church. A different cloud was appearing, and a different black dog was now barking in my head.

One of the pieces of feedback that I had from my wife from her crisis centre was that they encouraged her to keep me away from support groups for married gay men. In their experience, they told her, men who joined usually ended up finding a partner quickly. Trying to be respectful of my wife's request, I stayed away. I did wonder if this was the right thing to do, but my insecurities were having a huge impact on my decision-making skills.

In my mind, this also played into the conversations around cohabitation, which I had agreed to consider until our daughter had also finished high school. What I knew, after considering this option, was that it would not be appropriate to bring any man I met into our home. That would be unreasonable and totally unfair on my wife and my kids. So, my need to explore who I was socially—even at a minimum—remained unmet. I noted to myself that I was in a no man's land. I was out of the closet ... but at the same time, I was not. I felt like some kind of U-turn had taken place, which had never been my intention. In many ways, it felt like I had walked out of the closet but into an empty and closed room.

With a little hope in my heart, I had thought that telling my wife would at least have opened the closet door some more, giving me headway towards having the courage to reveal my newfound sexuality to the world. This seemingly was not the case. Confusion reigned supreme in my head, surrounded by the multi-layered clouds. I wanted to meet people, I wanted to meet gay men, but now I'd had this new alarm placed in my head that made me need to avoid meeting someone that could lead to a relationship—this was something my wife had told me she did not want me to have for the next two years while we cohabited. No doubt she was thinking of our daughter and that our cohabiting would provide her with a stable environment while she completed her Higher School Certificate. But ...

Is she being fair to me though?

I felt even more trapped than before. Even with my own feelings, I empathised with my wife. Could I blame her? When she had married me, it had been for better or for worse. Of the two, I imagined this was probably the latter, and dealing with my transition was definitely not easy for her.

It's Time:
Breaking the News to My Kids

Crunch time hit. The final exams were over for my son, and he was about to leave the nest for a year. It was time to tell our kids. I talked it through with Michael, and we discussed possible reactions and repercussions—the potential rejection or tolerance and acceptance of the situation—and practically everything else. The Friday night after our son's final exam was to be the night.

So, did we tell them at the same time or separately? There were arguments for and against either approach. I had a preference for together, but I took the lead from my wife. She requested that we talk to them separately, as they were different kids, with different interests, needs and views of the world, and I agreed. My son was first. We gathered another chair and put it in our study. Then, we brought my son in. I wondered what he was thinking because this was not a usual pattern for us. For me, once again, it felt like the night I came out to my wife. The room felt like it was closing in and getting darker despite its large size. We are all tall people, and our son is much taller than me, so when there were three of us sitting in our narrow, but long study it suddenly felt excruciatingly crowded. I sat at my desk, but my chair was swung around, and my wife sat on a chair in the entrance way.

My son sat in a chair between our desks.

'We have some difficult information to talk about,' my wife said. 'I'll let your dad explain.'

While we had talked about the approach, we really hadn't talked exactly about who would say what and when. I wasn't quite ready, but in another sense, I was as ready as I was going to be. 'Well,' I said, stumbling over my words and not sure exactly where to look although I knew I needed to look at him. I could feel the shame encroaching, making me cower, so I struggled to look up and into his face. 'Well,' I said again, 'I have been going through a really rough time. It has been very challenging, and I have come to realise—'

Oh, here it goes again.

In the articles I had read and the videos I had watched, I had heard that coming out is actually a lifelong process, and not a one-time event. I still hadn't comprehended this fact, but that night, during my confession to my children, I started to get a glimmer of it.

'—that I am gay.'

My wife then stepped in and said, 'It is our intention to live together until your sister has completed her schooling.'

My son was mentally exhausted and wasted after the long, draining processes of the Australian school examinations. He was also a nearly eighteen-year-old teenager, and his communication skills were not his strongest asset, as many parents of an eighteen-year-old lad would appreciate. I didn't see any noticeable response or reaction, so we asked if he had any questions. He didn't. So, we told him that it was no longer a secret; if he wanted to tell anyone, he could, but it would be helpful for us to know so that we could decide if there was someone else we needed to tell. In our previous discussions, we had decided that we wanted to tell people ourselves rather than have them find out from others. He told us that he didn't feel he needed to tell anyone.

My son has had anxiety for a lot of his life, and he'd had his own therapist for a while. At this point in time, we hadn't gone with him for a couple of years because he had taken ownership of the process for himself, which made us proud. We now offered a suggestion that, if he wanted to talk to anyone about this, he could maybe have a chat with his therapist. He acknowledged this but didn't seem keen.

It was over so quickly. We stood up and cleared the passageway out of the study to the kitchen. My son gave his mum a hug and moved on. I wondered if he had already pushed me out of his life in one instant, and my heart missed a beat. Was I being rejected? But … in the very next heartbeat, he swung around, came back and gave me a hug too. My son, so much taller than me, was willing to give me a hug despite this life-changing information. There was hope that our relationship could continue. I was overwhelmed and humbled by his gesture, and I felt a deep sense of love. He moved out of the kitchen to his bedroom, and my wife went to get my daughter. So, back into the study I wandered. Back into the gloom, but I was reminded that the first discussion had gone as well, if not better, than I could have expected.

My daughter had turned sixteen three months earlier; she was growing up so fast. As she sat in the same chair her brother had vacated, we started again—the quick hand pass—and I was a little more ready to catch the ball this time. 'Well,' I stumbled, yet again, still not sure exactly where to look, but I made myself look at her. However, this issue of shame was still strongly there, still towering over me. It was a struggle to maintain her eye contact. 'Well,' I said again, 'I have been going through a really rough time. It has been very challenging, and I have come to realise'—I paused—'that I am gay.' My wife once again finished the dialogue by telling our daughter that we would stay living together for the next two years until she had finished school.

This time there were tears. While you can have a plan, you never really know what is going to happen or how anything is going to work out. Our daughter, an up-and-coming elite athlete, has never really been a crier. A few years earlier, she had played in a three-day state netball championship with a broken arm. She had wanted to keep on playing. The last time I had really seen her cry was in a fall on the last day of that competition when she smashed the same arm she had injured on day one. So, this wasn't one of the scenarios that I had expected.

Think.

Breathe.

What might be going on here for my beautiful daughter?

'Why the tears?' my wife asked gently. 'What is happening for you?'

The response was one that astounded me, and it still does today. Our strong-willed sixteen-year-old said, 'At the end of the day, I want the two of you to be happy, whatever that looks like.' We explored some more, very gently, not sure where this might go. It turned out that she didn't want the pressure of us staying together any longer than we wanted to, or ought to, for her. The emotional intelligence this young woman had was amazing, and it certainly didn't come from me.

Again, we told her that it was no longer a secret, but we asked her to let us know if she did want to share the news with anyone. We talked through some examples, as it was her wider friendship circle and connections whose parents also had a connection with my wife.

Again, it seemed over very quickly. We stood up, and my wife and I both received a hug from her. Then, my daughter left. But, a short time later, she came back when we were still debriefing each other in the kitchen. She asked if she could tell a particular friend. We said that that was fine, and thanked her for checking in. During the debrief with my wife, we agreed that the process had gone well; there didn't appear to be any immediate crisis with the kids. We agreed to monitor this over the next days and weeks.

The emotional energy in telling this news to those so critically close to you is exhausting. Looking back, I think their responses were pretty much predictable, but that negative voice in my head still always wants me to know that danger and crisis lurk. I think this is why I get so exhausted: I have a basic underlying presumption that everything will be a disaster.

After an hour, I needed to go to bed. I checked in with the kids, but they didn't have any follow-up questions, and life seemed to be continuing with their electronic devices and books.

Two more people down, but how many more to tell and how many more to go? This coming out really was a lifelong exercise, and at this point, I was getting it, but I still didn't fully understand it yet.

Extremely fatigued, I retired for the night.

Every few days, I checked in on the kids, but after a few weeks, they seemed to get agitated by my doing this even though it was primarily based around my concern for them. It took me some time to understand that, unlike my wife and me, they seemed okay about the news that they had received. Well, perhaps not 'okay' about the situation but not distressed by it. I didn't get any follow-up questions, which I found rather surprising. Was this, possibly, their way of showing acceptance?

The one person that my wife insisted I communicate

with regarding our situation was my mother-in-law. I was a very lucky man in that, supposedly unlike many husbands, I got on well with my mother-in-law, and we enjoyed each other's company. My wife and I were also very fortunate that, every Wednesday, my mother-in-law came down and helped out with the kids before they went to school. When they were in primary school, she helped with school pickups and also odd activities around the house, including helping with the washing. It was a routine that worked for all and a great benefit for us. However, although I had a great relationship with my wife's mother, I felt like it was my wife's responsibility to tell her first. In truth, I believed that it was inappropriate for me to come out to her before my wife had had a chance to share what was going on.

Juggling Act: The Executive, Father and Husband

My coming out journey had begun. I should have felt relieved, and the burden of revealing my truth should have lessened; however, the next steps were proving to be more arduous as I contemplated whom to tell next. The days blurred into weeks. Home and work were visions of static movement in which I felt disconnected and unfocused. Numbness overcame everything around me and within me. My focus was on trying to make everything appear normal at home, especially for the kids, and the years of being someone who hid things about himself— being a lifelong actor—were proving useful. But, as every actor knows, complex scenes requiring the management of emotions are draining if you're going to pull it off and pull your audience in. I didn't know how long I could go on pretending to be someone I was not.

I was so grateful to my wife, as this whole episode was as distressing for her as it was for me. I suspect her training as a teacher was helping to hold her up because, in one sense, a teacher is also something of a trained performer, putting on a calm face each day in front of a class, no matter what the strain.

My wife remained concerned that if I joined an LGBTIQA+ group, I might instantly meet someone, fall in love and then refuse to continue to cohabit until our daughter had finished school. Everything seemed to be off limits. But, I needed to find my tribe; I needed to find people like me to try and validate my very existence. *Were* there other people like me? Was I even like other people?

Hungry for knowledge and a sense of belonging, I continued to research organisations and support groups. I eventually came across an organisation called the Sydney Gay and Lesbian Business Association. For my whole life thus far, I had not been willing or able to find a way to integrate my separate identities, which now spurred my ongoing research. This included stumbling across an organisation called Freedom2Be, which was a group that provided a safe meeting space for gay Christians in Melbourne and Sydney. Once again, the questions started to bombard my mind along with the hammer in my head.

Who am I?

How do I reinvent myself?

How can I integrate myself into a wholeness that has been hidden from me for all of my life?

I continued to see my therapist, Michael, and realised that my life was traversing through issues that were quite multidimensional, so I required support in many areas. We discussed themes of recovering from the stress of my coming out, how to integrate this new identity alongside my faith, how to manage both my perfectionism and my work and career demands and what this new identity meant for me and those I cared about. Perhaps, most importantly, I started to wonder about expressing my sexuality. Having never had a true encounter with another man, but having accepted my sexuality, I began to feel tension around the fact I had not touched another male's body for nearly forty years, and back then, we were boys. I began to desire the answer to some underlying questions that were now a new hammering in my head.

So, do I just go to a gay sauna, or do I go to a male prostitute?

I felt like I was seventeen all over again; my hormones seemed to be driving me all over the place, and these unanswered questions bombarded me constantly. Michael and I had begun to dive into so many of my uncertainties, and it felt good to be supported in my pursuit of answers.

What are my ethics?

What men should I be allowed to have sex with?

If sex is legal and consensual, why am I so worried?

Where is this voice coming from?

I kept wondering about this voice that I was hearing in my head; the voice that was asking the questions and making me second-guess my decisions. Was it a repressive, Christian influence that also might say, *'You need to be a virgin to get married?'* I believed it was this voice that kept me 'pure' or 'protected' from my true sexuality.

As the acceptance of LGBTIQA+ people was evolving in society, and as some Christians were failing to justify their gay conversion therapy, others were backing away from this abusive treatment, which was also becoming visible to the wider society. The trade-off for some conservative or fundamental Christians was to accept that LGBTIQA+ people existed but that they shouldn't act on their sexuality. Really, it was another form of abuse from Christians to say that a class of citizens were excluded from sexual activity for no real biblical reason.

This voice in my head had nearly destroyed me many times; it resounded in me daily, and it was ultimately the voice that encouraged me into marriage. Was this voice truly real, and was it actually helpful … or destructive?

The issue of sexual ethics kept coming around and around, both inside and outside of therapy. Michael didn't set the ethics, but instead, he helped me to explore my relationship with them and to find a way I could ultimately live with my decisions. It has to be said that I struggled with them although I suspect this is the very nature of ethics. Tension and struggle, and getting it right some days but failing on others: learning, failing, learning, discovering, thinking, overthinking. However, this overthinking, and my endless desire for perfectionism, was also providing a shade of gloom.

I suspect that tied up in this somewhere was the concept of forgiveness, which had been twisted by some evangelical Christians and other church-related perspectives I encountered. They often wanted to avoid any discussion on the reality of sex and sexuality, and they preached a message that sex and anything to do with sex was immoral—except within a very strict code—which became the basis for control, exclusion and, importantly, unforgivable failure. This was what I kept coming back to: my 'failure' in the world of sexual ethics because the old voice of Christianity was not willing to let go. But over time, I would find my own way.

Shame.

The voice resonated in my brain. Shame launched itself as a massive issue once again for me and, I imagine, for my wife too although I can't speak for her as we have never talked about it. Many people feel shame simply as a result of a divorce, let alone facing our situation, but fortunately, the Christian denomination we are members of does recognise that marriages break down for a variety of reasons. Members typically recognise that there can be more harm done to people through forcing a marriage to remain intact rather than to find a different pathway forwards.

I do wonder what my wife felt about our situation, but I hope she knows that I didn't intentionally mislead her. I imagine some of our community of friends might wonder whether she saw some signs but elected not to address them. Perhaps she dreaded feeling the gaze of family, friends or work colleagues who might have said, 'How could you not see this?' At least for this last issue, I think we are fortunate that our circle of friends understands our history, the context of the time we live in and the social stigmas for gay men. This sort of disparaging response was common in the past, and it still happens in Australia and around the world today, so I think we are both lucky to have the friends we have.

No matter how supportive people are, though, internalised shame is a powerful and damaging force. Shame can be subtle one day, but the next it can be like a sledgehammer bashing you up and making you cower in fear of who you are. In the midst of my pain, I knew I still needed to find sympathy and compassion for my wife; how well I achieved that, I will probably never know, but I imagine it was probably never enough. I tried to allow her the space to grieve and to express her hurts and fears. To her enormous credit, she never directed her anger at me, and for that I am immensely grateful. But she felt frustration with me, and that was apparent; it was to be expected.

Our previous conversation around the options of what a family life might look like were no doubt very confronting for her, and one particular night there was another set of confrontations for each of us in our own way as we further explored the options. At this point in time, I was still a gay virgin—I had never kissed a man and never had a man bring me to orgasm or vice versa. The idea of me exploring my sexuality while we were independently living together was another shock for my wife, and this did lead to her recoiling. But again, there was no anger.

For her, it was yet another area of unchartered territory.

In our society, the religious right wing has been trying to stop any LGBTIQA+ anti-bullying programs in schools as well as disallowing the concept of providing effective sex education to all children, let alone LGBTIQA+ kids. Even worse, in Australia, they still sometimes try to reduce or refuse basic heterosexual education in schools, regressing back to the prudish mentality that no knowledge is the best knowledge. This trend can still be observed globally. In fact, I would suggest that, at the time of writing, there is a significant attempt to roll back LGBTIQA+ rights— despite them being so recently obtained—often under the banner of 'religious freedom' or, as I prefer to call it, 'religious privilege'.

Christianity does have a lot to answer for in taking one of the most important parts of who we are almost off the table for discussion. I had a head start because I had been practising open discussions with Michael in my therapy sessions, but they weren't appropriate conversations to have with my wife. I don't know if her therapist prepared her for these as well, but I hoped they did.

My wife's first response to my comment about needing to consider potential sexual activities in a cohabiting environment was, 'What would God think?' At this stage of the conversation, I definitely wasn't going to respond because I really didn't know what God thought. The silence of my response wasn't helping either of us, so when she didn't get the answer she was expecting or needing, she changed tact, graciously stating that she couldn't see how I would hold up—'remain intact' or 'be perceived positively'—if it was known that I was sleeping around. I found this frustrating, as again, this was a religiously driven thesis, but I couldn't blame her. These conversations needed to be had, and our understanding of our sexuality was influenced by our faith, for good or for bad. When all was said and done, she was concerned for my moral integrity and for my future.

Integrity was certainly a conversation that I was having with Michael. What surprised me was that it was possible to have both integrity *and* sexual expression. I was still on the journey of discovery before I could get to acceptance, but beliefs, faith, knowledge, history and ethics were all colliding.

The topic of my minister came up again with my wife, so perhaps she thought my sexual ethics and integrity needed additional input. My acting skills were required again as I tried not to show exasperation.

Over time, I came to realise why I was struggling to provide the definitive commitment to two years of cohabitation. With the breakdown of our marriage, it meant the breaking of what I held as very significant: my marriage vows ... a promise. I realised this had become the issue for me through talking with Michael and being able to reveal my truths. As I was in the process of breaking what I believed to be a critically important vow, I didn't know if I could make another pledge to my wife because promises were incredibly important to us both and to our family. Different people have different understandings of a promise, but once I make one, I don't have the intention of breaking it. This is one of my values; it's my sense of ethics. However, not knowing who I was or what the short-term future held gave me pause for thought.

Can I offer a promise I'm not sure I can keep?

I explained this to her, and there was some acknowledgement and recognition of what I was saying and why. I think it provided some help for her to realise I was not just being a self-centred twit but that I was seriously considering issues and perspectives. From her perspective, however, there was a difference, and it was clear that I needed to listen to her point of view as well. She was asking something without ever actually asking it explicitly: 'Can't you wait just two more years?'

This was so hard for me. On one hand, I understood where she was coming from, and the repressed Christian voice in my head said, 'Of course I can.' But I was still on the way out of the closet, which was very old and starting to break down. The door was ruined because it was crumbling and deteriorating, and it probably wouldn't hold me if I went back into it for another two years.

As my hormones now freely raced around my body, my head and elsewhere, I began to accept my natural self. In some ways, I was now experiencing the real puberty that I had suppressed when I was a teenager and these hormones were being reactivated.

A few times in the latter years of our marriage before I came out, the thought of actually exploring the physicality of my sexuality had crossed my mind, but I had made a decision to be faithful to her because of the promise from our wedding day. So, on the one hand, her request seemed reasonable. I had not engaged with any males in the last twenty years of my marriage, nor during the fifteen or so years beforehand, so two more years wouldn't matter. On the other hand, though, the lid on the box had been smashed opened; the closet door was ajar sufficient for the light to stream in and it was spotlighting the wonder of who I actually was. My mind and body were now in a different space entirely from the last forty years, so another two years seemed like an eternity. And, at the same time, loneliness was setting in. The more I was navigating the journey of coming out, the more isolated I was actually feeling, and I was experiencing so much intensity and so much pain. Conversations with people I had known for many years became challenging, and the actor in me was now providing Oscar-winning material.

The issue of faith did come into the conversations between my wife and me with some regularity. She wanted to know if I had told my minister. When I shared that I hadn't, her reply was always that she thought I should.

With Michael's professional help, I already had a plan in place, which included discussions with my minister as per the timetable Michael and I had specified, but my plan was now subject to other voices. While this was an added frustration for me, I was no longer the only person this was directly affecting. So, out of respect for my wife, I agreed to bring forward my conversation with my minister.

About nine months earlier, my parish had restructured its pastoral care program, and they wanted to ensure that every person had someone to check in with. There were announcements in church over a period of time to help with the transition, and I received a letter confirming the change and the person nominated as my pastoral carer. Yet, when I looked at it, it made me extremely uncomfortable. I was about to start a journey with a person I didn't really know, and therefore I had no idea whether or not I could be real with them about my journey of deep acceptance. This was not a reflection on them but more a reflection on me. The voices in my head were calling out again.

Fear!

Shame!

There will be more rejection!

A few days passed, and I looked at the letter again as it sat on my desk.

How am I going to respond?

Eventually, I sent a brief email to my minister to say I still wasn't sure if I wanted a pastoral carer. This didn't seem to set off any flags—which I am not sure was right or wrong from a pastoral care theory perspective—but for me, at that point in time, being left alone was a good thing. But now, I had to face the pressure of telling my minister.

How am I going to do this?

I definitely want to do this at coffee after church.

I had never really reached out to my minister before. I liked him and the parish; it seemed a safe place and, in reality, it was. But still, my fear from deep within reared its ugly head.

Will they really accept me when they discover who I really am?

The fear I still had of accepting myself was driving how I saw everyone else's perspective; I was superimposing my own expectations of how they would react without having any idea how they would actually respond.

When considering how to approach my minister, I knew he was a person who liked to meet people over coffee in the shops. That would provide a level of safety, as conversations could be kept quiet and the environment would ensure any bad reactions would be kept to a minimum. The positive was that I had seen other LGBTIQA+ people at the Church who had been well accepted by him, so I hoped he wouldn't have a bad reaction to my news. My analytical brain was trying to override the emotional side that was predominately in control, and it was suddenly speaking to me and giving me hope. So, I sent an email to see if he was available to catch up, and we agreed a time at a coffee shop close to church one workday morning—the benefit of owning my own company was that I could be flexible with my time.

Once we settled at a table inside the coffee shop, we participated in the small talk that Aussie males do so well to avoid so much. I decided that I didn't want to beat around the bush too much, so I told him I was really struggling and that family life was very difficult at the moment because I had come to accept that I was gay. There was almost no immediate reaction; he had always been careful with his words. And then, when he eventually started to speak, I struggled to listen because I feared what he was saying. Even a relatively short period of time later, I still couldn't really remember his words. Yet, what I do remember to this day is the slowness, the carefulness, in how he spoke to me; there was no rejection. It was an acknowledgement from the minister that my plight had been a hard one and that I must have been undergoing some difficult times. Slowly, and somewhat awkwardly from my perspective, we talked some more, and I saw that there was acceptance.

Eventually, I raised the issue of the pastoral carer scheme, and I revealed that the reason I didn't want one when the new system launched was because I knew this issue was going to come up soon. I told him I didn't know who I could trust with my situation because I didn't know people well enough yet in the parish. My minister acknowledged my perspective with quiet, gentle support. 'If you wanted someone in particular,' he asked, 'who would it be?'

'There is someone,' I said, 'but I fear they may be too close.'

The person I wanted was a chaplain and a lesbian, and she worked in the area of mental health. But I was concerned that all of this from me might be too close to her own existence and experience. However, my minister nodded and noted that she, the chaplain, was 'very good with boxes', which made me hesitate. Boxes? I knew a lot about boxes, but he didn't know about *my* boxes. Where was this going?

My minister seemed to recognise my rising anxiety, and he consoled me by saying, 'She is able to partition her life into various boxes and keep those boxes very separate. I could ask her on a no-name basis if that helps and see how she responds?'

Could this be the faith support that I am looking for?

I reported back to my wife although I wasn't sure the response was what she had been hoping for. However, I confess that I didn't share all of my thoughts and fears. Instead, I told her that, for me, it was a supportive meeting.

A week later, I got a message back from my minister

to say that the chaplain was open to being my pastoral carer. Somewhat ironically, she and I then skipped church the next week to go out for coffee to get to know each other better. This was the start and foundation of building a critically important relationship and a much-valued friendship, which became pivotal to my survival. I gave a quick back story to set some of the scene, and the chaplain provided me with some resources online and the names of some other gay Christians who I might want to talk with.

There was one funny side to this meeting: after my minister had asked the chaplain on a no-names basis if she would support someone pastorally, quite appropriately she had spoken with her partner. They had a very busy home life, and she wanted to ensure from their family's perspective that taking me on wouldn't take too much time away from her own family. Her partner's response was, 'That has to be Jason!' She was the only person who picked me out as gay in advance.

My wife then decided that we needed to talk with someone together from a faith perspective. Interestingly, she suggested my minister over the one at her church. In one way, that was good, but it surprised me. So, we scheduled a meeting with my minister, and this time we held it in a meeting room at church. It was awkward, but at least we were both talking about the same issue with the same person, and there was not much that I wouldn't talk about.

We talked a little bit about theology, but my minister's strategy was not to provide any definitive answers; instead, he provided frameworks for thinking and reflection as we prayed and journeyed towards our own conclusions. Then the major theological question came up from my wife as she said, 'If God knows us, why did he allow us to get married?' I think this was the foundational faith question that she had, and I suspect that this was one of the major risks to *her* faith.

For me, I had been able to disentangle this through my emerging understanding of faith from an LGBTIQA+ perspective. Many of the conservative, evangelical churches are very black and white when it comes to sexuality, LGBTIQA+ people and their theology, and I would say that there isn't much in the way of any good news. We, however, were members of the Uniting Church, and, as I've said before, it has a far more nuanced understanding of these areas than many other denominations. I personally think this is its greatest strength, but at times when you are seeking urgent answers, it can be frustrating.

For her, on the day that we spoke to my minister, there was not a quick, clear or concise answer, and there certainly wasn't an answer to justify putting me back in my box for the next two years. And while my faith was holding, albeit with a fragile struggle, I became concerned that her faith had been severely shaken through my coming out journey. I was also fearful that she now doubted her own judgements as she possibly wondered how she could have allowed herself to marry a man who turned out to be gay.

We left the meeting, and there was not a lot of conversation between us on our way home. My wife had been seeking and needing those elusive, definitive answers; answers that had to have a high level of precision. Maybe she was also seeking a strong rock to hold onto, but, sadly for her, no direct guidance had been provided.

As my wife and I continued to work out our new situation, there were still very few people who knew what was happening. Fortunately, through a connection that had become aware, someone reached out to let us know that they might be able to introduce us to a family who were about five years further down the pathway than we were. My wife thought she would like to meet with the woman, and a meeting was set up. Fortunately, they agreed, and I think it was good for my wife to meet another woman who had experienced this same journey. Apparently, her ex-husband had become a party animal and hadn't been fair with their financial split, so I took this as a warning to not go out and neglect my family. Yet another confusing, confronting piece of information for me to take in; but then again, did being gay necessarily mean becoming a party animal?

I reached out to a colleague of mine, who had a highly successful professional career and who also had split up with his wife after a long marriage to then openly identify as gay. It took a while for us to actually meet up at his office. To be honest, I felt a little pissed off with him because, when we had caught up at an earlier time before my own coming out story had begun, he had known he was gay, but he hadn't told me. I had thought our relationship was strong enough, so this made me sad. However, when we met up this time, he told me that he couldn't tell me at the time, and now, I understand. It's not always a case of not wanting to tell people; sometimes, you are not always *able* to tell people.

My friend's office was large, with a huge working desk, a lounge area and a meeting table. We sat in the lounge area, and I heard some of his story, and then I told him some of mine, which was a new learning experience for me. After a while, we started discussing sex, and he told me that gay sex was very different to hetero sex. He suggested that I should start experimenting, to slowly find out how it worked and what I liked. He also recommended finding a family lawyer that was not adversarial, and he provided me with the contact details of his lawyer. He and his ex-wife had worked out the details and then had the lawyers do the legal work.

I found it odd talking to him, particularly about sex. I knew that talking about it was not a bad thing, but it was so new for me although I felt that I needed to be open to the conversations. There was much to learn. My sex education from my father had been no more than five minutes, with me naked in my room after a shower. There had been a brief discussion on mechanics, nothing about protection and, most importantly, 'Don't get a girl pregnant, and be careful of young girls who want young men for sex.' I had never talked about sex with any of my school friends either, but now, it seemed like I absolutely needed to talk about it.

I set up a meeting with the lawyer my friend recommended. She was a bit old-school, but she had experience in this area. We talked about options regarding the kids, my obligations—particularly in relation to my daughter, who was under eighteen, and less so my son, who would soon be turning eighteen—and the various legal approaches that could be taken. She provided me with a list of documents that I needed to submit, particularly around my financial situation.

So much was going through my mind, and I couldn't stop thinking about my need to experience male-to-male touch. For me, I now understood that male-to-female touch met a social construct, and for most of our marriage, I was the one avoiding sex. However, my mind and body were now aligned and, as with most people, intimacy was important to me. I craved that sensual touch; those trembling hands that sent the tingles through your body and the smell and scent of the other that enlivened other parts of your brain. I was in my fifties, and I had not had this naturally. Sex was perhaps what the Bible had always taught me: centred on procreation rather than being a pleasurable experience.

I continued searching the Internet, and there seemed to be lots of options, from saunas to male prostitutes to erotic massages. It took me a long time to work out what to do, but eventually, it seemed like a massage might be a good way to start. I knew that I needed to start slowly and build up from there.

One day, I sent an email. The man was based in the Blue Mountains, and he offered erotic massages. I had a free day before I flew to Armidale in New South Wales in the evening, where I was running a course the next day for a client. The man responded pleasantly, and he asked me to let him know if there was anything I was looking for. Fortunately, the date I requested was free, so I replied, letting him know my back story and explaining that I just wanted a gentle time. He confirmed the details to get to his workplace, his payment methods and his willingness to support my needs.

When I woke up on the day that I was going to meet the erotic masseur, I was surprised by how I felt. I was in a relatively relaxed state as I prepared and packed to head to Armidale via the Blue Mountains, and I liked that I actually felt something; I wasn't numb. It was also surprising to me that my longing to know and feel touched in the way that I wanted was starting to feel natural and normal. I had not followed that want or desire before because I had wanted to remain faithful, but the natural 'me' was finally starting to surface. I was finding my inner soul and was finally managing to be brave and listen to my body. Those innocent times when I was ten and fourteen years of age were coming back, and I could feel the excitement brewing of being with another male.

It was nearly a ninety-minute drive, and following his directions, I found the place with ease. I knocked on the door and was greeted very pleasantly. I was ushered into a room in a very relaxing way, and after we did the introductions, the erotic massage process started. Rather than tensing up, I relaxed and went with the flow. The touching was gentle and caressing, and there was kissing and an exploration of my maleness in a way I had never experienced before. I felt free. What transpired was tender and natural, and it was comfortable.

This is me.

I could hear these gentle words flowing through my mind because I had finally discovered what gay pleasure could feel like as an adult. I didn't feel strange or like an outcast. This had been a much-needed, fact-finding mission and an experience to allow me the self-understanding to move ahead; there was not going to be a friendship here, as I saw this for what it was.

That day in 2015 was the first time I really knew for sure.

This is me.

It was no longer a hypothesis. This wasn't an experiment or a phase; this was my reality, and I was now at peace with myself. After the connection, I showered, hopped back into my car and drove for two hours to Sydney Airport to get my flight to rural NSW. During the drive, the flight and then that night in the hotel preparing for the lectures the next day, there was no regret, embarrassment or fear. Yes, I was still married, but the marriage was over and, although I still cared for my wife, it was in a well and truly different way. I can talk about it now, and I am able to write about it, which clarifies to me that it was something I knew I had to overcome. My innate self had been stirred.

After the pleasures of that day in the Blue Mountains, which seemed almost a magical time, I tried to continue family life as best as I could, but the experience only reinforced my understanding of the journey that had commenced. I was reminded of my conversations in the therapy room with Michael: there was no 'roadmap to follow'. Essentially, I was experimenting with life again, and I needed to find other signposts that might help me along the way.

My list of contacts continued to swirl around in my head, and I realised there was a particular business leader with whom I needed to have a conversation. One of my fears was how to manage the information around my sexuality in the business community. This business leader was gay and held a very successful career. Our paths had crossed a few times, and he always seemed happy to chat. We had reconnected a year earlier on a flight to Melbourne when I was travelling to see my daughter in her national school's netball competition. So, I made an appointment to see him, as I thought he would be the perfect person to talk to, especially after my encounter in the Blue Mountains.

When I arrived at his office, I was taken from reception into a meeting room. He was happy to see me, and we made small talk initially. Then, I felt it was time to get to the reason for my visit. 'I am not here for the purpose you might expect,' I said. 'I am here, really, on a personal matter.' Again, I started to stumble; I had not yet developed the internal strength around the system of revealing my truth. Each coming out was, and still can be, hard even when I knew it was completely safe to do so. The internal shame was still very high. 'I have come to realise that I am gay.'

It seemed that starting with the same opening line was a good pathway to begin my conversation, and I received an almost excited response as my friend said, 'Welcome to the community.' I had been aware of the Christian community and the LGBTIQA+ community, but this idea of another community—in business—was new and part of the discovery that was yet to be fully made. We talked about the pink mafia, which is slang for gay business people, business and politics and how he was willing to guide me through that. Previously, I had heard of the 'pink dollar', which is a term used in the tourist trade for LGBTIQA+ tourism, and now I was being educated in the pink mafia and the network of LGBTIQA+ people in business.

In many business circles, there are semi-hidden networks; you see members of certain Catholic Church communities wearing a particular ring on their small finger—the subtle sign of a community or an influence. And as I said before, even my own dad joined the Freemasons to get a promotion because he either needed to be part of the Catholic's 'mafia' or the Freemason's 'mafia'. Fast forward to this moment in time, and here I was about to join the pink mafia. My friend and I talked about the importance of connecting with such groups because the isolation that I was feeling was real. I accepted that it could be part of the answer, but one positive comment on this day was not going to alleviate the whole issue for me. However, it was a good meeting, and it added to my confidence in the process, the value of having a reason and my purpose in telling someone about my situation and my story ... or, at least, part of it. But as we wrapped up, he left me with a challenge when he said, 'I want you to find a group and march in Mardi Gras next year!'

Mardi Gras? No way!

I pictured a group of free, gay men reflecting their true identities, and the initial thought made me shudder as I imagined the glaring eyes of others and the Church chastising me. The Sydney Mardi Gras has been around for just under forty years, but I actually knew very little about it. I knew it was a big event and that a large parade of LGBTIQA+ people marched through Sydney's gay district, but no more than that. I had never watched the Mardi Gras—probably out of internal fear of seeing something of myself amongst the participants—but there was no way I could picture myself walking the streets of Sydney in a large parade while being watched by huge crowds. I was thinking 'baby steps' at this point in time rather than being that far out of the closet. For that reason, I nervously laughed and responded, 'I think that is very unlikely.'

So, a chosen few came to know of my journey, and they provided the proverbial 'flight maps', indicating points along the way that I never knew existed. Like a pilot, I began to navigate my way and trust this small, but growing, group of confidantes and the new routes they provided me with for the next part of my life. It was now just a matter of time before my journey of acceptance needed to take the next step.

A Life of Fulfilment: My Children

Now, as a 'split, yet living in the same home' couple, my wife and I were focusing on our son, who was in the final stages of preparation for his gap year, where he would be working in a school in the UK. Visas, airline tickets, travel arrangements, baggage and clothes for the very different environment he would be living in were on our very long checklist as he prepared to leave the heat of the Australian summer for the cold of the English winter. This was the buzz and the stresses and strains in our home during this period. In one sense, it was good because it provided a different focus away from me.

Summer was well underway that December, which also meant that Christmas was edging closer and various events would be happening. Still, hardly anyone outside of the family knew about our situation, so how well would we navigate the festive, social gatherings? There were some men I knew who were the other husbands linked to the mother's group, which had been created with the birth of all of our first-born children. Therefore, these men had been in my life for a long time. Our children had gone to primary school together, and the group had since expanded by meeting other fathers through the sports our children played at school. We got together once or twice a year for a drink, often in the lead up to Christmas.

I was looking forward to catching up with this group of guys, but again, the questions and my insecurities started to play havoc in my mind, and the badgering questions began.

Will I tell them?

What will I tell them if I do?

Yet, when thinking this through properly, I kept coming back to the main principle.

For what purpose do I tell them?

Critical advice I had received from my pastoral carer and from Michael was that I did not have an obligation to tell anyone that I was gay. If I did, I should be asking myself, what purpose and what benefit is there for me in telling them? This was a lifesaving piece of advice. Even so, in the run up to our gathering, I ran different scenarios in my head. What would I say? How would they react? What would they say? How would I respond? These thoughts kept revolving around and around in my mind, and all this overthinking was making me dizzy.

Then, the wave of anxiety crashed full force again the day before the drinks when my wife asked what I was going to do and say. 'I really don't know,' I said. 'If it seems right, I will say something, if not, nothing. I can only plan, but I can't predict the actual outcome.' We talked back and forth about whether I needed to say anything at all, but it felt as though I was being gently pushed back into the closet; I felt like I was being controlled again.

Eventually, we came to an agreement. Since the kids knew and it wasn't a secret anymore, I would go with the flow. I would decide at the time if it felt right to reveal my truth. However, even though there was an agreement to this, I still sensed nuances of reluctance from my wife. It would be a while until I understood where that reluctance came from ... if I ever did at all.

The next day, she and my son drove me to the bar where I was going to meet the other fathers, and soon, the conversation restarted in the car. 'Are you going to say anything, Jason?' my wife said. 'Or just let it be?' My wife looked worried again, and part of me wondered if she was making this just about herself. It could be that she was concerned I was not functioning well and might make a complete meal of it all, causing more confusion and challenges for the family. But, it made me feel annoyed again because my response remained the same. There had been a number of times when I had not been happy with the directions and approaches used by my wife, and I was sure she had felt the same about me—probably more so—but this was one of the times that hurt me the most.

She then turned the conversation to my son and let him know that two of the dads I would be with at the drinks gathering had sons who had been his friends from primary school and junior high school. Since moving to another high school, there had been limited contact between the boys, who were now all young men. On the few occasions they had got together in the latter years of their high school, they had been glad to see each other, and they enjoyed each other's company, but none of them had made any effort to reach out to each other since then.

My wife asked our son how he would feel if I disclosed the family's situation to the dads. His immediate reaction was neutered, which was not unusual, but she wouldn't leave it there and pushed again. Perhaps to avoid any further discussion, he stated—maybe he had been guided—that he would prefer nothing to be said. At this point, I felt that the situation had been manipulated. 'Selfish' was the only word that came to mind when looking at my wife that day, but I was certain she was mirroring the same feeling to me.

My biannual meet ups with this group of men helped us to network, talk about our kids and hopefully make valuable connections for them later on in life. The group participated in soccer, rugby union and rugby league. For the most part, I felt I was the listener in this crowd, adding stories to participate rather than to initiate them. But, they were indeed our friends, so why shouldn't they know about our new family dynamic? Frustration was again building up as I felt myself being pushed into the closet again; however, I felt that the cupboard was continuing to disintegrate, and there were splinters all around it.

Mental health experts regularly comment that one of the major contributors of poor mental health for Australian males is that we don't talk when we have issues. We keep it in, and eventually it bursts, often with devastating consequences. My mental health was still in a challenging space. Nevertheless, I decided, with a steadfast resolve, that if some of my male friends wanted to discuss my new life, then I would answer in the best, most truthful way I could. But, there was no reason for them to know the change of situation, so probably there would not be a conversation about it unless I started it. Growing up at home, Dad had taught me to play snooker, and now I felt snookered. Yet, as I had done before, I acquiesced, so perhaps I only had myself to blame.

I arrived at the bar and went inside. It was a typical 1950s suburban pub, and if it wasn't for the fact that this was our usual meeting place, I wouldn't have gone there. I was the first one to arrive, so I bought a drink. Apple cider was generally my choice with this group because I can't drink beer due to my gluten allergy. I love wine, but it is relatively more expensive. Also, I wanted to appear 'normal', and apple cider looks like beer because it is served in the same type of glass—this was my own insecurity raising its head and not a reflection of my drinking friends. I was always trying to fit in, and when you are not able to be your true self, that adds to the tension and the stress.

I found a large table in the middle of the main bar and

ensured there was enough room for when everyone turned up. The pub didn't have a huge clientele and didn't stay open very late by Sydney pub standards, but that didn't matter because we were catching up soon after lunch. I sipped away at my drink, and time slipped by. No one else arrived, leaving me free to become more agitated by the conversations I'd had with my wife about coming here; they were really starting to bug me, as I realised how hurt and frustrated I was by them. Again, I had agreed to the needs of others over myself.

My drink was nearly empty, yet still no one else had arrived, so my frustration levels continued to rise, and my hurt turned to anger. As I took the last sip from my glass, I checked my calendar on my phone and realised that my mind really was not functioning as well as it should have been.

Fuck.

The gathering was scheduled for the following week, which was why no one else had turned up. All of the conversation, frustration, pain and hurt, and it wasn't even the right week. I left the pub and walked the block to catch the bus home. Frustrated and angry, I entered the house. I was trying to understand why my state of mind at the moment was such that I couldn't even read a calendar correctly. Those little things added to my sense of worthlessness: if I couldn't even do a simple task, how could I really do anything.

Am I really worth anything?

Having Michael was helpful, and my pastoral carer at church was great, but neither of them were my friends—although later, my pastoral carer became a crucial friend. What you need in your crisis are your friends, yet I felt estranged from them. I was hurting.

Another awkward week went by. As the following Saturday got nearer, I realised that I had to attend a basketball umpiring course, which was being held at

Sutherland Stadium—the opposite end of the city for me and an hour's drive away. I let one of the key people organising the drinks gathering later on the same day know that I would be about an hour late. It would limit the amount of drinking time, so I negotiated that my son could come and collect the car from the pub, and I would either get the bus home or walk. It was a long walk—about forty-five minutes—but I had done it once or twice before.

On Saturday morning, I woke up quite stressed due to my continuing frustration of being gently and partially pushed back into the closet, and these negative feelings were taking their toll on me. It was so bad that I didn't eat that day, and I wasn't sure if I could even make the hour-long drive to the basketball stadium. But, I headed off because I needed to do the umpiring course in order to fill in for junior representative competitions, if required, for my local basketball association. It was not a stadium I had been to before, but I eventually found it. As I was tired and not feeling particularly well, I opted out of doing the fitness test; I just was not up to that.

I sat through the updates of the basketball rules and the interpretations for the major youth league in Sydney, and then I left as soon as I could. During the hour's drive back, I became even more frustrated; I couldn't talk to anyone. I heard the voices in my head that would be at the pub.

How are you Jason?

It has been a while since we caught up. What's been happening?

I had always tended to be the person who was not the focus of attention; maybe that has always been part of the act. But now, I had something that I wanted to say—that I needed to say—and that had been out in the open for a little while now. But I was in a situation where I wasn't free to say it.

I started to feel sicker and sicker and, as I got closer to where I was to meet my friends, I came to a junction that was the same distance either to the pub or to home. I needed to make a decision quickly: should I go home and crash in bed, or should I confront the questions that would be presented to me? My insides were churning, but I was not sure that I wanted to be in the company of those fathers and not be able to tell them I was coming out of the closet. The pressure built in my head and my body, and the hammer and the shame made themselves known; the self-imposed shame. I headed home, where I simply said that I wasn't feeling well, and I went to bed, staying there for the rest of the day.

Now nobody knew how I was truly feeling and what was going on in my head. I had also purposefully put myself in a situation where I didn't have to say anything about my truth. Was the closet door banging shut on me again? Was my life taking a U-turn after all I had been through with my family?

Christmas was approaching, and preparations were abounding. We generally had the holiday at our home, with my wife's mother coming down from the Blue Mountains to join us. At our place, I usually did all the catering because I liked putting on a spread for Christmas: usually ham, chicken and another meat—beef or lamb—plus multiple salads and lots of desserts. My own childhood family tradition had been to have Christmas cake for breakfast, and it was something that I had continued even though no one in the family seemed to want to join in.

The holiday season always seemed to be the right time to open up the home to people who didn't have any family of their own to be with on the day. This was the first time the opportunity to have guests outside of our family had appeared since the change in our family dynamics, and it was great to have extra people at our Christmas table. However, once again it was clear there would be no discussion around our family situation—it had become almost a decree. Also, there was still this idea that I had the sole responsibility of telling my wife's mother that I was gay and what was happening in our family, but it was clear that Christmas Day was not the day to do it.

We prepared for the celebrations as usual and organised presents for our kids, but there were to be no presents between myself and my wife, at her request. I agreed, as this would seem fake on my part knowing that the present would be a gesture rather than from the heart. Then, final preparations started the day before Christmas Day. As much as there was tension in the air leading up to this, the kids knew the plan, and it all seemed to work. As usual, the large table on the back deck was covered by my late mother's large white linen cloth, and then a colourful Christmas runner was laid lengthways down the table. Our best cutlery and crockery were set, with alternating green and red cloth serviettes at every place. Wine and water glasses were added to the table, and a bon-bon—also known as a Christmas cracker—was placed on every plate. The finishing touch was Christmas bush, which I call the Australian Christmas holly, creatively laid out on display amid the table settings. Spaces were left for the platters of meat and bowls of salad, which would be followed by Christmas pudding and a pavlova for dessert.

On Christmas Day, having others at our table for the first time helped to take the focus away from us. Maybe this was God's hand in trying to create a useful diversion to help us get through what can be a very stressful day for families in any circumstance, let alone what was going on for us that year.

After everyone was gone and the cleaning up had

been completed, tiredness crept in and then, inevitably, exhaustion. I collapsed into my bed early.

On Boxing Day, hardly any shops were open in our area, so it was a relatively slow day. We worked through the checklists for all the items our son needed for his year away and what needed to be done to send him off on what I hoped would be a wonderful journey and experience.

By the time New Year's Eve arrived, everyone was still tired, so I was the only one who stayed up to watch the fireworks from our first-floor balcony. The position of our house was on a high point in North Ryde, and while we couldn't see the bottom half of the Sydney Harbour Bridge with the usually amazing waterfall effects, we could see the fireworks that were set off from the top of the structure. So, where I stood was always one of my favourite places during this, one of my favourite times of the year.

Over the years, Sydney has become famous for its New Year's Eve fireworks, and the harbour provides something like nine individual firing points around its perimeter. From our place, we could see about four. The display is set to music, and there are quiet periods with simple and more delicate firings, building up to a grand finale with displays off the Sydney Harbour Bridge itself. All nine firing points shoot massive fireworks into the dark sky, with huge sounds and immense bursts of colour sequences as millions around the world watch in amazement.

That year, while I watched, the fireworks became quite overwhelming. So much sound. So much colour. It blended, and it morphed … seemingly like my life in that moment, inside my head. So much noise, so much colour; yet, the fireworks momentarily became a distraction for what had been going on for me over the last few months.

The first of January, 2016, arrived. It was a new year, and there was a sense of joy and sadness with my eighteen-year-old son, who was fresh out of high school and about to leave the family home for almost twelve months. I was pleased he was going to work in a boarding school that had students with the same challenges he had, so the staff were more likely to understand him.

Final packing was finished, and in the early afternoon we drove to Sydney International Airport as a family. We took photos before we saw him though the entrance to departure and immigration, and then we bid him farewell. The drive home was sad, as it would be in any family situation when you watch your child leave the nest. Doubts started to encroach in my mind: as a parent, had I made the right choice in letting my child, who was now by law an adult, journey off by himself for twelve months without my ever-present guiding hand? I had to believe that I had.

When we got home, it was not long before the sadness spiralled into chaos. During another kitchen conversation, the stress levels reached breaking point, and my wife suddenly blurted out, 'When are you going to tell my mother what is happening?'

I had been thinking about this for a long while, and I had finally realised—and gained the courage to tell my wife—that this was not my issue. So, I responded as truthfully and respectfully as I could by saying, 'I don't think it is my responsibility to tell your mum, and I also don't think it is appropriate. In my opinion, there are things that you and your mum would need to be discussing, and it would be far better for you, as her daughter, to have that complete conversation without me first.'

We talked about this for a little while, and eventually there was an agreement that it would be better for my wife to tell her mum. I was starting to see this reluctance from my wife as being linked to not wanting to have the conversation with anyone. I could only reflect on this and surmise that it was because—similar to her own parents— we were going to end up getting a divorce.

We then went over old ground again, and the subject of me agreeing to cohabit for the next two years. I kept reminding her that I would try, but I couldn't promise that it would definitely happen. The emotional energy of Christmas and then seeing our son off for the next twelve months made these conversations between my wife and me so much harder. I was aware of that, and I was sure the same was true for her too.

Then came a bolt out of the blue.

What? Wait!

My wife suddenly announced that she couldn't go through the process of telling twenty people, one at a time, what was happening in our family, so she had decided to write an email and tell everyone that very evening. This had never been discussed before, and the hammer in my head started pounding like a ferocious beast. Send an email?

Nooooooo!

My journey had been about working out who I wanted to tell, when and why, but shame, fear, the unknown and the embarrassment might well have been too much for my wife to bear for her to then face these sensitive conversations one by one. In hindsight, I can see how the face-to-face conversations would have been quite scary for her, and I feel for her; the journey of acceptance is raw and real.

However, for me, the idea of a mass email was sterile, and my head started pounding some more because I wanted to tell her that her tactic was wrong. But how? How could I be so blunt and tell her that it could be perceived as cold and emotionless by others? So, in the end I didn't, and I worked to make the best of it. Michael was teaching me that each of us had to deal with our situation in our own way. For me, it was about being tactical and telling people for a reason that would ultimately have a purposeful outcome for me. For her, I could see the pain of having to go through the same conversation time and time again, where she would have to relive whatever hurt she might have been holding on to at that point in time.

As I have said before, I had started to see the challenge of 'coming out' as a forever experience. Yet, for her, there was the 'coming to terms' shift with her family and friends; she would not have the 'always' experience, but I was sure that there would be regular conversations and questions from various people for many years to come.

The challenge I had was that I was already emotionally drained before this news was dropped, and I didn't have the best family negotiation skills at the greatest of times. I definitely didn't have the energy to challenge her, and I certainly didn't have the skill to try and suggest this was not the best time to broadcast such an important announcement. I suppose for her, however, the beginning of a new year was the perfect time to announce that we were going down a new and unexpected path, and I really had to respect that.

So, I simply asked if I could have a look at the email and the people she was sending it to. This was important to me. There were about twenty women on the list, but in reality, there were only three that I could see who might cause a challenge for me: the husbands of those women were people I wanted to reach out to first. So, while she was drafting her email, I worked out how I wanted to communicate with those people and also what I wanted to say. I thought I would send a text, so the men would know reasonably soon, or at least around the same time their wives received the email.

My wife's email was short and to the point, and I only asked for one thing to be changed. I decided that this was *her* message and perspective, and while I was not in full agreement with all of its contents, I had to let it be hers. I also now had to agree to the impersonal use of electronic message rather than the face-to-face human connection, but life is a balancing act, and sometimes you just have to go with the flow. So, I sent the following text to three of my friends:

> *Sorry for the slightly impersonal nature of this communication; however, there is some information that I thought would be important to get to you quickly, and [my wife] is sending an email to her friends, which may include some of your partners.*
>
> *As some of you know, I have been struggling with a bout of depression for three years. About 15 months ago, I started to think that I was gay, which, as you can appreciate, caused some immediate turmoil for me. Around May last year, I accepted that I am gay.*
>
> *I first discussed this with my doctor back in June, as I was not progressing with my depression with my psychologist, and we found a new psychologist to work through this. I am still seeing him at the moment.*
>
> *Back in August, I let [my wife] know, and together we told the kids after my son finished his HSC.*
>
> *This has been a distressing period of time for [my wife] and me as we have been working through this.*

Our focus has been to get [our son] through his HSC and off to the UK. We are also focused on ensuring [our daughter] has a stable environment through to her HSC (and her sport!).

This will lead to a significant change for [my wife] and me. We have a lot to work through, but unfortunately, at some point in the future, it is most likely we will separate.

We both hope that we can continue our friendships with you, and this is probably more important now as we work towards the future.

I would be happy to chat/coffee/drink at any stage to answer any immediate questions/ concerns/thoughts/comments that you may have.

Looking forward to being in touch more personally soon.

Thanks for your concern.

Kind regards,
Jason

The responses were pretty immediate.

Jason, can we catch up very soon, preferably involving some good red liquid? Your journey in recent years has been far from easy, and your message is very unexpected. Any thoughts haven't yet settled. I have shared it with [name withheld] though. Hope that's okay. We are in [rural town] for the next week, so remote. Will call?

++++

Wow! Huge news for the new year. Please be 100% assured of my support for you, especially, and for your family. Let's meet sometime soon. You are welcome any time.

++++

G'day, mate! My first thought is of sadness for the stress that this must be putting on you and your beautiful family. My second thought is of pride in your courage to 'find' yourself, come to terms with it and respectfully inform your family and friends of the situation. I just want you and your wife to know that you all have my wife's and my support through this period and into the future. Jase, you will always be a dear friend to me, mate, and I want you to know that we will always be here for 'Team Masters'. I assume [your wife] and you will need a little bit of space, but we should try and catch up soon, whenever you are ready. I will be in touch, or feel free to contact me anytime, mate.
Yours sincerely,
[Name withheld]

++++

Australian men aren't particularly known for their emotional responses, but the immediacy of these three text responses was critical for getting me through the

283

next few days.

Then, the next morning, I received an unexpected email:

> Hi Jason,
> We got an email from [your wife] today announcing that your marriage is ending. I'm really sorry to hear that, and I can only imagine how much pain has littered the road to this decision. Hang in there; this too will pass, and hope will rise.
>
> I have to note that there was no sign that you co-wrote this announcement. For that, I am sorry for you. [Redacted]. Be assured that we are keen to hear from you, when you are ready, on how you are travelling and to support you as only old friends can.
> Blessings.

I responded with the following email:

> Thanks [name removed].
>
> I was surprised that [my wife] wanted to send out a communication last night, but I have felt it important to support her in what she needs to do (or not do) through this challenging period. I did have a chance to review it and asked for a small change, which was upsetting for her, but I felt she needed to communicate from her perspective.
>
> I sent the following text to a small number of my friends but wasn't sure of your mobile phone number. The following was my text from last night ...

The following response was also really nice to hear from another of my married, male Christian friends:

> *Hi Jason,*
>
> *Glad to hear your side of this. As expected, you are acting with truth and grace. You both have to move on now. Each of you has already begun in your own ways. Wade through the swamp of it all.*
>
> *We are here to support you in prayer or any other thing.*

Thus, I was set on a trail towards a number of coffees, lunches and dinners. Each was unique in their own way. One friend opened up that he had a gay uncle and a lesbian aunt. Another commented that it was difficult, as he had worked through his own divorce—we had journeyed together on that—and this was bringing back difficult memories. Another response ended with a massive dinner and huge quantities of red wine—both of us rather drunk at the end of the night—with salutes to my future boyfriend.

The days turned into weeks, and the outpouring of support for me was immensely appreciated. My wife finally decided to spend time with her mum, and from what I heard, it went 'well' for those types of conversations. I received a telephone call from my mother-in-law, and she explained that she wanted to keep the lines of communication open. I knew she was concerned for me as well as for her daughter because she was also my friend. I felt somewhat better having that conversation.

However, when I needed to contact my brother-in-law a few days later in relation to some financial concerns I had for my mother-in-law, he seemed to take a long time to answer. I imagined he was deciding whether or not to answer my call, and I heard deep breaths when he finally picked up the phone. It was a challenging conversation, and eventually, the discussion turned to the issue between his sister and me. It started well, as he stated he wanted to be open-minded because he hadn't heard my side of the conversation. I appreciated that. Then he added, 'But I will be keeping a close eye on my niece and nephew.'

What does he mean by that?

He sees it as his right to somehow protect my kids?

Protect them from what?

I tried to contain my internal reaction because some of my wife's relatives had not invested much in our kids, and it was often our side of the family who had driven the family activities. But this comment burrowed deep into my psyche for over a year. Eventually, I let it go because I never heard from them again, so I assumed that my actions with my children showed there was no real or present danger. I do hope that one day in the future there will be a family event where we can all attend, as I will be fine, and I just hope they will be too.

I flew down to Melbourne to catch up with my best friend from early-on in my career. This time, I was visiting because my daughter was competing in a national volleyball competition. His third relationship and marriage had broken down many years before, and he took the primary responsibility of looking after their three kids who, for the last several years, had all lived permanently with him. We always had open conversations, so when we were talking in his kitchen, with me sitting on the kitchen bench—a regular spot with a glass of wine in hand—I felt that I wanted to bring up my news. Conversations were going back and forth with ease.

His son, who was the same age as my daughter, was sitting on the bench as well, working on the computer as he listened to us and engaged, like he always did. It was comfortable as it always was. So, I felt I could listen to my instincts—there was a high level of trust between my friend and me, and we had worked on many projects together. He was my first professional boss, and we had a deep bond and friendship. There was also a bond of trust between his kids and me. His son was well-balanced, honest and reliable, as were my friend's older daughters. I thought that he would be okay with the news. Anyway, he wasn't moving anywhere, but why should he?

I realised that there was only so much time left if I wanted to seize the moment. So, listening to my instincts to move forward with coming out, I changed the direction of the conversation and spoke about my depression, finding the trigger and coming to accept that I was gay. No one seemed to flinch. There was appropriate questioning, of course, which was presented with honour and respect due to our thirty-seven-year-old friendship. His son also engaged intelligently with the conversation, reaffirming for me that, as with most of his generation, sexual orientation and gender diversity was not going to be the large issue it was with my generation. That day helped me to realise that the generation after me had the power to evolve. I felt at ease knowing that this would also be a better path for young LGBTIQA+ people; hopefully, society would be more tolerant towards them in the very near future.

I realised after the New Year celebrations that I needed to do more than just potentially join the Sydney Gay and Lesbian Business Association. There was so much going on globally where the LGBTIQA+ community simply didn't stand a chance for freedom. The debate around marriage equality in Australia was heating up, but the pathway for Parliament to resolve the issue had not been determined. I was becoming more attuned, and I felt the impact of LGBTIQA+ people being the political plaything of politicians and a number of religious leaders.

In February, I decided to go to a meeting of Freedom2Be, the Christian-based organisation providing support to LGBTIQA+ Christians. It was at the building of ACON Health, the organisation formerly known as the Aids Action Council of NSW that was set up as a not-for-profit LGBTIQA+ health provider and advocacy organisation in Sydney to support people with HIV. They had an entire floor in their building available for community groups to meet. In one sense, it was heartening to know that such an organisation continued to advocate for the health of LGBTIQA+ people and support those with HIV. During the HIV and AIDS crisis, many of the conservative Christian leaders around the world indicated that HIV was 'God's wrath' on the gay community, but interestingly, it was often the Catholic nuns who provided considerable practical and pastoral support. Nevertheless, ACON welcomed Freedom2Be to use their community meeting spaces for LGBTIQA+ Christians to socialise. I had found some semblance of connection—and they were Christian.

As I entered the vast building, I received a warm, friendly smile from a passer-by, who then asked me, 'Are you looking for Freedom2Be?'

'Yes, thanks,' I said, and into the lift we went to find the meeting space. Then, I was ushered into a large room with about forty chairs and some standing space.

I facilitate the Company Directors Course for the

Australian Institute of Company Directors, and in one of my courses the previous January, I had met the president of ACON Health. During that course, I'd talked to him about what I perceived as a potential lack of support programs for kids of LGBTIQA+ parents coming out. He was the guest speaker at the Freedom2Be event that night, so it was encouraging for me to be there and to be meeting up with him again. While he didn't talk much about HIV, he talked passionately about his advocacy around the issues confronting LGBTIQA+ people, locally and around the world.

I had found an amazing group of Christians, many of whom had been rejected by their churches, and some of whom had found a place to be in a church that was not fully accepting. The friendliness at Freedom2Be was what I found missing in many of our churches across Australia and internationally—a real concern for the LGBTIQA+ community. Fortunately, my own parish was supportive, which was critical to my own journey of acceptance.

As a first-time visitor, people wanted to chat and welcome me, and after the session, we headed down to a local pub for dinner. I shared a little; I heard a little. But, how much should you share the first time you meet someone? This has always been a challenge for me, particularly when dealing with my sexuality and orientation. Yet, there was a safety here that I hadn't experienced before. This was another dimension to the coming out process where I was surrounded by a group of Christians who were also LGBTIQA+ and who each presented their own unique story. No matter what their circumstance, they were connected to the Christian faith.

I got home late that night, later than expected, and my wife wanted to know where I had been. She made a beeline for me as soon as I walked through the door. This hadn't happened before, but I suppose her eagerness was a testament to the more obvious secrecy of my activities, and she knew that I had never intentionally kept any secrets from her in the past. I knew she didn't want me to meet up with other LGBTIQA+ people for fear of me suddenly meeting a future partner and destroying her plan for us to cohabitate for the next two years. So, I stumbled through, trying to formulate something, and said, 'Out with some people from work.' After that sentence, I made my way up the stairs and went straight to bed.

It wasn't a good end to a good night. What had become of me? I was sneaking out and not telling her where I was going. Even though it was a Christian organisation, I felt awful. I had never intentionally lied before, but now I had. Was it all worth it? I was starting to stew inside, and the pressure of the last year was really building up. In one way, this might seem like such a small incident, but for me, it became huge.

Can I be trusted anymore if I am intentionally lying?

My wife's reaction was a challenge, but compared to many, we were working through things with grace. The reaction from my kids had been wonderful, and the reaction from my friends, when I was forced to tell them, was supportive. Furthermore, the reaction from my minister and pastoral carer had been more than I could have hoped for. But, none of this was enough. It seemed that years of fear and loathing could not be undone in a short period of time, and now I was finding myself sneaking around and lying. The voice in my head did not let me go to sleep that night, and the suppressed shame that had also been bottled up with my sexuality burst dramatically onto the scene. As I tossed and turned, I could hear the questions rattling around in my mind.

Oh, God, how can this be?

Shame.

Is this really worth all the pain?

Shame.

As the night went on, I still couldn't sleep, and shame

continued to drive my restlessness. My mind became more and more stirred up.

Is this life really worth living?

Shame. Shame. Shame.

Now that I am partially out, why do I still have to sneak around?

How can I resolve this shame?

Shame.

Is this how I now exist?

Is this a life worth living?

The answer was no. This was surely not a life of acceptance, and suicidal thoughts once again entered my mind. I had been on anti-depressants for a while, but they were at a relatively low level. I thought about taking all the tablets I had, but I had a strong suspicion that the total amount wouldn't be enough.

Then, my mind shifted to the boxing bag I had put in the shed for my son. I knew the strength of the roof structure, and I had rope in the shed too. But ... What would the impact be if one of the kids found me hanging by a noose? The tablets seemed better, but I was convinced I didn't have enough—was that my understanding of the medication, or was that the other part of me trying to stay alive? Options went back and forth. Every way I wanted to do it, I felt like I needed to minimise the impact on the kids. Eventually, I dropped off to sleep.

The next morning, I awoke rattled. The things that had protected me the night before were my kids. I knew of suicides, and I knew of the impact on the family. The pain might subside sometimes, but it never goes away. My kids were young and, at the end of the day, I couldn't create a lifetime of hurt for them when they seemed to have accepted me. Maybe the reality was that I hadn't really accepted myself at this point, but if I could, then maybe the pain that I was going through would go away. The tension was so high for me at that time, and the shame was growing as it fully enveloped my brain and body. In my mind, things didn't seem to be getting better since coming out. In fact, in many ways, they seemed to be getting worse. My distress had increased, but I really hoped that the hurt would diminish if I could find a way to make everyone better off.

Looking at the coming out videos on YouTube for inspiration, almost everyone said things got better for them. The obvious exceptions were the young people who had been kicked out of their homes. But although the videos, in the main, showed a growing acceptance, they were all about young people. Where were the videos of people my age coming out?

The next few days were horrible; the constant lying to myself and living behind a false mask of strength was catching up with me again. I just wanted to die, but I now knew this wasn't an option for me.

One Monday evening, heading home from what was the beginning of a wasteful period of work, I realised I needed help. So, I called Michael and got an urgent appointment. We talked through the situation, and he wanted me to see my doctor urgently. So, the next day, I was able to get an emergency appointment to see my doctor, and he, too, was concerned. I appeared numb, and this was to be the beginning of another period of major haze in my life. The doctor ramped up my antidepressants, and he wanted me to check what support structures I had. He reminded me to call him during the day if I was in crisis, or in the evening, I was to go straight to the emergency department at our local hospital. Then, when I saw Michael over the next couple of days, I was not allowed to leave his room until I had the telephone number for LifeLine Crisis in my phone contacts and on the speed-dial list.

Unfortunately, I found that the ramped-up antidepressants affected my head so much it meant I couldn't think or work properly. They might have been helping me to refrain from killing myself, but I couldn't function at the level I needed to. Being a self-employed consultant, I billed clients by the hour for the work I did, but if I couldn't think or focus, then, obviously, I couldn't bill anyone and therefore couldn't maintain my income.

Can I survive this?

Is the treatment almost as bad as the issue?

I am now threatened with having no income and no livelihood!

For the next six weeks, I felt like I was a walking zombie, barely surviving, yet trying to hide this from the family. If I worked at home, I struggled to motivate myself to do anything; if I managed to get myself to the office, I just sat there, flicking through the Internet, but I had no concentration and found it nearly impossible to undertake any tasks. Eventually, becoming even more distressed because of this, I headed back to the doctor. We talked through how I had been feeling, where my suicidal risk currently sat and the increasing risk of not being able to function. I convinced him that the risk had lowered, but part of the problem was that I wasn't sleeping well. As a result, my doctor felt it was safe to lower the dosage of my medication and to try a new mix to see if that helped with sleeping. This would then hopefully also reduce the levels of depression and allow me to function at work.

Coming out was supposed to take the load off my shoulders, but in this moment of my life, I seemed to have more weighing me down; I often wondered if I should have been born in a different generation. One thing that I knew for certain was that I had to wholeheartedly accept and own my story. That was going to be essential for my survival.

The Next Transition

With our son now in southern England starting his gap year and our daughter back at school, we continued the discussions on how to move forwards. It was becoming more evident that cohabiting for the next two years would not be healthy for me, nor did my daughter want us to do it just for her. So, we started to discuss how our separation might be managed, and I suggested my wife use the family lawyer, if she preferred. The partner of the firm we had been using had recently retired, so he referred her to another person in the firm, which she accepted. I was happy to use the lawyer my friend had put me in touch with earlier. We both knew we didn't want an expensive family dispute; we would work through as much as possible ourselves and only use lawyers for the bare minimum, to cover the legalities. One of the pieces of advice I received along the way was that lawyers generally aren't good at the accounting side of separation, so it was important to double-check everything.

After a while, I didn't find my lawyer to be that responsive, so I found a new one in a more prominent, midsized firm via LGBTIQA+ media, to which I had now subscribed. They too, were more than happy to support the approach we wanted to take in managing the separation. This was fortunate, as my new lawyer found a financial mistake in my wife's lawyer's updates in the final settlement papers. The error provided a significant benefit to me, but I was able to recalculate the numbers and asked my wife to have her financial advisor double-check the calculations to be inserted by my lawyer. To help minimise costs for my wife, I also offered to pay for all the documents that needed to be created for the family court.

As we worked through everything, the property market in Sydney was getting quite hot, so it seemed the optimal time to sell our house to maximise the value each of us could realise from the family home—even though it still had a reasonable mortgage. Initially, the reaction from my wife was that I was trying to get out of living together until our daughter had finished school, so I suggested that she speak to her financial advisor. Fortunately, when he analysed the market, especially where we lived, his advice was that this was probably the most advantageous time to sell before a downturn.

To prepare for the sale of our house, we moved some furniture out to open up space and, fortunately, we had recently repainted the interior and replaced the air conditioner, making the home nice and fresh. We initially thought the real estate agents bidding for the contract to sell the house had put a price that was too high on the potential sale. So, we selected an agent who we felt comfortable working with and who was from a reputable firm. However, while they did not suggest the highest price, their proposal was still much higher than I had expected.

The sale process was a four-week marketing campaign, with an open house twice a week and then an auction on-site at the end. When we had our final briefing with the agent before the first open house, which was to be held a couple of days later on a Saturday morning, they commented that if there weren't requests for ten copies of the contract after the open house, we would have to revise the price as the market was starting to head down.

Bloody agents! was my initial thought. *Trying to set false expectations to get the business and then wind everyone down.*

However, one of the unexpected resale benefits of our property was the wide frontage, as it met the requirements for a duplex or apartments to be built.

When the morning of the open house arrived, I woke up in horror because a huge storm had gone through Sydney in the early hours. The dark clouds remained, and it continued to rain for the rest of the morning. The temperature was also quite cool. When I went outside, our driveway was flooded, the lawns had puddles of water covering them and the swimming pool was overflowing. I began to panic, and black thoughts started to roll through my brain.

No one will come to the open house.

The agent will use that as justification to lower the price because they will be after a quick sale rather than an optimal price.

I will miss out again.

This will have a negative impact on my finances for the future.

Is this the price for accepting who I am?

As the hammer continued to pound, out into the rain I went—and I hate getting wet. I turned on the pool pump to remove water from the pool, and then I got the wheelbarrow and shovels to try and remove the large pools of water in the carport before the open house started. I did what I could; I wanted to do more, but it was all I could do in the time I had. It had to be good enough.

The agent arrived, and my wife and I left just as a car pulled up for an inspection. We drove around the neighbourhood for the next thirty minutes of the open house, nervous to hear if anyone else came. We were pleasantly surprised that, in such inclement weather, a total of six prospective buyers turned up to carry out an inspection. But it wasn't the ten contracts we needed, and the negative thought processor in my brain went off. However, the agent then mentioned that they had also received four contract requests from developers, so we had hit our ten, and the property could remain listed at that higher price.

On Sunday morning, we received an unexpected call from the agent. Two families were interested in the house and wanted to purchase pre-auction. The agent wanted to know what we thought. Unbelievably, it seemed likely that the top-end price would actually be achievable.

The following twenty-four hours were crazy, with two more unplanned inspections by the interested parties. We did a quick tidy up, got out for those second inspections and then waited. Offers were made: one was willing to offer more, but they didn't have all their finance in place; the other wanted to structure the transaction, but one of the companies wasn't registered. Negotiations continued during Monday and Tuesday, and by Tuesday night, a contract was executed. When the agent received the deposit, we were shocked, but I was pleased because this was a crucial part of starting my new life and my wife hers. We had about a twelve-week settlement, and in that time, we had to each find new places to live, split furniture and move. I hadn't rented property since the early 1990s, and unfortunately, things had changed ... and not for the better for renters.

Parallel to selling our home, my wife and I also started working on the child support agreement. With my daughter's concurrence, we decided that she would move between our future homes week in and week out. So, we both decided to remain close to where we had been living to make it easier for our daughter to get to school, and ideally, to be not too far from each other. A place was identified, and it was initially earmarked for me as it looked like my wife would be able to rent some rooms in a home that belonged to a relative of one of her friends. However, as we got closer to moving out, those rooms didn't eventuate, and knowing she would need the certainty of a place to live straight away, I was happy to move into a motel or hotel for a few weeks or months until I found a rental. So, my wife signed the rental agreement. Unfortunately for her, though, while it was a convenient place, she didn't have a good landlord.

The following weekend, I went out looking at rentals and found two that would be suitable. I applied for both, with a preference for the one that had just come on the market because its public transport links were so much better. I was offered the one that had been on the market for a few weeks, so I had to stall them until I heard about the other one. Luckily, I was accepted for the one I wanted, which made me feel so relieved.

My wife and I were able to make the moves slowly, about ten days apart. We helped each other, and we each had friends who helped with the packing and unpacking. My move came second, and it was strange being in a half-empty house by myself for those ten days. When it was my turn to pack and unpack, some of my gay friends, both men and women, came to help. I think my wife was very gracious to be around so many gay and lesbian people after everything that had happened.

The only problem we had was when we called our son to let him know about our new addresses. When he had left six months earlier, he'd expected to come back to the same home. But instead, he was very concerned that something terrible had happened between us. We both had to spend time assuring him that it was purely a financial benefit to separate earlier than we had initially stipulated. He seemed to accept it, but did he really?

And so, another transition in my life was well underway.

The Lid on the Box: My Evolving Life

Of all the times to come out, I really could not have chosen a worse time. I think the younger you are, maybe the more chance you have with time on your side.

Several countries had already enacted legislation to allow same sex people to marry, and in 2004, a couple who were married in Canada petitioned for their marriage to be recognised in Australia, just as male and female marriages overseas were recognised. The Marriage Act in Australia was actually silent on who could get married, but this petition led to an outcry from the Christian community. Ultimately, in 2004, the Howard Liberal-National (Conservative) government changed the Marriage Act to specify that marriage was between a man and a woman, so Australia would not recognise same gender marriages from overseas. This was simply enacted by an amendment bill in Parliament without much—or any—consultation and with the support of the opposition Labour Party.

In 2013, the government of the Australian Capital Territory (ACT) enabled legislation for same-sex couples to marry, and thirty-one couples used the seven days to do so before the Howard federal government challenged the ACT legislation in the high court. Eventually, the government won, and the marriages were then voided. Yet, pressure from long-term advocates for marriage equality and changing the attitudes towards LGBTIQA+ people and marriage was building.

In 2015, an even more conservative Catholic was elected as the Australian prime minister. His term of office was spectacularly unsuccessful and very divisive, and eventually, just as with the prior Labour government changing prime minister midterm, he was removed from office by his own party. One of his last acts was to try and delay the momentum for marriage equality in Australia by suggesting that there should be a plebiscite—a technical term in the Australian constitution that allows for a compulsory national vote, but the outcome is not binding for the members of federal Parliament. The last thing the minority LGBTIQA+ community needed was for a matter of social justice to be put to a public vote, with the expense—not only financial, but also personal and health—to be borne by the community. But the new, more progressive Prime Minister Turnbull, while personally supportive of marriage equality, felt he 'owed' it to the conservatives in his party, who had helped him to gain the prime ministership, to hold a plebiscite on marriage equality.

The opposition Labour Party, and enough of the minor parties, were now fully supportive of marriage equality, and they believed that Parliament should develop and pass legislation and not 'outsource' the process to the Australian public. Every attempt to pass enabling legislation for the plebiscite was blocked in the senate.

In 2017, having made a commitment to a very public voting process on marriage equality, the prime minister and his advisors determined that the Australian Bureau of Statistics had legislation that enabled them to 'survey' the Australian public on any matter. So, using 'spare budget' that didn't need parliamentary approval, the prime minister launched the devastating 'Marriage Equality Postal Survey'—a voluntary vote from every person on the

Australian electoral roll. Votes would be counted at both a national level and also an electorate level to provide guidance for members of Parliament when it came time to consider subsequent legislation. I even put some of my own money into various campaign groups as well as discovering the ability to post my own commentary and have it promoted as paid content on Facebook, focusing on my local electorate and surrounding areas.

The lies from the 'No' campaign advocates—primarily the Christian groups—were horrendous. I hated that my fellow Christians put so much rubbish, mistruths and misinformation into the public domain via television advertisements and paid social media to continue keeping the LGBTIQA+ community excluded from marriage.

In a bid to counteract this, I put personalised leaflets in my neighbourhood's letterboxes, and I placed a 'Vote Yes' sign in the front window of my home. I also went door to door by myself, which worried many of my friends due to some of the assaults that had happened during the campaign. Some of my Facebook blogs had over thirteen hundred comments, and some of them were atrocious. I had to moderate them. Some had images of guns pointed to a head and the words, 'Go and kill yourself.' There were pictures of nooses and alongside them were the vile, echoing words, 'Go and kill yourself.' There were even comments such as, 'All LGBTIQA+ kids should die.' Facebook was making a fortune during this campaign, but I ended up stopping my reports of abuse to Facebook because each of the dire posts apparently didn't breach the site's rules.

There was a campaign tactic from the 'No' side around 'Think of the Children', which inferred that LGBTIQA+ people could not be good parents. Posters supporting this element of their campaign were hung upon electricity poles around the main street near my home, which infuriated me, and I wondered how my kids now felt being part of a rainbow family. As if marriage equality meant that married, same-sex couples would somehow easily be able to produce children! Sadly, for same-sex couples to become parents, it requires not only enormous time, but enormous amounts of energy and money too. And contrary to the 'Think of the Children' aspect of the campaign, studies have actually shown that children in same-gendered parent families are as socially well adjusted as their peers, sometimes better. The 'No' campaign once against demonstrated their appalling ignorance of LGBTIQA+ people, their relationships and their families.

After months of campaigning, and on the 15th of November, 2017, I stood in what has been renamed Equality Park, near Sydney's Central Station, with ten thousand other LGBTIQA+ people. This was the day of the announcement of the plebiscite's results—this nonbinding, government-initiated postal survey. There were many people I knew there. There were couples, and there were singles. ACON health had a support tent ready, just in case the vote went badly. I also noticed a number of boys from several local high schools in their uniforms coming into the crowd—I don't know if their school gave them permission or if they skipped class.

Wow! How things have changed from when I was in high school.

There was an air of anticipation, hope and nervousness. In recent elections, pollsters had been inaccurate with expected results, and since then, their ability to predict election outcomes had deteriorated further. There were large, outdoor screens around Australia in capital cities and in major centres, like parks. Many corporations allowed their staff to go to their boardrooms and lunchrooms, where there were televisions, to watch the live announcement of the postal survey results. Never in our history had the Australian Bureau of Statistics (ABS) had such a high profile.

Australia was now only the second country in the world that had held a public vote on marriage equality. Ireland had to, as marriage was defined in its constitution. However, our public vote and campaign happened because, in my view, conservative politicians abrogated their responsibility, placing the physical and mental health of the LGBTIQA+ community at severe risk. In effect, Australia's politicians failed the LGBTIQA+ community, failed Australia and outsourced their responsibility.

As we all arrived in the park, there was some music to entertain the ten thousand people who had gathered. Then, there were some preliminary comments before a nervous hush descended over the park as 10 a.m. rolled around for the big announcement ... Suspense was brewing. The picture on the big screens moved from the main stage to the broadcast room where the Australian government statistician would announce the survey results. This was his moment; one an Australian statistician has never had before. He came to the podium, and he started with the role of the ABS. He then explained the process of the postal survey, which we all knew because we had just lived through it. His speech had only taken several minutes by this point—as my son reminded me later that evening—but it seemed to take an eternity.

For goodness' sake, give us the bloody results!

Then the statistician started with the numbers. He gave us the total number of valid postal surveys received, and I quickly worked out the 50% mark. Then he gave the total number of 'Yes' votes. We had done it, but my brain wasn't quick enough to work out how well. Then, the percentage was announced: 61.6%! It overwhelmingly confirmed what had been known from polls for many years: that 61.6% of Australian people supported Parliament amending the Marriage Act to allow for the marriage of two people, regardless of gender. With that percentage, there was one hell of a loud roar from the assembled crowd, and there were tears rolling down my face as the statistician continued to announce the results.

After that, we looked on our mobile phones for how our electorates had performed. New South Wales—despite having the largest LGBTIQA+ population—had the lowest 'Yes' vote in the country, although it was still over 50%, and my electorate had voted 'No' by a small margin. I was sad about that, but it wasn't unexpected. The 'No' campaign had targeted the non-Anglo community well, and perhaps we on the 'Yes' side hadn't communicated well enough in that space. My electorate had been moving from an Anglo-Saxon to a more diverse community, welcoming in many Asian families. Unfortunately, the 'No' campaign had specifically targeted the Asian and other migrant communities using fear and misinformation, which led to some of their own community leaders strongly supporting the 'No' campaign.

However, now there were speeches, singing and celebration, and we slowly dispersed around lunchtime. I sat and ate with some friends and colleagues for lunch as we recapped, reflected and, to an extent, collapsed. This was truly a historic day in the Australian political landscape. There were plans for a celebration that evening in Oxford Street, which is the main street that passes through the gay bars and restaurant district, and it forms part of the Sydney Gay and Lesbian Mardi Gras Parade route.

The New South Wales police hadn't taken notice of the leaders in the LGBTIQA+ community, who had earlier requested that Oxford Street be closed that evening if the result was positive; it appeared there hadn't been a lot of planning. However, the vote was so clear, and the LGBTIQA+ community in Sydney wanted to party that night, so the police really had no choice. Taylor Square was the designated meeting space, and as I boarded my bus to head from my office to where the celebrations were being held, I could hear instructions over the radio to the driver that Oxford Street was being closed at 6:30 p.m. It gave me confidence around the ability of our police force to respond to a major situation, as they were closing major roadways in the city in response to the will of a large number of people in peak hour.

We gathered at Taylor Square and joined a celebratory march back down towards the city to Hyde Park. There were so many people that the march pretty much took up the entire length of this long street. It was full of different people, who were all part of the LGBTIQA+ rainbow: sportspeople, musicians, teachers, Christians. I kept moving from group to group amongst an abundance of hugs and kisses.

Once we reached Hyde Park, I decided to walk back up to Taylor Square, where I ran into another group of my Christian friends. I ended up doing something I had never done before, even as a young man. I bought several small bottles of champagne from the local liquor shop—it was doing a roaring trade—and sat in the park by Taylor Square as I drank straight out of the bottle. We chatted for hours. The bars were so full, you couldn't get in. Drinking in the street and in the parks were the only options. Probably illegal, but who cared? Certainly, the New South Wales police were now being very sensible, protecting the people celebrating, and by doing so, protecting the crowd rather than trying to enforce laws that, at that moment in time, were not relevant.

It was a time of celebration, freedom, love and, finally, acceptance. The people of Australia had said that we were acceptable and should be able to marry. Triumph on one level ... but, the celebration was short. The 'postal survey' was just that; it wasn't binding although each member of Parliament now knew exactly where their constituents stood. Importantly, rural Australia was very supportive—to the surprise of many members of Parliament who seemed to be completely disconnected to the will and views of their constituents. But unfortunately, we were all aware that members of Parliament didn't *need* to vote now in accordance with the survey.

After a tortuous number of weeks of parliamentary debate regarding a bill that changed the Marriage Act to allow for two same-gender people to marry, it was passed in the senate on the 29th of November, 2017, with none of the amendments from the conservative senators being successful. The news was full of these debates every day. Fortunately, in the senate, the bill passed relatively easily. It then went to Lower House—the House of Representatives—with a further tortuous number of days of attempts to modify the bill by conservative members. As a community, we needed to listen to outrageous statements from some conservative members under parliamentary privilege, which meant they couldn't be challenged even though they were spreading some outright lies.

I often sat in my office working, or trying to, with the live feed from Parliament House on my computer screen as I took notes of the contemptible comments that were being made. It seemed that some of the conservatives wanted to use their parliamentary privilege to repeat the lies that had been said during the same campaign that had caused so much hurt and harm. Eventually, the bill passed on the 7th December, 2017, with many joyous scenes in Parliament. Part of this bill was the automatic recognition of overseas same-sex marriages. Only four members of Parliament had enough confidence in their own position to vote against the bill. And, as much as I disagreed with them and their reason, I respected them for doing so. After all, that is democracy in action.

Unfortunately, ten members of the House of Representatives refused to be present in the House for the final and historic vote: Deputy Prime Minister Barnaby Joyce, former Prime Minister Tony Abbott, future Prime

Minister Scott Morrison, Andrew Hastie, Stuart Robert, Michael Sukkar, Kevin Andrews, Rick Wilson, Bert van Manen and George Christensen. They had all campaigned against us, hurt us, and now wouldn't do us the honour of voting in Parliament after rejecting what their own electorate was saying. This made me furious. The only opposition member who was not in the chamber was Wayne Swan, who had a reasonable excuse because he was attending a United Nations conference in Bangkok. He is on the public record, however, as stating that, had he been there, he would have voted yes.

My own MP had fallen foul of an issue for many members and senators in the Australian Parliament in recent years over their right to be in Parliament due to dual citizenship. Just before the vote, he had been forced to resign, so unfortunately, we weren't represented, but he did declare that he would have voted for marriage equality. Soon afterwards, he was re-elected to Parliament.

So, marriage equality had arrived, but there was still so much inequality to be resolved. A number of my friends tried to comment that LGBTIQA+ equality was fully resolved; however, that was far from the truth, and as I pointed out areas of inequality from my list, they would usually ask me to stop because they 'got the point'. Yet, many people believed what they had. However, it took another twelve months for transgender people in Australia to have full marriage equality, and to this day, private schools can still discriminate against LGBTIQA+ children, teachers and staff in their schools.

Coming back to the beginning, after the Marriage Equality legislation, the Uniting Church, at its National Assembly, agreed to allow a conscious decision for our ministers and parishes to decide if they would officiate and allow the use of their parish churches for same-sex marriages. This was a major achievement, but the decision-making process at the Assembly came at a personal cost.

Since then, the road for equality for LGBTIQA+ people continues to be at risk on a daily basis, not only in traditionally conservative countries, but also in progressive ones like Australia. My future now lies in being a father, hopefully a lover once again, a businessman and an advocate against many injustices, but with a definite bias for LGBTIQA+ rights. There are days when I'm campaigning that I have to remind myself that not everyone knows my story, and other campaigns can be very misdirected. One such campaign was when we supported transgender people who were being unreasonably attacked by a major news corporation. I was 'discovered' by a particular subgroup of feminists, who rejected transgender women. They decided that I was a misogynist and a homophobe, and they thought that my daughter needed a better father. For those who know me, this is completely laughable— but that is the world of social media: the additional space for social activism.

I am the same person I have always been. I know who I am, and from reading my memoir, you will have a better understanding of who the real and authentic Jason is. This is a new world blossoming open for me, and I am now in my own space. I am on a new journey, so please feel free to walk and journey beside me.

Where I Am Today: Forever Evolving

A few years on from the start of this journey, I am still working on dealing with my companion, shame, but every day it gets a little better, and messages from people are helping me on this road of recovery. The shame comes from so many sources: the rejection of who I was as a teenager and adult; hurting others, including my now ex-wife, because I couldn't accept who I was; coming out so late and receiving the benefits from those who came out in the 1970s, 1980s, 1990s and 2000s; not being able to support those who were murdered, bashed up, spat upon or rejected, or to help those who struggled and lost their battles with AIDS ... those who fought the social and political fights when I was not able to. It has been a difficult journey, but I am here now.

I am forever reminding myself of the analogy that Michael gave me: that my life is like the stock market, generally going upwards. There will be the odd dips, but I am hoping that the crashes I've had over the last few years mean there won't be another for a long time even though I am much better prepared for that eventuality. I am also getting better at hearing my own internal warning signs and taking preventative action earlier on.

I have evolved as a person, and I'm still very much evolving. At this point, I don't have a lover although that's something I hope to have one day. I know I still have bad habits that keep me from doing things I want to do—when you establish a pattern of life that protects you, and then you journey through into a new unknown one as I have done, some of those protective mechanisms serve you well, but they might also now hinder you and keep the future at bay. Through my reflections of my journey, I have discovered that one of the mechanisms I used for survival in my twenties was to travel. I was thus concerned when I was sitting with Michael one day, and I said, 'I'm finding myself wanting to travel again. What am I escaping from?' The response he offered suggested that maybe now I am looking to escape *to* things. Maybe travel has changed from something that used to help me to escape from challenges to now allowing me to escape into pleasure. Now, I can escape into life, laughter and living.

'I'm going back to places that I have visited but not seen,' I decided one day. It had been very convenient for me to travel for business even when I was married and had young kids. To those looking in from the outside, all this travel might seem glamorous, but it's actually not, and often it is quite stressful. I could tell you about airports all around the world, particularly in my region, Asia-Pacific and America. I could tell you about hotels, and I could tell you about corporate offices. But, could I actually tell you about the beauty and the wonder of the cities? Could I tell you about the joys, the history and the passion of the people? Not so much.

Over the last few years, I've journeyed back to these places. I met my first boyfriend when travelling to Wales, and although it was short lived—as can be the case with long-distance relationships—we connected by travelling to spend time together, and this gave me an opportunity to go back to Singapore. When we were there, I saw a different side to the country that I'd never known. I got to discover it at a pace that didn't involve running for meetings or getting up early for corporate breakfasts. It was nice to just be myself and explore the city from a different perspective with somebody who meant something to me.

In 2018, I went back to Shanghai and stayed in the Old Quarter. Seeing the old buildings, the history and a different sort of hustle and bustle opened my eyes to the intricacy of the Chinese culture. I saw the new part as well, and I was able to visit the new towers and contrast the old with the new, divided as they are by a magnificent river. New versus old resonated with my own sense of growth.

Then, in 2019, I travelled back to Seoul, a place I'd been to on many occasions, but apart from the airport bus, hotel, offices and one or two occasional meetings with a friend, I had seen nothing of it. So, I found a hotel near Seoul Station. Among much other exploration, I went to the gay bar district, but I discovered that this area didn't start pulsing until quite late at night, and I was getting a bit tired. However, I found contentment in being present even though there were not a lot of gay guys around. There, I also saw some of the continuing cultural rejection of Korean LGBTIQA+ people: the Korean gay community still came out very late at night, just as in Australia pre the 2000s, so they are not visible to others that might have known them. I have noticed that this is true worldwide; the gay bars often happen late at night and into the early morning so that people hopefully wouldn't be seen or recognised.

Working on this book has also given me the opportunity to visit Bangkok. It wasn't really going back to a place I'd been to, but it was a wonderful opportunity to see and experience Bangkok as a local rather than as a foreigner coming in and doing the touristy things. It helps to have friends in places you've never visited! Needless to say, I visited the vibrant gay bars and clubs, dancing away late into the night. This was the first Asian city where I experienced some fun with the LGBTIQA+ community, and they were more open and more readily accepting. Around this time, Taiwan had also passed legislation for marriage equality.

I've come to realise that one of my worst traits when trying to survive is to keep busy; I've always needed to be busy. If I'm busy, I don't need to feel pain. Therefore, I don't have to feel anything, and that needs to change. As I went through considerable trauma during the last few years, it was still a technique I fell back on, which unfortunately made it harder to connect with people, but this is still an area in which I am evolving. For example, during one of the editing sessions for this chapter, I flew back from Auckland, New Zealand, where I had been for a few days on some professional development. I realised that my frustration in not having the Internet for the last night and morning meant it was hard to distract myself, and it put me out of sorts. So, this continues to be very much a work in progress, as I find it challenging to be able to switch off and 'go with the flow', which probably makes it much harder for me to meet my future lover.

Now, I'm at a time in my life where I can physically and spiritually feel the pull to slow down, knowing that there will still be the ups and downs of life, but this is going to take some time. Hopefully, there won't be any more major traumas. There may be other traumas on the way forwards, but I want to live an open-minded life in which I take full ownership.

There have been some wonderful *journey* people on the road. My psychologist for one, but also the president of ACON Health, who asked me to come and join the finance, audit and risk committees of ACON, which connected me to a whole different aspect of the LGBTIQA+ community and the associated health issues. I have connected with many other people and particularly with an author of another book regarding a journey of coming out as a married man in Australia. Listening to his story, and hearing his concerns that mirrored mine, humbles me. Joining Freedom2Be in my first year of coming out and finding some kindred spirits in the group have been some of the key milestones in my life and for my mental health.

Several years ago, I was challenged to go to my first Mardi Gras, and I thought that was a crazy idea. However, in 2019, I ended up being one of the coordinators of the Uniting Network's—the LGBTIQA+ community within the Uniting Church—entry into Mardi Gras. A fantastic group of mainly young people helped to organise that. It involved people who were genuinely passionate about how God loves LGBTIQA+ people and who wanted to get that message into the churches and into the community. I've had some wonderful conversations with them, and some great care and compassion has come my way from this group too.

But, to everyone out there, I think it's important to remember that, when the going gets tough with LGBTIQA+ issues and fights, we often don't have the energy to care for each other. We actually need our community of allies to step up to the plate, and I'm thankful for those of you who are my allies and friends; you have always been there for me.

There have been so many other things on this journey that have revealed to me who I am. For instance, I've always been a person who cries at movies and YouTube videos, and I think we all ought to allow ourselves to accept and recognise our emotions. I'm cool with that now, whereas before, I was very embarrassed.

Another example is when I was put on antidepressants leading up to my coming out. I agreed only on the basis that it would be for a very short period of time, but now, many years later, I've actually found peace with the place that antidepressants have in my life. I'm not quite sure if or when I'll be off them, but at this point, they're now at a fairly low dose. Most importantly, I'm no longer embarrassed about being on medication for my mental health.

In an organisation where I was leading in an interim capacity as their CEO, we put on a new employee assistance program (EAP). In the cemetery industry, it can be difficult work, especially with other people's grief being front and centre all of the time. I thought, *If I'm no longer embarrassed about my mental health, can I use that for the advantage or benefit of others?* So, at the work sites, I used an opportunity to introduce the new EAP program to talk about myself and my regrets from my time in the railways when I had my first mental health breakdown. I talked about when I was too embarrassed to go to the EAP provider to get help because I was fearful that I would no longer be accepted as an executive if people knew I had mental health issues. But, this was my issue, not theirs. I stood up and said, 'As a leader of this organisation, I am very committed to having an effective EAP service, and that's why we're putting this new one in place.'

If, as a CEO and a leader of an organisation, I can't be honest, how can we expect our employees to do the same? I have taken ownership of being true to myself and my feelings, and this is how I encourage people to shy away from shame.

Working on the personal issues at the level of intensity I had experienced became very exhausting. I was quite lucky that I had a role for the first couple of years of my coming out as an executive chairman for two or three days a week, which kept me financially secure. Some other board roles also provided me sufficient income to traverse through my early coming out process, and they provided me with the time and space I needed. As I gained people's trust, my CEO and I started having some more personal conversations. I'm grateful that when he saw my mental health was deteriorating, he was willing to speak up. This is one of the fundamentals of the 'R U OK?' campaign, and it usually meant going back and catching up with Michael, which is something I still do today.

Once, I had been searching through a myriad of educational programs, partly for interest, partly for professional development and continuing professional education (CPE), when I came across a program at Stanford University for LGBTIQA+ leaders. It was an executive leadership program that encouraged people to see the executive world through an LGBTIQA+ lens. I applied and was accepted; it was quite a seminal program for me. I found myself in a room of fifty of the most significant LGBTIQA+ leaders from around the world, and only a third of the group was from outside the US. I remember one of the professors coming up to me and saying something along the lines of, 'We are so glad you're here. You have the business and the academic background that we were hoping to draw to this program.'

Another one of the professors said, 'One of the things you need to be aware of here is that you are at Stanford, one of the top business schools in the world—we think the best—and some of you have a background where you have doubted yourselves. During this course, this doubt may come up, and you might think you don't deserve to be here. Let me remind you, you have all met the entry criteria to come to the Stanford Graduate School to do this executive leadership program. You are here. Be fully here.'

I'm so glad he said that because, the very next day, I had that very doubt. There I was, a person who had always struggled with his own acceptance, at one of the grandest and most prestigious business schools in the world. I was learning from some of the greatest professors of business alongside some of the most phenomenal LGBTIQA+

business leaders of the world. Did I deserve to be there? According to that professor, yes, I did deserve to be there. So, I stepped up to the plate and was fully present, which was something I had struggled with for my entire life.

Because of this journey, though, I now feel I have some knowledge to contribute to society. I have things to learn and I have networks to build, and, in a way, the week with those global leaders was an amazing turning point. There were many important and seminal moments, but, to turn to something that on the surface seems quite trivial, I had, some years earlier, bought an Apple watch. I decided to buy a number of changeable wristbands for it, which would, in my view, display my acceptance of me and my new community. One wristband was a blatantly rainbow-coloured flag: the community's banner. I only wore that occasionally and definitely only in gay environments. Other times, I had a metal wristband that shimmered. I knew what it meant, but it may have been too subtle for others. Now, when I got to Stanford, I thought, *If I can't wear this for the entire week, then I haven't accepted who I am. I haven't accepted that I am a gay executive.* And so, I put on my rainbow wristband, and I wore it all week. I received some welcoming feedback from a fellow student when they told me that they found encouragement from me wearing something that was obvious when nothing else really stood out. I took that encouraging comment positively and made a decision that it would be the wristband I would wear all the time after Stanford. And I did.

Over time, I told my own staff, and I came out to them one by one, with my executive assistant being first to hear. Each person was very supportive and accepting in their own genuine way, and there was even some fun during the process. For each team member, I worked on when and how I would tell them, yet each time, I felt nervous as I continued the 'coming out' process. One of the last staff members I told arranged to meet me in a coffee shop. I was running late and texted through my usual order of a 'large decaf soya flat white.' When I eventually turned up at the table in the café, the coffee was waiting for me. The staff member nonchalantly mentioned how 'gay' my coffee order was, and I was not sure how this conversation might go. So, we talked business around a new client, and he drew attention to the fact that the senior executive of the client was very nice and that he was gay.

My goodness! What is happening here?

But in the end, I needed to trust my instincts in trusting my team members, and I considered how I might broach my news. So, I said something like, 'You know that coffee order? That's me!' The look from that staff member was unforgettable; it's a good story and has become a friendly banter between us years later.

I don't look like your stereotypical gay person—whatever the hell that is—but I am happy to stand tall in my community … no pun intended! That, of course, gave me the ability to develop who I am. I'm not waving around my flag, but I'm not hiding who I am anymore either. And it's interesting. I have committed to being more open, transparent and honest, and, for some reason, people seem to be more open and honest in return. Rather than avoiding telling people what I am doing now with my time when they enquire, I say, 'Mardi Gras is on, and I'm going to see a queer film this evening,' or, 'I have a meeting tonight to organise our float for the Sydney Gay and Lesbian Mardi Gras parade.' With Mardi Gras being a big deal for my newfound community in Australia, this shift in confidence is profound. That would have never happened before.

A senior staff member who'd been through the loss of a child came to me saying, 'I wish there was something more we could do … I see so many gay suicides. You know, the other week, we held a funeral and buried a man, a dentist in his mid-thirties, who was gay. The Church and his family wouldn't allow the funeral service to be held in their parish church. His partner is still not fully recognised by the family.'

The fact this still goes on hurts me, but it does go on. On another occasion, we had to deal with a grave licence holder for a grave of her lifelong partner. Her late partner's family members objected to them being remembered as a couple and would deface her tombstone. So, you see ... acceptance of LGBTIQA+ people still has quite a way to go.

The worldwide ongoing trends towards re-marginalisation of the LGBTIQA+ community should not be ignored, and those places moving forward to recognise basic human rights for all groups, sexual orientation or otherwise, should be celebrated. I look at my own denomination that has said, 'Yes, we'll allow ministers and parishioners to make their own determination if they'll allow LGBTIQA+ people to be married in the Church, but ministers and parishioners still have the right to say no.' In Australia, we're having a political debate about whether or not religious schools should have the right to discriminate against LGBTIQA+ kids and teachers. Really? Should this even be considered in today's society?

In Chechnya, the government is rounding up gay people and putting them in prison, potentially executing them. Transgender people are still being murdered in huge numbers around the world. One of our very Australian national newspapers has been running a multi-month campaign over a year with, at times, weekly articles against the transgender community. On more than one occasion, their material has led the Australian prime minister to criticise transgender people directly or the processes in place to support them.

In Australia, we're a little bit unusual in that we have

the 'I' in 'LGBTIQA+', but I'm certainly very supportive of the rights of intersex people—people born with more than XX or XY chromosomes, or who are of indeterminate gender, or who have multiple gender parts, and so on. There are still doctors around the world, including here in Australia, who want to cosmetically 'fix' an intersex child before they actually know which gender they are, but this causes all sorts of consequences or issues in their formative years.

There is also still more work to be undertaken around the world regarding HIV, which is not caused by homosexuality or any other orientation even though it is sadly linked to it in public discourse, mainly by misguided religious leaders. We're also struggling with religious organisations, which are campaigning against the use of contraceptives when condoms—that are a significant tool in the reduction of HIV everywhere—could have a major impact in third-world countries.

So, while I have reached a positive point in my own acceptance journey, my own acceptability, there is still a way to go for LGBTIQA+ people to be completely accepted as full human beings in the eyes of religion, in the eyes of society and, in many places, in the eyes of the workplace and the sporting field. During my journey, I have gained allies, and I have become willing to talk about my experiences because, for the first time, I'm happy being me. Furthermore, accepting myself and who I am assists in the advocacy work I'm passionate about, such as the examples mentioned above.

In 2018, several years after my coming out journey began, I spoke about a small part of my story at the Asia Pacific Rainbow Forum in Hong Kong. I received lots of support as I discussed that I was an accidental advocate, but I now realise that statement is not true. I kicked open the solid wooden door at the Box Hill Town Hall in rage. Now, it is time to 'kick down more doors' intentionally as an advocate, and to shine the light on the systematic and institutionalised discrimination, injustices and hate towards the LGBTIQA+ community.

I have seen many minority groups through my Christian journey: those who are homeless; youths in prisons that, quite frankly, I wouldn't put a dog in. The needs of our Pacific Island nations are great, and Australia should be so much more generous as a developed nation, especially with the additional challenges from climate change. We should recognise the benefits of microfinance led by women in developing countries who can have so much impact in their communities. We should support advocating groups who are highlighting the need for climate change and how the moral role of global corporations and governments have failed us in this fight so far.

I learnt in my youth how to be a Christian advocate. But I was always the advocate from the majority—generally the white, Anglo Saxon perspective—that felt called to respond to the Gospel of Jesus. I was never part of the disaffected, the rejected or the minority. But now I am, in so many ways. I am a gay Christian, and I am a member of the LGBTIQA+ community. However, although I have been made amazingly welcome by them, I am occasionally rejected by a small number of the community because of my Christian persuasion. Indeed, I have been fully aware of some nervousness in the LGBTIQA+ community towards us 'queer Christians'. I can fully understand this. What communities of faith have done and continue to do— including in Australia—to LGBTIQA+ people is, at best, abuse and the total opposite of what our faiths are calling us towards. I hope for those in the LGBTIQA+ community who still struggle with the physical and mental anguish from what faith communities have done to you, that us queer people of faith can be part of your healing, however small our part may be.

For me, I have been lucky in my own parish and, in

much of the Church, I continue to be fully welcomed and included. I know there are some in my own denomination and in broader Christianity who believe I don't belong and can't be a Christian because of my 'lifestyle'. What I would like to write about these people I know won't pass the editorial process, so I will leave that to your imagination. I suppose my politically and editorially correct statements are that, 'When you reject us, you are rejecting Jesus,' and, 'My lifestyle is not a choice; this is how God created me.'

I have moved from accidental advocate to intentional advocate. However, I am learning my place in this area of advocacy. At the moment, I am a bit of a scattergun, hence why this is an 'emerging memoir'. Five years of journeying into *accepting* who I actually am; five years of *showing* the world who I actually am. I really am not much different. I have just accepted that I am drawn to men rather than women. I am moving into another phase of my life and, in spite of this story, I have had a good life so far. My hope and prayer is that the next phase will be better for everyone I am connected with … and for me.

One of the other realisations through writing this memoir about me and the LGBTIQA+ community is around resilience. Unfortunately, some don't make the journey. I almost didn't, but I have, and so have many others. I don't know where my resilience has come from, and perhaps that is an area for me to work on, making it a more intentional focus for the future. Even writing this book has required additional resilience. The release has been delayed on more than one occasion. There were legal issues raised by some of the organisations mentioned in my book, and it ended up with more than one chapter having to be re-written—limitations were put on what they felt I could say to ensure confidentiality of meetings was maintained.

Then COVID stormed the globe, and although Australia

fared better than many countries for the first 20 months, I had a major fall when out undertaking my permitted 'lockdown exercise' walk and severely injured my left shoulder. Six operations later, a non-operative procedure that put me in intensive care for several days and a post-operative infection that required surgery, with six weeks of hospital treatment on multiple strong antibiotics, and finally a reverse shoulder replacement, requiring seven weeks of hospitalisation, I am finally starting to get there. There may still be more operations to come, and I still don't have a working left shoulder. I have also ended up with a permanent disability in my left arm. All of this medical treatment was undertaken during some of the worst of the COVID outbreak, meaning extensive isolation for me during, and outside of, the lockdowns.

As a result, all of these events had a significant mental health impact, so it was time to focus on myself, and this journey had to be put aside for a while. Sometimes, simply surviving to the next day is the best that we can do.

For my LGBTIQA+ community members of faith, may our God guide us and continue to remind our faith community of inclusion. My prayer is for our wholeness and for strength in our ongoing cries for full acceptance.

For my LGBTIQA+ community, thank you for your heartfelt welcome, and I am looking forward to working together with you globally for our rights. I deeply hope and pray this type of memoir will no longer need to be written because there won't be stories like mine anymore. Unfortunately, due to people of certain political persuasions and fundamentalist faiths, I suspect there will still be a number of people following the journey I have travelled. Please remember that you are so valuable and precious, no matter how little you value yourself or how low others value you. You are much loved.

I suspect each of us, in some way, continue on a

journey to acceptance, and my hope and prayer is that the journey will become calmer and smoother for each of us as we journey forwards. My time has come, and sharing my story is part of this time. I will advocate for my community, no matter how uncomfortable that might be for some others who advocate against us or who are simply silent because silence provides strength to those who oppress others.

My message as a basketball coach for others is now relevant for me, each and every day moving forwards.

'I can't change the past, but I can influence the future!'

Acknowledgements

The Father sent the Son to be the Saviour of the world.
1 John 4:14

A book doesn't just happen; there are many people behind the scenes.

While not naming any individuals, there were some amazing people who helped me in the beginning and during my coming out phase; they helped me survive, and they guided me towards the amazing LGBTIQA+ community. There were a number of them who, early on, and for reasons I never understood, said, 'Stories are important, and we need more stories. Would you please write yours?' I am not sure why they thought my story was important or why so early on they thought I would even contemplate writing it. In the end, however, it was the gentle encouragement from them that ignited a small spark in my head and ultimately led to this book being written.

I was in Hong Kong—speaking for the first time about part of my journey—when I met Jules Hannaford, author of *Fool Me Twice* and a top-ranked interviewer in Asia with her podcast *Confidential*. She heard that I was thinking about writing my story sometime in the future, and her response was, 'You must, and you have to, talk with Pashmina P. from the Online Author's Office.' So, I embarked on an amazing journey with Pashmina, who is a gentle soul with a fierce desire to ensure that we authors get the best out of ourselves and that we receive support when the going gets tough. Thank you so much, Pashmina, for your wisdom, love, support and encouragement.

Behind Pashmina is an amazing team: Charlotte L. Taylor, who edited and reworked the manuscript with me; Gemma Purnell, who helped me to create my ICT presence; Felicity Simister, who created my meaningful cover and formatted my interior; and Ari Silva, who is responsible for my amazing illustrations.

Thanks also go to my EA and Business Manager, Michaela Burkitt, who had to cover for me from time to time as I either disappeared into writing or into the depths of darkness and beyond.

My thanks go to fellow author, Anthony Venn-Brown, too, whose book, *A Life of Unlearning: a preacher's struggle with his homosexuality, church and faith*, was the first of its kind in the Australian context. It helped me to appreciate that I am normal to be both gay and Christian. Thank you for checking in on me to ensure I was okay, as it really is a mental and personal challenge writing such a memoir.

To my numerous friends who have provided gentle encouragement to stay on track and get this completed, thank you.

Finally, thank you to my children, Joshua and Kate. Thank you for putting up with me as I disappeared into my study space or disappeared on retreats to work on the book. Thank you, too, for understanding my sometimes challenging moods as I worked on difficult parts. I love you both very dearly.

About the Author:
Meet Jason Masters

Executive, Author, Independent Board Member, Church Leader

Managing Director, Jason Masters runs a boutique management consulting firm based in Australia. Focusing on the integrity of commercial transactions, he is an independent board member across a wide number of industries: financial services; medical regulations; pharmaceutical start-ups; cemeteries; and corporate giving programs. He also chairs numerous audit and risk committees for the government and not-for-profit or private sector organisations.

Jason has a Bachelor of Economics (Economics and Computer Science) from Flinders University in South Australia and is a graduate and Fellow of the Australian Institute of Company Directors. He is also a Professional Fellow of the Institute of Internal Auditors (Australia), certified in the Governance of Enterprise IT (CGEIT) (ISACA), certified in Risk Management Assurance—from the Institute of Internal Auditors—and in the Association of Certified Fraud Examiners. He previously co-authored the international landmark book *Computer Security in Australia.*

Writing his book, *A Journey Towards Acceptance: An Evolving Memoir,* has tapped into Jason's passion as an accidental activist, which stems from his desire to help those in need—especially those who suffer prejudice within a minority group. Coming out as a 'gay executive' while also a Christian has been a long and arduous journey. However, through writing his memoir, he uncovers how the road to success is to live a life of acceptance by breaking down stereotypes, crossing boundaries and believing in the fundamental truths of survival.

As an author, Jason shares a story that will not only help executives across the globe, but will empower the youth of today to live a life they were born to have and to own. As a basketball enthusiast, he has inspired his community with his coaching. As a church leader, he has been a Sunday school teacher, a youth leader and an elder in his local parishes through regional, state and national council roles.

Jason the executive, and now Jason the author, hopes to offer his story as an inspiration to those who fear the unknown as he did. His life journey led to his passion for social justice being more focused on the needs of the LGBTIQA+ community in addition to other justice issues. He has worked hard to reintegrate his life as a family, religious and business man, and part of his road to success has been finding his own unique voice in all components of his existence. Coming out as an author—and his bravery as a Christian to publish his story—has driven Jason to live a life of fundamental acceptance for himself and for the world around him.

Printed in Great Britain
by Amazon

19485168R00188